REA

FRIENDS
OF ACPL

S0-BHW-366

# Dandies

# Dandies

## *Fashion and Finesse in Art and Culture*

EDITED AND WITH AN INTRODUCTION BY

## Susan Fillin-Yeh

*New York University Press*

NEW YORK AND LONDON

NEW YORK UNIVERSITY PRESS
New York and London

Library of Congress Cataloging-in-Publication Data
Dandies : fashion and finesse in art and culture /
edited by Susan Fillin-Yeh.
p.   cm.
Includes bibliographical references and index.
ISBN 0-8147-2695-X (cloth : alk. paper) —
ISBN 0-8147-2696-8 (pbk. : alk. paper)
1. Dandies—History.  2. Men's clothing—History.
3. Fashion—History.
GT6720 .D35  2000
305.31—dc21            00-012369

New York University Press books are printed on acid-free paper,
and their binding materials are chosen for strength and durability.

Manufactured in the United States of America

10 9 8 7 6 5 4 3 2 1

*For J. and K.*

# Contents

# Illustrations

# Preface

An image wisp from memory has persisted as this book took shape: a woman who steps briskly out of her door very early in the morning. She is wonderfully turned out—hat, gloves, burnished shoe leather. The time is the 1930s or 1940s (my mother's history enters in here). Her stocking seams are perfectly straight. She passes by weedy, brick- and trash-strewn vacant lots and the streets on which she walks are dingy and unprepossessing, for few people enliven them and the stores are not yet open. She is resplendent.

But is she a dandy? In conventional thinking, no. She almost certainly has never experienced the leisure time supported by money historically implicated in dandyism. (If you want to be a dandy, make sure that you are rich, Charles Baudelaire advised.) And she doesn't trace a lineage back to the fantastically dressed eighteenth-century English Macaronis, or to George Bryan "Beau" Brummell, whose austere elegance of costume and demeanor positioned him as the cynosure of royalty. But, as with Brummell, her clothing is her armor, and her presence and presentation are gifts to those who look at her. Her apparition invokes one task of *Dandies: Fashion and Finesse in Art and Culture*: to suggest a new paradigm for dandies, a robust and diverse "outsider" paradigm of sartorial finesse detached from Western European upper-class dandyism—traditional, mainstream, and gendered as male (see "Introduction: New Strategies for a Theory of Dandies"). This paradigm is imbued with realizations gleaned from a generation's measure of feminist scholarship, though its shortcomings are my own. Such a paradigm can render my memory woman's unrecognized dandyism visible. And other dandyisms as well.

This book has come into being thanks to its contributors, Jennifer Blessing, Rhonda K. Garelick, Joe Lucchesi, Kimberly Miller, Robert E. Moore, Richard J. Powell, Carter Ratcliff, and Mark Allen Svede. Their enthusiastic participation and thoughtful scholarship have produced essays on late-nineteenth- and twentieth-century artist dandies; dandy fashion stars, African dandies, Native American trader-tribe dandies, African American dandies, and Latvian dandies. Their work has affirmed my conviction that a project of this scope, with roots in art history, cultural history, literary scholarship, material culture, and anthropology, and a theoretical lineage in postmodernist, postcolonialist, and feminist theory, queer theory, and fashion history, finds its most evolved expression and far-reaching impact as a joint effort. As does clothing itself. A text, as Roland Barthes pointed out, is a tissue. The essays in this volume remind us that garments—in actuality and metaphorically—are constructs, and that in studying them, one carries out deconstructive tasks.

The idea for the project originated in a conversation with Whitney Chadwick, whose broad vision of scholarship is inspiring. Robert Farris Thompson was encouraging at a very early stage, as was my editor at New York University Press, Eric Zinner, whose belief in this project has been essential in its evolution. I thank Harriet Watson for her support and help in engineering leave time to work on this book, and Silas B. Cook for serving as acting director of the Douglas F. Cooley Memorial Art Gallery, Reed College, in my absence. Joan and John Shipley lent their beach house. I was inspired by lively exchanges with friends and colleagues Robert Moore and Mark Svede and thank Julia Ballerini, Kate Mai-lan Fillin-Yeh, and Lena Lencek, who generously read the manuscript and offered a great many valuable suggestions. I thank Kate Fillin-Yeh for the deconstruction discussion, and Jennifer Robertson for the photograph of Anna Jun. Naomi Sawelson-Gorse was instrumental in organizing preliminary editorial tasks of the book, and Christina Houstian has been a meticulous and cheerful editorial force, as was Nadine Fiedler. Despina Papazoglou Gimbel, managing editor at New York University Press, was gracious and thorough, as was indexer Julie Kawabata. I thank Professor Kathrine French for generously helping me edit a chapter. Aaron Jones and Sarah Hamill fed lists of books to the Reed College Interlibrary Loan Office, whose staff was unfailingly helpful. Marv Dunn untangled computer languages. The College Art Association offered me the opportunity in 1997 to organize a session on dandies that introduced me to new contributors. Amy Jo Fillin supplied me with *New York Times* clippings. I thank Jen Yeh for finding me books, and for his love and constant support; this project could not have come to fruition without him.

# Introduction
## New Strategies for a Theory of Dandies

### Susan Fillin-Yeh

> Dandyism is a mysterious institution.
> —Charles Baudelaire, 1863

For a while when he was in his twenties, Charles Baudelaire impressed Bohemian friends with his dandyism. Dressed completely and startlingly in black ("the necessary garb," he wrote, "of our suffering age"), in elegant clothing tailored to his own instructions, Baudelaire set out to address dandyism in his writing.[1] His review of the Salon of 1846 drew on Jules Barbey d'Aurevilly's study of quintessential dandy Beau Brummell to popularize dandies as the aloof new heroes of 1840s Paris.[2] Later, in 1863, in Le Figaro, Baudelaire introduced his readers to the newspaper artist and illustrator Constantine Guys and gave them an artist-dandy, almost an alter ego, to contemplate. Like Baudelaire a dandy who actually worked at a profession and cultivated only the appearance of dandiacal leisure, Guys, Baudelaire proclaimed, was an utterly original personality.[3] More than an artist, he was a man of the world gripped by a passion for contemporanaeity: "[H]e wants to know . . . everything that happens on the surface of our globe."[4] Guys was a dandy in "his subtle understanding of the moral mechanism of this world," and in his search for that shifting, up-to-the-minute quality that "you must allow me," Baudelaire says, "to call 'modernity.'"[5]

Baudelaire offers us jumping-off points for a discussion of dandies: cosmopolitanism, presentation, spectacle, "moral mechanism[s]." His dandyism conjoins clothing—personally intimate and literally "material"—and the passionate pursuit of an original selfhood that makes its own rules: "Dandyism, an institution beyond the laws," he wrote.[6] It is no accident that Ellen Moers began her classic study of dandies with the revolutionary antihero Yankee Doodle Dandy, the American descendant of the Macaronis of 1760s London, and his song that poked fun at provincialism, vulgarity, and pretentiousness. "From the beginning," Moers noted, "*dandy* had the power to fascinate, to puzzle, to travel, to persist and to figure in an ambiguous social situation in a revolutionary climate."[7] Ambiguities encourage dandies, who seem constantly and irrepressibly to reinvent the mode of behavior. When in 1910 Coco Chanel appeared in a man's suit at a society event, the Paris races, she sought—and achieved—the power of a dandy's glamour; the clothing she chose to wear defied societal restrictions imposed on her by class and by her status as a mistress. Caroline Evans and Minna Thornton have written about a snapshot taken of Chanel: she looked "sporting, tasteful and energetic, with that added touch of personal style, almost insolence—the man's coat and tie—which calls her status into question and yet gives nothing away."[8] Appearance can be a political act; it is always a social one. Chanel's—and all dandies'—ensembles are the "social things" that Karl Marx described in identifying the "fetishism of commodities," that is, "a definite social relation between men, that assumes . . . the fantastic form of a relation between things." In this sense, dandies' clothing is a "social hieroglyphic" that hides, even as it reveals, class and social status and our expectations about them.[9]

Might Baudelaire have recognized Coco Chanel as a kindred spirit? Perhaps not, although he came close to suggesting that dandies and women were alike in their cultivation of artifice.[10] But contemplating an imaginary encounter between the two sheds light on some of dandyism's possibilities, while building on a historic definition that juggles fact and fluidity. Dandies—deliberately and always—everything that others are not, Barbey d'Aurevilly claimed.[11] When Baudelaire elaborated on Barbey d'Aurevilly's description of the dandiacal attitude, he spoke of the dandy's "joy of astonishing others." For Baudelaire, dandyism was a déclassé achievement based on talents that work and money cannot buy.[12] Writers on dandies have noted another intriguing aspect of dandies' elusiveness: their presentation as spectacle. Dandyism is more than an art of dress, though cloth is the dandy's material. Barbey d'Aurevilly's rejoinder in 1845 to Thomas Carlyle (who once called dandies clotheshorses) is still instructive: "Dandyism is . . . not a suit of clothes walking about by itself! On the contrary, it is the partic-ular way of wearing these clothes which constitutes dandyism."[13] It is in this "particular way of wearing . . . clothes" that dandies transform their bodies into art. Clothing rests close to the body; it is not surpris-ing that dress has its somatic reverberations in disguise and displace-ment, and that it can be the material of self-transformation and artistic transformation. In fact, as Barbey d'Aurevilly's analysis of Brummell's dandyism reminds us, the dandy is both artist and living art: his pres-ence has a doubled density. Appearance is ephemeral, but dandiacal appearance can imprint on the memory. A dandy's impact is dia-chronic. Cumulative and played out over time, dandyism is lived, and it is performative.[14]

Why study dandies? Certainly because new ones continue to flour-ish. Dandies' resistance to norms has found many outlets in the twenti-eth century; contemporary life and events have invoked (and provoked) dandyism. (Andy Warhol's downtown style that blended punk, camp parody, and glamour identifies him as a dandy; Madonna's seemingly endless parade of invented selves is dandyesque.)[15] But many dandies, including historical ones, have remained invisible. The conventional notion of the dandy as a Western European man-about-town is in need of refurbishing. This study encompasses and moves beyond the notion of a dandy as a Western European man to offer a cross-cultural view that introduces new dandies from other places, and female as well as male manifestations of dandyism; it examines unrecognized dandiacal constructions of appearance, including cross-dressed ones. *Dandies: Fashion and Finesse in Art and Culture* looks back to—and forward from—Barbey d'Aurevilly, who praised dandies for their hermaph-roditic "twofold and multiple natures" and for their "eternal . . . Caprice."[16] In directing attention to overlooked dandies at particular times and specific places who have devised sartorial strategies that forge new identities and selves, *Dandies: Fashion and Finesse in Art and Culture* juxtaposes theoretical models, evocative images, and ac-tual clothing. Style is a mode of confrontation. Multivalenced perspec-tives in diverse approaches and subject matter offer new insights into the obstreperous phenomenon of dandies, for one thing, noting their courage.

It has taken the vast changes in thinking about identity offered by feminist theory, queer theory, and other studies of women subsumed under the rubrics of deconstruction and postmodernist discourse to recognize and understand these different dandyisms.[17] New tools at hand for fresh exploration into the affect of dandies' finesse can be found in theoretical strategies and analyses that question the "either/or" limitations of gender binarism and examine the politics of gender. The observations introduced in feminist film theory demonstrating that identity is shifting, multilayered, and, above all, constructed offer useful information for a field guide to dandies, for they are the perfect exemplars of self-construction.[18] Lacanian constructions of identity offer other tactics for breaking open monolithic notions of self. Using the Lacanian dyad, "an element in a larger chain," Marjorie Garber has considered the innovations of a third transvestite sex, many of them dandies.[19]

Other poststructuralist analyses bear directly on the clothed body and articulations of power, and contribute to feminist analyses of clothing as a field of intellectual study.[20] Roland Barthes gave dandies the status of a "rudimentary" sign "that can signify without recourse to . . . speech." Barthes may have prematurely announced the death of dandies: they were killed off, he wrote, by the fashion industry. At the same time, his musings on the dialectics of fashion writing ("there is a turnstile between person and garment") and his notion of a vestimentary "transformational myth" animated by ludic disguise and ambiguity offer up ground rules for the "game of clothing" relished by dandies.[21] Recent British cultural theories of resistance provide another lens for looking at dandies. Drawing on Louis Althusser's description of unconscious ideologies, Dick Hebdige, Stuart Cosgrove, and Angela McRobbie have identified subcultural groups for whom style is an oblique political act.[22] These cover ground explored by Michel Foucault in studies of the body submitting and resistant to societal and sexual pressures, and filiations of power: "a moving substrate of force relationships."[23]

Other theory maps the haunts of dandies. Writing in the 1920s, Mikhail Bakhtin defined aesthetic activity in terms that seem tailor-made for a dandiacal destabilizing stance. Locating cultural and aesthetic activity at "the intersection of various boundaries," Bakhtin enables us to make sense of dandyism as a mode of behavior by directing attention to the terrain dandies inhabit. Remember that, as Ellen Moers pointed out, dandies "travel." Dandies are observant strollers; they are flaneurs.[24] In Baudelaire's and, later, Walter Benjamin's Paris, people are out walking. Dandy flaneurs "botanizing on the asphalt" are pedestrians who constantly, simultaneously, claim and relinquish urban sights.[25] If, as Benjamin noted, the street is home for the flaneur, Bakhtin illuminates our understanding of the street as a "cultural sphere." The street "is situated entirely on boundaries; boundaries go through it everywhere. . . . Every cultural act lives on boundaries; in this is its seriousness and significance."[26] Boundaries make creativity possible. Their abutments offer the physical sites for the resonance of many voices, for dialogue. In language that gives immediacy to the performance of aesthetic activity, Bakhtin enacts the visual dialogue of dandies, who, as observed and observers, raise the stakes of both enterprises.

Bakhtin's "cultural sphere," the dandy's turf, has a flavor that has also been described by others. Natalie Zemon Davis has written about "borderland[s] between cultural deposits that allowed new growth and surprising hybrids."[27] Analyzing the activities of "tricksters" among the western North American tribes who are dandy-like in their affinity for disguise, subversive independence, and ambiguous sexual status, Barbara Babcock-Abrahams has located a terrain preferred by dandies analogous to Davis's: "They tend to be associated with marketplaces, crossroads, and other open spaces that are 'betwixt and between' clearly defined social statuses and spaces or in which normal structures or patterns of relating break down—with places of transition, movement, and license."[28] Identifying a recurrent class of "betwixt and between" locales amplifies an important dimension of dandies' physical and psychic geography. Whether or not it is urban—that is, metropolitan—a dandy's border world is deeply cosmopolitan. In their decentralized mobility and elusiveness, in their dialogue, flaneur dandies energize that cosmopolitan world whose qualities have also been described by Guy Scarpetta: "an untenable position of systematic crossing over, of an essential exile, an endlessly recommended diaspora, of movement, of a tearing away of everything that keeps you rooted."[29] If Bakhtin's idea of the dialogic is closely related to his vision of boundaries, its exposition in Bakhtin's thinking brings us back to issues of dress, for the performative nuances of clothing are not created out of nothing, but are created socially, in dialogue. "All aesthetic acts," as anthropologists Mary Ellen Roach and Joanne Bubolz Eicher have pointed out in describing clothing and its uses in a variety of cultures, " are acts of speaking . . . what is said having meaning only because of relationships with other people."[30] These twentieth-century recognitions underscore Baudelaire's prescience in 1863, when he looked beyond Paris and London to find dandies in other times and in quite different places, in "antiquity, Caesar, Catiline and Alcibiades providing us with dazzling examples; and . . . Chateaubriand having found it in the forests and by the lakes of the New World."[31] It is to this inclusive dandyism that this study pays respect and which it will explore.

## A Note on Methodology

The strategies for recognizing dandies set out in *Dandies: Fashion and Finesse in Art and Culture* are grounded in art history, for they deal in the nuances of visual culture that Erwin Panofsky has called a history of cultural symptoms.[32] That the project takes in both images and actual clothing is its debt to an interdisciplinary net cast over the world of appearances, including Jules Prown's tactical studies in material culture.[33] The historiography of clothing offers scenarios such as Georg Simmel's, who in 1931 suggested ways in which dandies' dress can be rebellious. Simmel traced innovation in fashion to the demimonde, with perhaps a nod to the Baudelairean notion of a dandy's characteristic oppositional stance, where an aristocracy of self-made elegance replaces one of birth.[34] J. C. Flugel's analysis of clothing in 1930, the earliest Freudian investigation of the subject, charts the symbolic power of male dress, with attention to its positioning within the Freudian dynamics of sublimation and transference.[35] Published by Virginia and Leonard Woolf's Hogarth Press, his study has an intriguing connection with dandies, for Virginia Woolf's *Orlando,* with its dandified, crossdressed hero/heroine, had been published by the press just two years earlier. Orlando is the exuberant heir/heiress to fictional studies of the dandy's world by Bulwer-Lytton, Wilde, and Beerbohm that have shaped notions of dandies, and this study is indebted to them. But with Orlando there is a difference, for Woolf offered her readers a lively parade of selves differentiated by clothing within the body of the same person, introducing in 1928 the shifting, laminate conception of personhood we now refer to as postmodern. As Jessica Feldman has noted in her analysis of dandyism in literature, dandies offer anti-essentialist challenges to patriarchy "by advertising the self as nothing but the sum total of powerful, premeditated, costumed poses."[36]

Pioneering studies of the construction of meaning in clothing by anthropologists have contributed to a cross-cultural theory of dandies.

For Mary Ellen Roach and Joanne Bubolz Eicher to remind us that "adornment has long had a place in the house of power" is to offer a feminist corrective to a history of denigrating clothing as frivolous, trivial, and female.[37] Dick Hebdige, Stuart Cosgrove, George Melly, Stuart Hall, Jane Gaines, Angela McRobbie, Charlotte Herzog, Caroline Evans, Minna Thornton, Juliet Ash, Elizabeth Wilson, and Carol Tulloch have performed a similar service for British cultural studies. Hebdige's description of the "challenge to hegemony [by youth subcultures] . . . expressed obliquely, in style . . . [and] displayed . . . at the profoundly superficial level of appearances" offers a tool for recognizing twentieth-century, resistant dandyisms.[38] Cosgrove has explored historical connections between clothing and social action in writing on zoot suiters, the African American and Hispanic dandies whose spectacularly tailored and padded clothing was targeted in race riots in the United States in the 1940s:

> The zoot suit was a refusal . . . of subservience. . . . It was during his period as a young zoot-suiter that the Chicano union activist Cesar Chavez first came into contact with community politics, and it was through the experiences of participating in zoot-suit riots in Harlem, that the young pimp "Detroit Red" began a political education that transformed him into the Black radical leader Malcolm X.[39]

Cosgrove identifies other dandies as well. Octavio Paz's description of 1960s "pachuco," Mexican American street gang style, updates dandies' passion for originality. The "pachuco" attitude, wrote Paz, "reveals an obstinate, almost fanatical will-to-be, but this will affirms nothing specific except their determination . . . not to be like those around them."[40]

Recent ethnography, especially the work of social scientists who draw on anthropology and history to explore connections between dress and societal structures, offers new insights into dandies' concerns with surface, and expand these insights beyond Western society. Hildi Hendrickson notes in studies of colonial and postcolonial African societies that

> By taking the body surface as our focus, we investigate one of the frontiers upon which individual and social identities are simultaneously created. . . . The body surface . . . is a field for representation, which, being concrete, has lasting semiotic value. Being personal, it is susceptible to individual manipulation. Being public, it has social import.[41]

Such new, multiple lenses render dandies newly visible—not caught, but recognized. Dandies' relentless search for control over surfaces notwithstanding, dandyisms are elusive, moving targets. "The body," Hendrickson states, "is perhaps the quintessential subversive object sign."[42] Yet, as Hebdige has pointed out, quoting Volosinov in his exploration of oppositional style, "When a sign is present, ideology is present, too."[43]

## A Digression on the History of Dandies

Inexcusably, in all his ghostly elegance, [the dandy] haunted the Victorian imagination.                                     —Ellen Moers, 1960

The European imagination abounds in dandies. Their visibility began in 1760s England when, so the story goes, Coke of Norfolk, a rich British landowner, came to town dressed in riding clothes, the future dandy's uniform, to successfully petition King George.[44] His example set the stage for a specialized history of the species. By 1798, when George Brummell—"Beau" Brummell—took his place at the center of the powerful, insular, aristocratic world of the London *ton*, his lively, haughty presence ushered in "dandy . . . independence, assurance, originality, self-control, refinement . . . all visible," Ellen Moers noted, "in the cut of his clothes."[45] That Brummell, the son of a civil servant, set standards for the aristocracy was predictive of the alluring, risking behavior of dandies; Brummell's "terrible independence proclaimed a subversive disregard" for class privileges.[46]

Dandies quickly took on identities as challengers to convention. The years after Brummel produced a cavalcade of French and English dandies whose activities speculated on a complicated mix of aesthetics and class hierarchies. It is tempting to speculate that the up-and-coming American painter Washington Allston could have been inspired to emulate Brummell when visiting Benjamin West and London's Royal Academy en route to Rome. In a self-portrait of 1805, Allston's taste for melodrama and stories of Italianate "banditti" joined the artistic and literary tenets of Romanticism with the traditions of dandyism and with his own artistic ambitions. He depicted himself against a background of mountains and ruins, dressed in stark fitted black clothing, with a white cravat whose seemingly casual but elaborate starched folds rival one of Brummell's own creations.[47] In the 1830s in England, Disraeli brought the attractions of dandyism to his campaigns for political office, while at the same time his novels described the lives of fictional dandies.[48]

Flux and volatility are characteristic of Western Europe and America in the years around 1800 when dandies were newly visible and Brummell, Disraeli, and Allston were men operating in an unstable social, political, and artistic climate. In 1863, when Baudelaire's essay "The Painter of Modern Life" was published in installments in *Le Figaro*, it brought new diversions and new surroundings to the dandy's mode of being. If Brummell's London stamping ground had included St. James and the streets and avenues near Buckingham Palace, Baudelaire's dandy's involvements brought him to Paris streets and crowds. ("Anyone who is capable of being bored in a crowd," Baudelaire reported Constantin Guys as saying, "is a blockhead.")[49] Another attraction of Baudelaire's Paris was the shopping arcades, which, as Walter Benjamin has described them, constitute a liminal zone between street and interior space.[50]

Benjamin's ruminations on Baudelaire are a gift to any account of dandies, providing a dandy's guide to tactics for negotiating city life (the ability to recognize human motives and interests from fleeting encounters); shopping ("The bazaar is the last hangout of the *flâneur*");[51] dandified "attitude" ("His leisurely appearance as a personality is his protest against the division of labor which turns people into specialists. . . . Around 1840 it was briefly fashionable to take turtles for a walk in the arcades. The *flâneurs* liked to have the turtles set the pace for them");[52] and especially a dandy's mobility, elusiveness, and resistance: "The *flâneur* . . . stood at the margin, of the great city, as of the bourgeois class."[53] Benjamin's analysis highlights a crux of thinking not only about nineteenth-century dandies, but about dandies of all kinds. For if, as Baudelaire maintained, dandies create themselves, still their acts of self-construction are specific, embedded in time. Benjamin is instructive in reminding us that "[w]hen we read Baudelaire, we are given a course in historical society." He traced the dandy's impassive, blank-faced appearance to the quick but hidden reactions demanded of early stock market traders.[54]

The dandy is a creation of the English who were leaders in world trade. The trade network that spans the globe was in the hands of the London

stock-exchange people; its meshes felt the most varied, the most un-
forseeable tremors. A merchant had to react to these but he could not
publically display his reactions. The dandies took charge of the conflicts
thus created.[55]

It was to such vast changes in urban experience that Baudelaire was referring to when he told his readers in 1846, "Dandyism is a modern
thing, springing from causes completely new."[56] And if his definition of
modern—a quality that is shifting and contingent—is one that we can
apply even to life and events producing today's postmodern dandies,
still, it reminds us that the conditions in which dandies flourish are varied—and historically grounded.

## Masquerade

The self is a condition of disguise.   —Linda Nochlin, 1994

I am looking at a photograph taken in 1968 for the cover of *Takarazuka Gurafu*, a Japanese fan club magazine devoted to the popular
all-female theater company Takarazuka Revue (since the 1920s the
counterpart to the all-male Kabuki theater) (fig. I.1).[57] The photograph
is dominated by the figure of a contemporary Brummellian dandy
whose double-breasted suit, tailored to impeccable effect with a doubled lineup of buttons, is set off by starched lace ruffles on a high-col-
lared shirt front and a dark figured tie. In spite of the attention directed
to clothing that is fashionable, even extravagant, it is the pose of the
head that dominates the photograph. A sleekly delineated shape, glossy
hair slicked back in an upsweep, the head is tilted forward, as if to lock
eyes with a viewer slightly below. The gaze is mesmerizing. It seems to
signal privately to a reader of the magazine, "This is *just for you*."

The magazine cover offers up an artificed theatrical world. It contains a backdrop: a medieval walled town, another European exoticism, an airbrushed piece of virtual reality complete with a crumbling
wall signaling the romance of the past. Poised at its center, the dandy's
image is nearly seamless, although there are some disruptive details:
cuffs and collar are a little too big (it is at this point that we realize that
the head almost floats, seeming to barely rest on the oversized collar),
and the interposed forearm and loose fists, stereotypic gender attributes in Japanese male body language, are seemingly extraneous coding.

*Fig. I.1.* Anna Jun, cover of *Takarazuka Gurafu*, 1968. Photograph by Jennifer Robertson. Reproduced by permission.

Until it becomes apparent that these details are deployed on a female body. This photograph of the actress Anna Jun, a Takarazuka *otokoyaku* (specialist in male roles), is the highly charged and sexually alluring image of a female dandy, with fan club purchasers of the magazine as witness to her popularity.[58]

What to say about female dandies in Japanese—or in Westernized—

culture? Some traditions argue that they do not, even cannot, exist. "No question of inventing the *flâneuse*," concludes Janet Wolff in her study of the French and English literature of modernity and its missing dimension: accounts of private, domestic life and the lives of women. "The essential point is that such a character was rendered impossible by the sexual divisions of the nineteenth century."[59] Wolff was looking at the dandy's historic manifestation as flaneur, the stroller in the city, the passionate observer admired by Baudelaire and Benjamin.[60] To those who would point to George Sand's example when she began her literary career, moving freely about 1830s Paris dressed like a boy in student's clothing, Wolff notes that such perambulations were possible only because Sand was in disguise. Sand was a female flaneur. "She could not adopt the non-existent role of a *flâneuse*."[61] Still, as a disguise, Sand's was effective, and it was dapper:

> I had made for myself a redingote-guérite in heavy gray cloth, pants and vest to match. With a gray hat and a large woolen cravat, I was a perfect first-year student. I can't express the pleasure my boots gave me: I would gladly have slept with them, as my brother did in his young age, when he got his first pair. With those little iron-shod heels, I was solid on the pavement. I flew from one end of Paris to the other. It seemed to me that I could go around the world. And then, my clothes feared nothing. I ran out in every kind of weather, I came home at every sort of hour, I sat in the pit of the theatre. No one paid attention to me, and no one guessed at my disguise. . . . No one knew me, no one looked at me, no one found fault with me; I was an atom lost in a large crowd.[62]

Sand's vivid pleasure captivates. Her words inscribe a contagious gusto for experience and more: a creative life carved out in freedom. "I could make up a whole novel," she recalled, "as I walked from one side of town to another."[63] And yet they tease the reader, and for good reason. Carolyn Heilbrun, who reminds us that Sand was repeatedly described as both a woman and a man, argues, "All who knew and admired her found themselves without language to describe or address her, without a story, other than her own unique one, in which to encompass her."[64] One reason the history of female dandies is elusive, and is one that needs to be teased out, is that stories of lives like Sand's tend to be untold stories. "How," Heilbrun asks, "can we find narratives . . . stories that will affect stories and, eventually, lives, that will [not] cause us . . . to throw up our hands in describing George Sand because we are unwilling to call her either a woman (under the old plot) or a man when she isn't one?"[65] bell hooks has described the sartorial and sexual inventions involved in "shaking up the idea that any of us are inherently *anything . . .* we become who we are."

> She pleaded with him: Just once—well every now and then—I just want us to be boys together. I want to dress like you and go out and make the world look at us differently and make them wonder about us, make them stare and ask those silly questions like, "Is he a woman dressed up like a man? Is he an older black gay man with his effeminate boy/girl/lover flaunting same sex out in the open?" Don't worry. . . . I'll make it real "Keep them guessing" . . . do it in such a way that they will never know *for sure.*[66]

These are stories that the career of the Takarazuka *otokoyaku* Anna Jun also tells. If the world of the Takarazukiennes is an imaginary dream world of the stage, it is also true that dreams can be powerful.[67]

Jennifer Robertson's study of Anna Jun and others like her in the Takarazuka Revue explores "a dominant gender ideology constructed, reproduced, resisted, and even subverted, sometimes simultaneously, by males and females whose private and professional lives confound tidy, universalist schemata."[68] It offers a demonstration of what one might call the pragmatic dimension of female dandyism that locates modes of behavior within a long history punctuated by volatile, shifting, gender markers. It's not surprising that there are many actress dandies. One could make cases for Sarah Bernhardt, Maude Adams (famous for playing male roles), Conan Doyle's Irene Adler. The twentieth-century careers of Katharine Hepburn (dapper in *Sylvia Scarlett*), Greta Garbo, and Marlene Dietrich also offer notable illustrations. Theater, as Marjorie Garber has pointed out, "recognizes that all the figures on stage are impersonators."[69] As with Anna Jun, Dietrich's performance in *Morocco* in drag in a dandy's tuxedo reveals shifting possibilities for sexual identity. "Clothes provide a way of carrying out a magical body change," notes Gaylen Studlar, who uses the psychoanalytic category of masochism (based on masochists' conviction that it is possible to be both sexes) to explain Dietrich's sexual ambiguity and to challenge a strictly Freudian interpretation of male sexual fantasy.[70] These portrayals evoke the fluidities of Virginia Woolf's *Orlando*'s shifting selves: Woolf's imaginary three-hundred-year-old but ever-young personage, elegantly, alluringly, neither a man nor a woman.

Even for her creator, Orlando was hard to pin down. As Woolf observed of Orlando in his/her eighteenth-century manifestation,

> To give an exact and particular account of Orlando's life at this time becomes more and more out of the question. . . . What makes the task of identification still more difficult is that she found it convenient at this time to change frequently from one set of clothes to another. . . . She had, it seems, no difficulty in sustaining the different parts, for her sex changed far more frequently than those who have worn only one set of clothing can conceive.[71]

Woolf's accounting of Orlando's rich, shifting store of selves plays itself out before the reader in terms of clothing. Her book even included photographic documentation of the putative Orlando for readers to admire. A sketch of a packed day has Orlando "spending her morning in a China robe of ambiguous gender among her books," then pruning trees in the garden ("knee britches were convenient"), receiving a lord's proposal of marriage in "a flowered taffeta," in court supervising her cases in "a snuff coloured gown like a lawyer's. . . . finally, when night came, she would more often than not become a nobleman complete from head to toe and walk the streets in search of adventure."[72]

Sartorial abundance inflects elegance. Woolf's portrayal points us toward the special shimmer that female dandies like Orlando, Dietrich, and Jun so often display, their presence so replete with selves that others seem thin. This, at any rate, is one definition of sexual ambiguity—many-layered density. In this sense, female dandies reverse the Tootsie syndrome, felicitously so-named by Naomi Schor after Dustin Hoffman's Hollywood character, which holds that the best woman is really a man.[73] The allure of female dandies insinuates that the better man is (also) a woman.[74]

Such claims contradict twentieth-century psychoanalytic conventions. Freudian theory has been dismissive of female dandies. Implicated in the most basic of Freudian scenarios, clothing, defined as the material of fetishism, hides the woman's lack of a penis and undertakes to disguise this "castration." Laura Mulvey, in demonstrating that Freudian scopophiliac erotics are gendered as male, uses Freud to argue that "women are phallic substitutes whose erotic spectacle is constructed to cover their lack."[75] Freudian women are imperfect men. Female dandies, in their Western manifestation at any rate, have been subjected to a common double put-down. A woman whose activities depart from stereotypically female ones is "imitating" male activity and is open to criticism and ridiculous. Not only is she not successful, she is not "womanly": she is "no longer a woman."[76]

Arguments refuting Freud where female dandies are concerned include the Lacanian concept of the third or "symbolic" dimension in human psychology, a critique of sexual binarism and rigid duality. As Marjorie Garber noted in her study of transvestism, it "involve[s] moving from a structure of complementarity or symmetry to a contextualization, in which what once stood as an exclusive dual relation becomes an element in a larger chain."[77] The third dimension, which as Garber argues is neither a "term" nor a "sex" but rather "a space of possibility," interrupts binary structure. "One of the most important aspects of cross-dressing," Garber has suggested, "is the way in which it offers a challenge to easy notions of binarity, putting into question the categories of 'female' and 'male,' whether they are considered essential or constructed, biological or cultural."[78]

Garber's transvestite's challenge is one aspect of the challenge offered by female dandies. It finds support in Barthes's analysis in *The Fashion System* of fashionable clothing's "transformational myth" of many selves.

> The multiplication of persons in a single being is always considered by Fashion an index of power; . . . [H]erein lies the ancestral theme of disguise, the essential attribute of gods, police and bandits. Yet, in the vision of Fashion, the ludic motif does not involve what might be called a vertigo effect: it multiplies the person without any risk to her of losing herself.[79]

Many selves multiply wants and needs. Defining fashion as "an image system constituted with desire as its goal," Barthes describes allure, critical to a definition of all dandies.[80] But dandies play contradictory roles in *The Fashion System*: seemingly set apart at the beginning of his discussion, they are linked with sports figures, the clergy, and eccentrics, whose clothing tends to identify them at a glance. "If we go beyond a few rudimentary signs (eccentricity, classicism, dandyism, sport, ceremony)," Barthes inquires, "can clothing signify without recourse to the speech that describes it?" However, dandies do not escape "the unavoidable presence of human speech."[81] They return to the discussion in Barthes's speculations on fashion and femininity, "two fundamental signifieds of an anthropological order: sex and the body." "Feminine clothing can absorb nearly all masculine clothing. . . . Fashion noteably acknowledges the *boyish look*."[82] Barthes gives examples of "certain forms of modern dandyism which tend to feminize masculine apparel." But if, for Barthes, modern dandies are androgynous, it is because "The *boyish look* itself has more a temporal than a sexual value." This is "a profound process of Fashion: it is age which is important, not sex."[83] For Barthes "Both sexes tend to become uniform under a certain sign . . . that of *youth*."[84]

Do non-youthful dandies exist?[85] Perhaps. The dandiacal facade could be said to encourage them, for its polish allows no signs of the passage of time. But if dandies stop time, they are in no way timeless. Rather they are repositories of time whose bodily appearance is the record of the hours of labor that went into the creation of the affect. Dandies are time capsules of sartorial events. Their appearance is a presentation of results and has the density, the history, of lived experience. Or, as Barthes commented on the details that fuse fashion with quotidian actualities, "Fashion rhetoric is paradoxically more real insofar as it is absorbed by a coherent reality dependent on an entire social reality."[86]

"Masquerade" is another paradigm contributing to a theory of female dandies, for it offers a way of questioning and going beyond the construct of the phallic woman that works to reduce "women," plural and various, to a monolithic and essentialist stereotype of "woman," that posits a stereotyped male spectator. Jane Gaines has mapped out a context and parameters for a masquerade paradigm that includes female spectators—"the woman in the audience" as well as "the woman in the text" (or, since so much of work theorizing gender identity as a construct has come from feminist film theory, "the woman on stage"). Masquerade is a critiquing mode, inherently deeply conscious of self-construction. It explores the "radical possibilities of what might be called spectatorial cross dressing," a vision that, as Gaines notes, "takes its inspiration from the socially subversive meanings and increased options of sexual disguise."[87] Since it is not only audiences but also the actors themselves who cultivate a new awareness of gender fluidity, its possibilities are double edged. In *Blonde Venus* (1932), as both Ann Kaplan and Gaylen Studlar have pointed out, Marlene Dietrich let her viewers know that she was completely conscious of how her image was fabricated and used. This knowledge shared by Dietrich's audience thus questions and adds new meanings to the movie's spectacle.[88] Studlar points out, "By creating herself through masquerade and performance . . . the woman gains power through her knowledge of how others see her."[89] It is with such new screen images in mind that Anke Gleber argues that in the 1920s movie theaters opened up new spectatorial territory for women, who could move into the role of the female flaneur: at the movies "women enter[ed] a world of images . . . long . . . denied to them on the streets."[90]

Barthes's ruminations in his essay "The Face of Garbo" offer another example of subversive self-knowledge, entrancing to its audience, for as Barthes noted, Garbo's "face is almost sexually undefined, without however leaving one in doubt. It is true that this film (in which Queen Christina is by turns a woman and young cavalier) lends itself to this lack of differentiation; but Garbo does not transform in it any feat of transvestism." Whether male or female, Barthes pointed out, Garbo is "always herself."[91] Building her analysis on possibilities offered by Deleuze's reinterpretation of masochistic theory, Studlar describes Marlene Dietrich as irreducible to anything other than her own selfhood: Dietrich's performance where she distances herself from "all her assumed costumes—whether the ambiguously male or the excessively feminine—is typical of masochistic masquerade in which the participants operate on the belief that sexual and social identity is as easily assumed and rejected as a piece of clothing." Her "trademark" male attire expresses the belief that "it is possible to become both sexes."[92]

If the masquerade paradigm is useful for a discussion of all dandies whose power is performative, coming to full expression socially as a form of dialogue, it is particularly serviceable as a tool for recognizing female dandies when their dandy's attire is not the male suit. Wayne Koestenbaum's interpretation of the iconic allure of Jacqueline Kennedy Onassis offers a notable instance of a dandy's elegance, rendered as female.[93] Koestenbaum speaks of "Jackie as Dandy . . . the artificer . . . an entrepreneur of appearances."[94] Throughout her life as Jacqueline Bouvier, Jackie Kennedy, and Jackie Onassis, she invoked dandies and dandyism, beginning with an essay she wrote in 1951 that won the *Vogue* Prix de Paris contest, in which she chose famous dandies (Baudelaire and Oscar Wilde) as the historical figures she would most have wished to meet. Koestenbaum sees Jackie as an artist, for she "produced a public persona that had the attributes of an art-work."[95] In fact, as he points out, Jackie adapted a dandy's pose in a fantasy of ideal behavior; she envisioned herself as "a sort of Over-all Art Director of the Twentieth Century, watching everything from a chair hanging in space" (and thus reminding us that in the early 1810s, Beau Brummell had been accustomed to view the passing London scene from his bay-window club chair at White's).[96] Throughout her life, Jackie reigned over "the realm of surfaces."[97] Koestenbaum's analysis directs attention to the participatory appeal of her dandyism: "Our contingent is, finally, partner and collaborator in Jackie's undercover dandyism. . . . As object of delectation, as pleasure-inspiring personage, Jackie turns us into dandies; loving Jackie, or indulging in our curiosity about her life, we participate in an aesthetic experience without borders or design."[98] Jackie was a Brummellian dandy in the sense that it was not only her attire, but her presence, a free-floating acting out of elegance and selves, that contributed to her dandyism. Her example also offers an alternate model for new definitions of female dandies that subsume a transvestite definition, without letting go of the rich aesthetic fabrications that enliven cross-dressing. One might even say that Jackie as dandy lived her life "in drag," if one uses the term as Parker Tyler once did in describing Garbo's image: "Garbo 'got in drag' whenever she took some heavy glamour part. . . . How resplendent seems the art of acting! It is all *impersonation.*"[99]

As Esther Newton has written of camp impersonation, "appearance is an illusion."[100] In this sense, the masquerade paradigm broadens the territory for androgyny while still allowing for a density of selves in play. Masquerade builds on the recognition of fullness and abundance in androgyny: androgyny can signal the presence of "'more' sexuality, meaning *both* feminine *and* masculine appeal."[101] Even in the many situations where, as in Caroline Evans and Minna Thornton's descriptions of the British club scene blitz culture in the 1980s, masquerade offers only the "traditional stuff of the feminine position," the paradigm works to tease out the *joie de vivre* of female dandies:

> Girls used the subcultural space of the clubs to have fun, especially through dressing up. . . . Dressing up offers the possibility of narcissistic speculation, curiosity, dressing up together in pairs, comparing, contrasting and giggling, a possibility of fantasy and exploration, not in any sense finding a "true self" but, rather, of exploring the shifting relation between being and appearance, seeing and being seen.[102]

## Women as Dandies: Sightings and History

New glimpses of female dandies take on definition seen through a refocused lens of theory and history. Their presence can be discerned in events that begin with the Industrial Revolution, when working-class women moved outside their homes to labor in factories; to stroll in parks, streets, and museums; and to enter the commercial public spaces of the new department stores. Theirs is a complex appearance for, as Rita Felski has pointed out, it exposes "the potential instability of traditional gender divides, even as their versions of these [male] discourses often reveal suggestive and interesting differences." Potential contenders for a dandy's mantle can be discerned in Felski's pragmatism: "It is . . . important to acknowledge the female presence within . . . spheres often seen as the exclusive province of men. . . . [r]ather than reading such strategies as pathological signs of women's subsumption into an all-embracing phallocentrism."[103]

Where can images of these dandies be found? It is intriguing to lead off a taxonomy with the description of one anonymous but highly visible figure: the tiny figure of a woman at the intersection of the rue de Miromesnil and the boulevard des Malherbes in Gustave Caillebotte's *Young Man at His Window* (1876). Crisply fashionable even at a distance, she seems to have paused before crossing from rue to Boulevard. She is central to the painting, even a hinge of the picture's meaning. In *Young Man at His Window*, Kirk Varnedoe claimed, "the perspective and the gaze itself draw us . . . [into] a charged relationship that is seemingly unprecedented. . . . In Caillebotte's oscillating image, the confrontation is . . . between . . . two different forms of . . . solitude."[104] Tamar Garb's analysis of *Young Man at His Window* emphasizes not solitude but surveillance. Directing our attention to "the elevated vantage point from which [the young man] peruses the street," she notes, "his gaze almost tangibly fixes on the passing figure of a woman in the almost deserted street below." Elsewhere Garb defines this woman as a Parisienne, "a generic term for describing the emergence of a particularly modern, particularly French form of femininity." This was a woman for whom "The city constituted her stage. It was here that she performed her part, always aware of being watched, always watching herself."[105]

But what constitutes surveillance? Is it necessarily complicit? Does it count as surveillance if, for example, as with the woman at the intersection in Caillebotte's painting, that person does not know that she is being watched? One might attempt to argue that the man in the window is not looking at the woman at the intersection (his head is turned slightly to her right), although it seems that Caillebotte wanted us to think that he was; he isolated the woman and centered her in her place on the sidewalk, a spot circumscribed by the boundary lines of the window balustrade, the sidewalk edge, and cast shadow. If I dwell on surveillance or escape from its purview it is because, in at least one important definition of a dandy's mode of behavior, the activity would seem to exclude women from dandyism, since they tend to be conventionally positioned as objects of male gaze. But dandies, though looked at (for, of course, it is being looked at that activates the private show and public spectacle of dandyism), look right back. They are looking subjects whose performative impact surrounds them like an aura; sartorial projection is protection. They are not simple (and not passive) recipients of a gaze. On the contrary. Looking goes in both directions. And even if it isn't a large portion of the sidewalk ("newly asphalted," Garb mentions, to accommodate her presence) that Caillebotte's woman occupies, still, as with the men, there is at least some space on the street for her as the female dandy flaneuse whose consciousness of being seen does not at all prevent her from looking back.[106] The nineteenth century has produced a few notable images of female dandies, among the most resonant Manet's paintings of Victorine Meurent, whose resplendent nakedness in *Dejeuner sur l'herbe* (1863) and in *Olympia* (1863) is its own form of dandyism. Victorine in *Olympia* offers what is perhaps dandyism's most radical and economical construction: no clothes, satin slippers, and a little black ribbon. As Eunice Lipton has rediscovered her for us, she is a woman whose naked body said, "See this? It's mine."[107]

Meurent's remarkable presence is, as Molly Nesbit has described her, "far more than a type":

> she stood for the city's women of whatever class so long as they were beautiful and a bit tart; finally she came to stand for the city itself. The city was forever confused with these women; the tourists were confused by them. One of Joyce's Dubliners, the gaudy Ignatius Gallager, summed up the wonders of the city by marvelling, "There's no woman like the Parisienne—for style, for go."[108]

And if, as Garb has suggested, "Her embellished person represented a femininity which was packaged for its display value" in a game of partnerings and marriages, it is "display value" that serves in a description of a dandy.[109] But she could be a dandy in other situations as well, as Léa de Lonval, Colette's courtesan heroine of *Chérie* (1951), could wittily have pointed out. Léa de Lonval (her name in dandified self-construction changed from the more ordinary Léonie Vallon) inhabited a world arguably like the one offered by Georges Seurat's *Sunday Afternoon on the Island of La Grande Jatte* (1884–86), a painting that offers a flaneuse dandy for our recognition: the severely elegant woman who walks a monkey on a leash as a complement to her outfit. With her top-hatted companion, she surveys the Sunday crowd on the island from a dandy observer's vantage point on the periphery—the extreme right foreground corner of the painting. Since, as with this couple, the majority of Seurat's leisure-seekers are depicted looking toward the sun and toward the water, it almost seems as if the painting's activities unroll from their gaze.

Leila Kinney has discussed *La Grande Jatte* from the point of view of the new forms of leisure that went along with industrialization—"a somatic awareness" that transformed French painting after around 1850.[110] Noting that the title of Seurat's painting gives both the place and the day—Sunday—she analyzes Seurat using Balzac's convictions about the importance of nuances, "the revealing signs of character and class," to direct our attention to the meaning of Seurat's Sunday scene.

> Balzac is precise: Sunday is the great leveler, the day on which the true man of leisure's distinction from his opposite becomes inoperative. . . . [O]n this day everyone amuses themselves and takes the air, everyone has a white shirt and clean suit, "l'homme comme il faut" could hardly do "comme tout le monde." On this one day of rest for the rest of the world, the man of leisure stays home.[111]

Seurat's *Grande Jatte* adds the profound, popularized dandyism of working-class men and women dandies to our compendium of dandies' appearances.

Kinney's analysis offers an avenue to pursue in a discussion of twentieth-century female dandies, among them, as Ellen Moers once claimed, the New Woman, "the lady . . . with a cigarette, a bicycle and a will of her own."[112] The twentieth century abounds in female dandies from all classes, such as those introduced in American painting: John Singer Sargent's portrait of Mrs. Isaac Newton Phelps Stokes (1897) confidently facing a new century wearing mannish starched tennis clothes instead of a ball gown, and John Sloan's exuberant crowds of working girls turned out to the nines who occupy center sidewalk in New York beginning in the 1910s.[113] All of these women break into new territory, and their clothing, chosen with care and worn with bravura and panache, is very necessary equipment for their new adventures. Even in adversity. George Orwell wrote of the dandyism of unemployed inhabitants of Lancashire and Yorkshire in the 1930s, "You may have threepence in your pocket and not a prospect in the world; but in your new clothes you can stand on the street corner, indulging in a private daydream of yourself as Clark Gable or Greta Garbo."[114] And with these dreams we are brought back to the Takarazukienne Anna Jun. Let us return to her photograph and take notice of the ground this dandy occupies: Bakhtin's boundaryland, the wonderfully generative margin replete with new dialogues and ways of being—outside the wall.

## Different Dandies: Sightings across History and Cultures

The dandies in every city look different.    —Adolf Loos, 1898

And not only in cities, although Adolf Loos's comment on diversity is trenchant. The essays in this volume offer their authors' investigations into unrecognized dandyisms in unexplored locales in North America, Western and Eastern Europe, and Africa. These are dandyisms with meanings activated, but only in part illuminated, by the late-eighteenth-century Brummellian example, although they retain aspects of Beau Brummell's mode of being deploying his fashionable body—his impeccable, unmatchable elegance of attire and demeanor—for social, economic, and political empowerment. This book's contributors demonstrate that dandiacal self-construction is not subsumed within Brummell's example, even if one takes into account his charismatic influence. They explore the sartorial staging that links constructed selfhood and cultural identity—the performative lives of dandies in operation visually both as sign and tool. Rhonda K. Garelick and Robert E. Moore observe the worlds of commerce and culture brokering. Carter Ratcliff, Susan Fillin-Yeh, Joe Lucchesi, and Jennifer Blessing analyze the various worlds of modernist and postmodern experimental art and sexually inflected artistic self-construction. Kimberly Miller hybridizes strategies drawn from anthropology, literary criticism, and linguistics to analyze the dandy-like ambiguities of gloriously clothed male Gelede dancers who are the embodiments of women in the socio-spiritual negotiations of 1980s Yoruba masked performance.

Richard J. Powell's and Mark Allen Svede's dandies enact political protest. Powell directs our attention to "black male sartorial expressivity" and the "black men who were called 'dandies'" in nineteenth- and twentieth-century America, who have been mostly absent from serious studies of race. Foregrounding methodology that interlocks social and political analysis with his subjects' "outwardly expressive, aesthetic selves," he quotes from Amiri Baraka to remind us that "Ideology and style are the same thing." Svede describes 1950s Komsomol (communist youth activist) attacks on subversive young *stiliagi* (stylish ones) sporting narrow-legged pants, checkered jackets, and Tarzan-style curled hair, who began to appear in Moscow, L'vov, Riga, and Tallinn after Stalin's death. He analyzes the improbable and varied *fin-de-Soviet* protest personae of Latvian dandy conceptual/performance artists Andris Grinbergs and Miervaldis Polis, beginning in the late 1960s.

The essays contribute to an expansive and cross-cultural materialist parade of dandiacal appearance and performance—the transcendent power of the adorned body as a source of critical knowledge—and they reward examination through many lenses. Moore's and Powell's essays are studies not only of dandies, but also of white anxiety when confronted with exquisitely dressed "Others." Moore asks, "Were these [Indian] performances of sartorial hybridity and cross-cultural dandyism something more aggressive—and ultimately more 'civilized'—than any of the European parties to these encounters could possibly afford to admit?" The activities of female dandies are subjects for Lucchesi, Blessing, Fillin-Yeh, and Garelick. Romaine Brooks, Claude Cahun, Georgia O'Keeffe, and Coco Chanel used the male dandiacal stance as a springboard to innovate distinctive modes of being and negotiate the territory of gender and art making along new paths. Brooks, Lucchesi demonstrates, reworked the figure of the late-nineteenth-century European dandy, and transformed its male cultural connotations in paintings that map a new site for lesbian sensuality. At the same time, Lucchesi notes, Brooks refused to accept the notion that her elegant "masculinely tailored" clothing was the outward visual sign of an inner pathology or, for that matter, the outward sign of anything at all except her own carefully orchestrated inventions of presentation and costume.

Such fluidity in gendered signification characterizes female dandies. As Garelick points out, Coco Chanel's vision for clothing design that was dandyesque in its spare elegance and "luxe caché" was a "Chanel revolution" in garments for women that were boyish and encouraged athleticism, and it was echoed in her celebrity status as a couturière "'garçonne' heroine." Claude Cahun, who, Blessing tells us, realized a dandy's "idealistic belief in self-creation" and artifice, made self-portraits in which multiple Claudes appear. In her art, she was simultaneously a male and a female impersonator, thus reminding us again that, as Judith Butler has demonstrated, all gender is impersonation. I discuss Georgia O'Keeffe's cross-dressed appearance in a dandy's austere black and white suiting as an activating counterpoint to her evolution as an experimental, modernist artist.

Carter Ratcliff casts an art historical net gathering in many of the great traditional figures of dandyism—Baudelaire, Whistler, Oscar Wilde—whose example fueled other artist dandies (Romaine Brooks's and Claude Cahun's pervasively dandiacal yet vastly different artistic modes were both influenced by connections with Wilde). Ratcliff switches focus to discuss not actual dandies but their behavior. He isolates the dandiacal austerities of blankness and acausality to construct a dandy's template for art making in avant-garde modernism beginning with Whistler and Manet. He singles out mid- and later twentieth-century American artists whose work offers "at least a shadow of resistance to the demand that a painting be a cause whose effect is a meaning that an institution can use." A useful observation. If there is anything that dandies share (as Mark Svede might put it), it is resistance to all manner of restrictions, even the inevitabilities of gravity and aging, time and death. "Style prevents you from being part of a group," the late Quentin Crisp told Rhonda Garelick. In offering readers instances of highly evolved and consummate dandiacal control over appearances, this volume's authors—and their subjects—exhibit the "finesse" of the book's title, a profound sartorial resonance.

NOTES

1. Charles Baudelaire, "The Salon of 1846," in *The Mirror of Art*, trans. and ed. Jonathan Mayne (Ithaca: Cornell University Press, 1965), 116–20. See also Ellen Moers, *The Dandy* (Lincoln: University of Nebraska Press, 1960), 272. For an account of modern men's tailoring and its allure, see Anne Hollan-

der, *Sex and Suits: The Evolution of Modern Dress* (New York: Kodansha, 1995), esp. chap. 4, "Modernity," 116–73.

2. Baudelaire, "The Salon of 1846," 128. Jules Barbey d'Aurevilly's *Du dandysme et de George Brummell* appeared in 1844.

3. Charles Baudelaire, "The Painter of Modern Life," in *The Painter of Modern Life and Other Essays*, trans. and ed. Jonathan Mayne (New York: Phaidon, 1970), 5. See also Rhonda Garelick's discussion of Baudelaire's vision of dandyism in *Rising Star: Dandyism, Gender, and Performance in the Fin de Siècle* (Princeton: Princeton University Press, 1998), 27–40.

4. Baudelaire, "The Painter of Modern Life," 7.

5. Ibid., 9, 12.

6. Ibid., 26.

7. Moers, *The Dandy*, 11–12.

8. Caroline Evans and Minna Thornton, "Chanel: The New Woman as Dandy," in *Women and Fashion* (London: Quartet Books, 1989), 124, for a analysis of the Chanel style.

9. Karl Marx, *Capital* (London: Lawrence and Wishart, 1983), 1:77–79. This connection between dress and commodities is discussed by Malcolm Barnard, *Fashion as Communication* (New York: Routledge, 1996), 7.

10. Baudelaire, "The Painter of Modern Life," 31, 33. See also Jules Barbey d'Aurevilly, *Dandyism* (1845; reprint with a preface by Quentin Crisp, New York: PAJ Publications, 1998), 64: "For Dandies, as for women, to *seem* is to *be*." See also Garelick, *Rising Star*, 34. For a discussion of dandiacal relations with women, see Jessica Feldman, *Gender on the Divide: The Dandy in Modernist Literature* (Ithaca: Cornell University Press, 1993), 6–10.

11. Barbey d'Aurevilly, *Dandyism*, 33–34 and passim.

12. Baudelaire, "The Painter of Modern Life," 27–28.

13. Barbey d'Aurevilly, *Dandyism*, 31.

14. Domna Stanton, *The Aristocrat as Art* (New York: Columbia University Press, 1980), 6, 43.

15. Source documents for the social and political roots of dandyism are Baudelaire, "The Painter of Modern Life," 28; and Barbey d'Aurevilly, *Dandyism*, 40. See also Max Beerbohm, "Dandies and Dandies," in *The Works* (New York: Dodd, Mead, 1922), 3–32; and Susan Sontag, "Notes on Camp," in *Against Interpretation* (New York: Laurel, 1966), 285, 289–291. For Warhol, see Mark Francis and Margery King, *The Warhol Look: Glamour, Style, Fashion* (exhibition catalogue) (Boston: Little, Brown, 1997).

16. Barbey d'Aurevilly, *Dandyism*, 78. Barbey d'Aurevilly's text concludes by identifying a hermaphroditic, classical Greek dandy, Alcibiades. For an account of Alcibiades' life, see Plutarch, *The Lives of the Noble Grecians and Romans*, trans. John Dryden (New York: Modern Library, 1932), 233–62, esp. 234, 243, 249.

17. See Danae Clark, "Commodity Lesbianism," in *The Lesbian and Gay Studies Reader*, ed. Henry Abelove, Michèle Aina Barale, and David M. Halperin (New York: Routledge, 1993), 188–89; 198 for insights into dandiacal behavior.

18. See E. Ann Kaplan, *Women and Film: Both Sides of the Camera* (New York: Methuen, 1983) and Tania Modleski, *The Women Who Know Too Much* (New York: Methuen, 1988). Important early articulations of the construction of gender include Joan Riviere, "Womanliness as Masquerade," *International Journal of Psychoanalysis* 10 (1929), reprinted in *Formations of Fantasy*, ed. Victor Burgin, James Donald, and Cora Kaplan (London: Routledge, 1986), 35–44; and Laura Mulvey, "Visual Pleasure and Narrative Cinema," *Screen* 16, no. 2 (1975): 6–18.

19. Marjorie Garber, *Vested Interests: Cross Dressing and Cultural Anxiety* (New York: Routledge, 1992), 10, 16.

20. For examples and discussion, see Elizabeth Wilson, *Adorned in Dreams: Fashion and Modernity* (Berkeley: University of California Press, 1987), 228–47; and also Angela Carter, "Elizabeth Wilson, Adorned in Dreams," in *Shaking a Leg: Collected Writings* (New York: Penguin, 1997), 138–41. See also Elizabeth Wilson, "Fashion and the Postmodern Body," in *Chic Thrills: A Fashion Reader*, ed. Juliet Ash and Elizabeth Wilson (Berkeley: University of California Press, 1993), 5–6; Evans and Thornton, *Women and Fashion*, 1–16; Linda Nochlin, "Whose Vision Is It Anyway?" interview with Thierry Mugler, moderated by Holly Bruback, *New York Times Magazine*, July 17, 1994, 46–49; and studies of dress by Mary Ellen Roach, Joanne Bubolz Eicher, and Ruth Barnes, among them, Ruth Barnes and Joanne B. Eicher, *Dress and Gender* (New York: Berg, 1992).

21. Roland Barthes, "Le Dandysme et la mode," in *Le Mythe du dandy*, ed. Emilien Carassus (Paris: Armand Colin, 1971), 314–15. See also Roland Barthes, *The Fashion System*, trans. Matthew Ward and Richard Howard (New York: Hill and Wang), 1983, 256.

22. See Dick Hebdige, *Subculture: The Meaning of Style* (New York: Methuen, 1979), 17, and passim; Stuart Cosgrove, "The Zoot-Suit and Style Warfare," *History Workshop* 18 (autumn 1984): 77–91; Angela McRobbie, *Zoot Suits and Second Hand Dresses* (Boston: Unwin Hyman, 1988); and Ash and Wilson, *Chic Thrills: A Fashion Reader*, 3–16.

23. Michel Foucault, *The History of Sexuality*, vol. 1, *An Introduction* (New York: Vintage, 1980), 93.

24. For essays exploring flaneurs' contributions to the understanding of both modern and postmodern conditions, see Keith Tester, ed., *The Flâneur* (New York: Routledge, 1994). For "the social life of city sidewalks," see Jane Jacobs, *The Death and Life of Great American Cities* (New York: Vintage, 1961), 55–73.

25. Walter Benjamin, *Charles Baudelaire: A Lyric Poet in the Era of High Capitalism* (New York: Verso, 1997), 36, 155.

26. Ibid., 37. See Deborah J. Haynes, *Bakhtin and the Visual Arts* (Cambridge: Cambridge University Press, 1995), 19, 85, 101.

27. Natalie Zemon Davis, *Women on the Margins* (Cambridge: Harvard University Press, 1995), 210. See also Sherry B. Ortner on "borderland politics" in "Borderland Politics and Erotics," in *Making Gender: The Politics and Erotics of Culture* (Boston: Beacon Press, 1996), 181–212.

28. Barbara Babcock-Abrahams, "'A Tolerated Margin of Mess': The Trickster and His Tales Reconsidered," *Journal of the Folklore Institute* 11 (1975): 155.

29. Guy Scarpetta, as quoted in Susan Rubin Suleiman, *Risking Who One Is: Encounters with Contemporary Art and Literature* (Cambridge: Harvard University Press, 1994), 236.

30. Mary Ellen Roach and Joanne Bubolz Eicher, "The Language of Personal Adornment," in *The Fabrics of Culture: The Anthropology of Culture and Adornment*, ed. Justine Cordwell and Ronald Schwarz (The Hague: Mouton, 1979), 7.

31. Baudelaire, "The Painter of Modern Life," 26.

32. Erwin Panofsky, *Studies in Iconology* (New York: Harper and Row, 1967), 15.

33. Jules Prown, "Mind in Matter: An Introduction to Material Culture Theory," *Winterthur Portfolio* 17, no. 1 (spring 1982): 1–19.

34. Georg Simmel, *Fashion, Individuality and Social Forms* (Chicago: University of Chicago Press, 1971), 311. See also Baudelaire, "The Painter of Modern Life," 27–28.

35. J. C. Flugel, *The Psychology of Clothes* (1930; reprint, London: Hogarth Press and the Institute of Psycho-Analysis, 1950).

36. Feldman, *Gender on the Divide*, 11.

37. Roach and Eicher, "The Language of Personal Adornment," 15 and passim. See also Mary Ellen Roach and Joanne Bubolz Eicher, *Dress, Adornment and the Social Order* (New York: John Wiley and Sons, 1965).

38. Hebdige, *Subculture*, 17.

39. Cosgrove, "The Zoot-Suit and Style Warfare," 78.

40. Quoted in ibid., 79.

41. Hildi Hendrickson, ed., *Clothing and Difference: Embodied Identities in Colonial and Post Colonial Africa* (Durham: Duke University Press, 1996), 2. For a useful analysis of "inhabited" clothing styles that "imply a radically reconfigured social identity, marked by the control over consciously acquired multicultural capital," see Johanna Schoss, "Dressed to 'Shine': Work, Leisure, and Style in Malindi, Kenya," in Hendrickson, *Clothing and Difference*, 183–84.

42. Hendrickson, *Clothing and Difference*, 15.

43. Hebdige, *Subculture*, 13.

44. James Laver, *Dandies* (London: Weidenfeld and Nicolson, 1968), 10–12.

45. Moers, *The Dandy*, 21.

46. Ibid., 17.

47. The painting is in the collection of the Museum of Fine Arts, Boston.

48. Ibid., 99.

49. Benjamin, *Baudelaire*, 37.

50. Ibid. See also Susan Buck-Morss, *The Dialectics of Seeing: Walter Benjamin and the Arcades Project* (Cambridge: MIT Press, 1999).

51. Benjamin, *Baudelaire*, 54.

52. Ibid.

53. Ibid., 171.

54. Ibid., 103, 96. There is an interesting analogy to be made with the vacant stare practiced in punk culture. See Hebdige, *Subculture*, 65.

55. Benjamin, *Baudelaire*, 96.

56. Baudelaire, "The Salon of 1846," 128.

57. See Jennifer Robertson, "The Politics of Androgyny in Japan: Sexuality and Subversion in the Theater and Beyond," *American Ethnologist* 19, no. 3 (August 1992): 419–42. Anna Jun's photograph appears on p. 434 of Robertson's pioneering study. See also Jennifer Robertson, *Takarazuka: Sexual Politics and Popular Culture in Modern Japan* (Berkeley: University of California Press, 1998), 47–88, and fig. 9.

58. The majority of Takarazuka fans are women. See Kim Longinotto and Jano Williams, *Dream Girls*, color film, 50 min., distributed by Women Make Movies, 1994.

59. Janet Wolff, "The Invisible *Flâneuse*: Women and the Literature of Modernity," *Theory, Culture and Society* 2, no. 3 (1985): 45.

60. Baudelaire, "The Painter of Modern Life," 5.

61. Wolff, "The Invisible *Flâneuse*," 41.

62. Quoted in Ellen Moers, *Literary Women: The Great Writers* (New York: Doubleday, 1976), 9.

63. Ibid. The painter Marie Blaskirtseff wrote in 1879, "What I long for is the Freedom of going about alone. . . . of walking about old streets at night." See Anke Gleber, "Female Flânerie and the *Symphony of the City*," in *Women in the Metropolis,* ed. Katharina Von Ankum (Berkeley: University of California Press, 1997), 73.

64. Carolyn G. Heilbrun, *Writing a Woman's Life* (New York: Norton, 1988), 35–36.

65. Ibid., 42.

66. bell hooks, *Outlaw Culture: Resisting Representations* (New York: Routledge, 1994), 210.

67. Robertson, "The Politics of Androgyny in Japan," 436.

68. Ibid., 419.

69. Garber, *Vested Interests*, 338. See also Annette Kuhn as quoted in Jane Gaines, "Fabricating the Female Body," in *Fabrications: Costume and the Female Body*, ed. Jane Gaines and Charlotte Herzog (New York: Routledge, 1990), 27.

70. Gaylen Studlar, "Masochism, Masquerade and the Erotic Metamorphosis of Marlene Dietrich," in Gaines and Herzog, *Fabrications*, 247.

71. Virginia Woolf, *Orlando: A Biography* (1928; reprint, New York: Harcourt Brace, 1960), 144.

72. Ibid., 144–45.

73. For a discussion, see Garber, *Vested Interests*, 5–9.

74. For a fashion world example, see Peter Lindberg's photographs of star models Linda Evangelista, Naomi Campbell, and Christy Turlington dressed in gangster style in *Vogue Italia*, no. 483–504 (February 1991).

75. Laura Mulvey, as discussed by Studlar in "Masochism," 231.

76. Deborah Cameron as quoted in Heilbrun, *Writing a Woman's Life*, 16.

77. Garber, *Vested Interests*, 12. See also Kim Michasiw, "Camp, Masculinity and Masquerade," and Carol-Anne Tyler, "Passing: Narcissism, Identity and Difference," in *Feminism Meets Queer Theory*, ed. Elizabeth Weed and Naomi Schor (Bloomington: Indiana University Press, 1997), 157–86, 227–65.

78. Garber, *Vested Interests*, 10.

79. Barthes, *The Fashion System*, 256–57.

80. Ibid., xii.

81. Ibid., xi.

82. Ibid., 257.

83. Ibid., 258.

84. Ibid., 257.

85. For a view of dandyism and youthfulness, see Oscar Wilde, *The Picture of Dorian Gray* (1891; reprint, Mineola, NY: Dover, 1993).

86. Barthes, *The Fashion System*, 284.

87. Gaines, "Fabricating the Female Body," 25. See also note 18.

88. Gaines and Herzog, *Fabrications*, 25–26; and Studlar, "Masochism," 242.

89. Studlar, "Masochism," 243.

90. Gleber, "Female Flânerie and the *Symphony of the City*," 84.

91. Roland Barthes, *Mythologies* (New York: Hill and Wang, 1972), 56.

92. Studlar, "Masochism," 244, 245.

93. Jackie wrote the account of another female dandy, her friend the fashion arbiter Diana Vreeland. See Wayne Koestenbaum, *Jackie under My Skin: Interpreting an Icon* (New York: Farrar, Straus and Giroux, 1995), 180, for a discussion of Diana Vreeland, "another inheritor of the dandy mantle." See

also Diana Vreeland, *D.V.*, ed. George Plimpton and Christopher Hemphill (New York: Da Capo, 1997).

94. Koestenbaum, *Jackie under My Skin*, 179.

95. Ibid., 182.

96. Ibid.

97. Ibid., 186. See also Hebdige, *Subculture*, 16–17, for his discussion of "the profoundly superficial level of appearances."

98. Koestenbaum, *Jackie under My Skin*, 186.

99. Parker Tyler, as quoted in Judith Butler, *Gender Trouble: Feminism and the Subversion of Identity* (New York: Routledge, 1990), 128.

100. Esther Newton, as quoted in Butler, *Gender Trouble*, 137.

101. Janet Bergstrom, as quoted in Robertson, "The Politics of Androgyny in Japan," 435.

102. Evans and Thornton, *Women and Fashion*, 42.

103. Rita Felski, *The Gender of Modernity* (Cambridge: Harvard University Press, 1995), 21, 24.

104. Kirk Varnedoe, *Caillebotte* (New Haven: Yale University Press, 1987), 62.

105. Tamar Garb, *Bodies of Modernity: Figure and Flesh in Fin-de-Siècle France* (New York: Thames and Hudson, 1998), 31, 87, 88.

106. Ibid., 87.

107. Eunice Lipton, *Alias Olympia* (New York: Scribner's, 1992), 15.

108. Molly Nesbit, "In the absence of the parisienne. . . ," in *Sexuality and Space*, ed. Beatriz Colomina (New York: Princeton Architectural Press, 1992), 308.

109. Garb, *Bodies of Modernity*, 88.

110. Leila W. Kinney, "Fashion and Figuration in Modern Life Painting," in *Architecture: In Fashion*, ed. Deborah Fausch et al. (New York: Princeton Architectural Press, 1994), 278. I am grateful to Bob Herbert for this reference.

111. Ibid., 279.

112. Moers, *The Dandy*, 309.

113. Sargent's painting of Mr. and Mrs. Isaac Newton Phelps Stokes is in the Metropolitan Museum of Art, New York. Among Sloan's paintings are *Sunday in Union Square* (1912), Bowdoin College Museum of Art, Brunswick, Maine. Among the etchings of the subject are *Return from Toil* (1915), also published as a cover for *The Masses* 4 (July 1913); *Sixth Avenue, Greenwich Village* (1923); *Shine, Washington Square* (1923); and *Easter Eve, Washington Square* (1926). See John Sloan, *New York Etchings*, ed. Helen Farr Sloan (New York: Dover, 1978), plates 31, 48, 49, 56.

114. George Orwell, *The Road to Wigan Pier* (London: Penguin, 1989), 81–82.

BIBLIOGRAPHY

Babcock-Abrahams, Barbara. "'A Tolerated Margin of Mess': The Trickster and His Tales Reconsidered." *Journal of the Folklore Institute* 11 (1975): 155.

Barbey d'Aurevilly, Jules. *Dandyism*. 1845. Translated by Douglas Ainslie. Foreword by Quentin Crisp. New York: PAJ Publications, 1988.

Barnard, Malcolm. *Fashion as Communication*. New York: Routledge, 1996.

Barnes, Ruth, and Joanne B. Eicher. *Dress and Gender*. New York: Berg, 1992.

Barthes, Roland. "Le Dandysme et la mode." In *Le Mythe du dandy*, edited by Emilien Carassus. Paris: Armand Colin, 1971.

———. *The Fashion System*. Translated by Matthew Ward and Richard Howard. New York: Hill and Wang, 1983.

———. *Mythologies*. New York: Hill and Wang, 1972.

Baudelaire, Charles. "The Painter of Modern Life." In *The Painter of Modern Life and Other Essays*, edited and translated by Jonathan Mayne, 1–40. New York: Phaidon Press, 1970.

———. "The Salon of 1846." In *The Mirror of Art*, edited and translated by Jonathan Mayne. Ithaca: Cornell University Press, 1965.

Beerbohm, Max. "Dandies and Dandies." In *The Works*, 3–32. New York: Dodd, Mead, 1922.

Benjamin, Walter. *Charles Baudelaire: A Lyric Poet in the Era of High Capitalism*. New York: Verso, 1997.

Buck-Morss, Susan. *The Dialectics of Seeing: Walter Benjamin and the Arcades Project*. Cambridge: MIT Press, 1999.

Butler, Judith. *Gender Trouble: Feminism and the Subversion of Identity*. New York: Routledge, 1990.

Carter, Angela. "Elizabeth Wilson, Adorned in Dreams." In *Shaking a Leg: Collected Writings*. New York: Penguin, 1997.

Clark, Danae. "Commodity Lesbianism." In *The Lesbian and Gay Studies Reader*, edited by Henry Abelove, Michèle Aina Barale, and David Halperin. New York: Routledge, 1993.

Cosgrove, Stuart. "The Zoot-Suit and Style Warfare." *History Workshop* 18 (autumn 1984): 77–91.

Davis, Natalie Zemon. *Women on the Margins*. Cambridge: Harvard University Press, 1995.

Evans, Caroline, and Minna Thornton. *Women and Fashion*. London: Quartet Books, 1989.

Feldman, Jessica. *Gender on the Divide: The Dandy in Modernist Literature*. Ithaca: Cornell University Press, 1993.

Felski, Rita. *The Gender of Modernity*. Cambridge: Harvard University Press, 1995.

Flugel, J. C. *The Psychology of Clothes*. 1930. Reprint, London: Hogarth Press and the Institute of Psycho-Analysis, 1950.

Foucault, Michel. *The History of Sexuality*. Vol. 1, *An Introduction*. New York: Vintage, 1980.

Francis, Mark, and Margery King. *The Warhol Look: Glamour, Style, Fashion*. Boston: Little, Brown, 1997.

Gaines, Jane. "Fabricating the Female Body." In *Fabrications: Costume and the Female Body*, edited by Jane Gaines and Charlotte Herzog. New York: Routledge, 1990.

Garb, Tamar. *Bodies of Modernity: Figure and Flesh in Fin-de-Siècle France*. New York: Thames and Hudson, 1998.

Garber, Marjorie. *Vested Interests: Cross Dressing and Cultural Anxiety*. New York and London: Routledge, 1992.

Garelick, Rhonda. *Rising Star: Dandyism, Gender, and Performance in the Fin de Siècle*. Princeton: Princeton University Press, 1998.

Gleber, Anke. "Female Flânerie and the *Symphony of the City*." In *Women in the Metropolis*, edited by Katharina Von Ankum. Berkeley: University of California Press, 1997.

Haynes, Deborah. *Bakhtin and the Visual Arts*. Cambridge: Cambridge University Press, 1995.

Hebdige, Dick. *Subculture: The Meaning of Style*. New York: Methuen, 1979.

Heilbrun, Carolyn. *Writing a Woman's Life*. New York: Norton, 1988.

Hendrickson, Hildi. Introduction to *Clothing and Difference: Embodied Identities in Colonial and Post-Colonial Africa*, edited by Hildi Hendrickson. Durham: Duke University Press, 1996.

Hollander, Anne. *Sex and Suits: The Evolution of Modern Dress*. New York: Kodansha, 1995.

hooks, bell. *Outlaw Culture: Resisting Representation*. New York: Routledge, 1994.

Jacobs, Jane. *The Death and Life of Great American Cities*. New York: Vintage, 1961.

Kaplan, E. Ann. *Women and Film: Both Sides of the Camera*. New York: Methuen, 1983.

Kinney, Leila W. "Fashion and Figuration in Modern Life Painting." In *Architecture: In Fashion*, edited by Deborah Fausch, Paulette Singley, Rodolphe El Koury, and Zvi Efrat. New York: Princeton Architectural Press, 1994.

Koestenbaum, Wayne. *Jackie under My Skin: Interpreting an Icon*. New York: Farrar, Straus and Giroux, 1995.

Laver, James. *Dandies*. London: Weidenfeld and Nicolson, 1968.

Lindberg, Peter. "Omaggio alle stile di Al Capone." *Vogue Italia*, nos. 483–504 (February 1991).

Lipton, Eunice. *Alias Olympia*. New York: Scribner's, 1992.

Longinotto, Kim, and Jano Williams. *Dream Girls.* Color film, 50 min. Distributed by Women Make Movies, 1994.

Marx, Karl. *Capital.* Vol. 1. London: Lawrence and Wishart, 1983.

McRobbie, Angela. *Zoot Suits and Second Hand Dresses.* Boston: Unwin Hyman, 1988.

Michasiw, Kim. "Camp, Masculinity and Masquerade." In *Feminism Meets Queer Theory*, edited by Elizabeth Weed and Naomi Schor. Bloomington: Indiana University Press, 1997.

Modleski, Tania. *The Women Who Know Too Much.* New York: Methuen, 1988.

Moers, Ellen. *The Dandy: Brummell to Beerbohm.* Lincoln: University of Nebraska Press, 1960.

———. *Literary Women: The Great Writers.* New York: Doubleday, 1976.

Mulvey, Laura, "Visual Pleasure and Narrative Cinema." *Screen* 16, no. 2 (1975): 6–18.

Nesbit, Molly. "In the Absence of the Parisienne . . ." In *Sexuality and Space*, edited by Beatriz Colomina. New York: Princeton Architectural Press, 1992.

Nochlin, Linda. "Whose Vision Is It Anyway?" Interview with Thierry Mugler, moderated by Holly Bruback. *New York Times Magazine*, July 17, 1994, 46–49.

Ortner, Sherry. *Making Gender: The Politics and Erotics of Culture.* Boston: Beacon Press, 1996.

Orwell, George. *The Road to Wigan Pier.* London: Penguin, 1989.

Panofsky, Erwin. *Studies in Iconology.* New York: Harper and Row, 1967.

Plutarch. *The Lives of the Noble Grecians and Romans.* Translated by John Dryden. New York: Modern Library, 1932.

Prown, Jules. "Mind in Matter: An Introduction to Material Culture Theory." *Winterthur Portfolio* 17, no. 1 (spring 1982): 1–19.

Riviere, Joan. "Womanliness as Masquerade." *International Journal of Psychoanalysis* 10 (1929). Reprinted in *Formations of Fantasy*, edited by Victor Burgin, James Donald, and Cora Kaplan, 35–41. London: Routledge, 1986.

Roach, Mary Ellen, and Joanne Bubolz Eicher. *Dress, Adornment and the Social Order.* New York: John Wiley and Sons, 1965.

———. "The Language of Personal Adornment." In *The Fabrics of Culture: The Anthropology of Culture and Adornment*, edited by Justine M. Cordwell and Ronald A. Schwarz. The Hague: Mouton, 1979.

Robertson, Jennifer. "The Politics of Androgyny in Japan: Sexuality and Subversion in the Theater and Beyond." *American Ethnologist* 19, no. 3 (1992): 419–42.

———. *Takarazuka: Sexual Politics and Popular Culture in Modern Japan.* Berkeley: University of California Press, 1998.

Simmel, Georg. *Fashion, Individuality and Social Forms.* Chicago: University of Chicago Press, 1971.

Sloan, John. *New York Etchings*. Edited by Helen Farr Sloan. New York: Dover, 1978.

Sontag, Susan. "Notes on Camp." In *Against Interpretation*. New York: Laurel, 1966.

Stanton, Domna. *The Aristocrat as Art*. New York: Columbia University Press, 1980.

Studlar, Gaylen. "Masochism, Masquerade and the Erotic Metamorphosis of Marlene Dietrich." In *Fabrications: Costume and the Female Body*, edited by Jane Gaines and Charlotte Herzog. New York: Routledge, 1990.

Suleiman, Susan Rubin. *Risking Who One Is: Encounters with Contemporary Art and Literature*. Cambridge: Harvard University Press, 1994.

Tester, Keith, ed. *The Flâneur*. New York: Routledge, 1994.

Tyler, Carol-Ann. "Passing: Narcissism, Identity and Difference." In *Feminism Meets Queer Theory*, edited by Elizabeth Weed and Naomi Schor. Bloomington: Indiana University Press, 1997.

Varnedoe, Kirk. *Caillebotte*. New Haven: Yale University Press, 1987.

Vreeland, Diana. *D.V.* Edited by George Plimpton and Christopher Hemphill. New York: Da Capo, 1997.

Wilde, Oscar. *The Picture of Dorian Gray*. 1891. Reprint, Mineola, NY: Dover, 1993.

Wilson, Elizabeth. *Adorned in Dreams: Fashion and Modernity*. Berkeley: University of California Press, 1987.

———. "Fashion and the Postmodern Body." In *Chic Thrills: A Fashion Reader*, edited by Juliet Ash and Elizabeth Wilson. Berkeley: University of California Press, 1993.

Wolff, Janet. "The Invisible Flâneuse: Women and the Literature of Modernity." *Theory, Culture and Society* 2, no. 3 (1985): 45.

Woolf, Virginia. *Orlando: A Biography*. 1928. Reprint, New York: Harcourt Brace, 1960.

## Chapter 1

# The Layered Look
## *Coco Chanel and Contagious Celebrity*

## *Rhonda K. Garelick*

Fashion murdered dandyism, claims Roland Barthes: "To inoculate contemporary clothing with a bit of dandyism, via Fashion, was fatally to destroy dandyism itself. . . . Fashion was, in a sense, given the task of neutralizing dandyism. . . . [I]t is in fact Fashion that killed dandyism."[1] While Barthes was right to see the profound connection between modern fashion and dandyism, he was wrong about the fatal nature of their confrontation. Rather than kill dandyism, fashion actually helped escort it from its nineteenth-century incarnation as a social and literary movement into its twentieth-century version: modern media celebrity.[2] We can attribute a large part of fashion's role in this transition to the work of legendary French couturiere Gabrielle "Coco" Chanel. Chanel's designs extended and developed dandyism's innovations, ushering women into dandyism's all-male inner circle. By borrowing heavily from dandyism's vocabulary of performance, Chanel revolutionized the way we perceive the female body.

### The Dandy

Long before the rock star and the motion picture idol, the dandy had made an art form of personality. As both a literary and historical movement (there are famous fictional dandies, such as Huysmans's Des Esseintes or Wilde's Dorian Gray, as well as famous real dandies, such as George "Beau" Brummell or the Comte Robert de Montesquiou) dandyism necessarily merges the realms of art and the everyday, blurring distinctions between the natural and the unnatural. Dandyism also dismantles social distinctions by creating an aristocracy of the self that does not require nobility of birth. The dandy exists in a parallel hierarchy based on personal attributes rather than genealogy or property.

British-born Beau Brummell (1778–1840) enjoyed meteoric social success despite his common birth. Brummell's theatrical originality won him the affection of the royal family and effectively launched dandyism in both England and France. His reign coincided with the Regency of the future King George IV (1795–1820), who was for a time Brummell's closest friend.

Brummell was known for his impeccable grooming, his exquisitely simple and elegant clothes, and his androgynous appeal. His meticulousness was such that he was known to have hired three glove makers at once: one to make the palm, one for the fingers, and one for the thumb. Brummell's greatest achievement, however, lay in his ability to provoke surprise, desire, and envy, while, on his part, evincing no emotion at all. According to Jules Barbey d'Aurevilly, Brummell's social power was such that he could sometimes persuade creditors to overlook steep gambling debts merely by agreeing to greet them publicly in the street. Presumably, the social status acquired by any man whom Brummell deigned to acknowledge would be far more valuable than money.[3]

But, of course, Brummell was not just a famous historical person, he was the inspiration for much of the literary dandyism of the nineteenth century. Balzac and Barbey wrote of him; Lord Byron was fascinated by him, as were Benjamin Disraeli, Bulwer Lytton, Carlyle, Stendhal, and Baudelaire. Dandyist literature, in turn, inspired more young men to adopt dandyist ways, creating a cycle of life and art imitating each other. As a result, a real, historical dandy such as Brummell or later, Baudelaire is always part literary or theatrical creation. In similar fashion, a dandyist *text* is often a striking blend of purely fictive and "real" or biographical elements. Balzac, for example, in his nonfiction essay "Traité de la vie élégante" (Treatise on elegant living), includes an "interview" with Beau Brummell.[4] In it, he recounts verbatim advice he claims Brummell gave him on how to write and how to dress. The interview lends convincing journalistic flavor to the treatise (originally published in the right-wing newspaper *La Mode* in 1830), but in reality, Balzac had never interviewed or even met Brummell. Balzac's description of his meeting with Brummell, then, adds verisimilitude to the text while turning it to pure fiction. This is the quintessentially dandyist touch, an extra-diagetic reference that adds an air of authenticity and turns out to be pure fabrication.

## *The Dandy and the Media Celebrity or Star*

As the twentieth century neared, dandyism's spectacle of a unique male personality performing for an elite began losing ground. Mechanical reproduction and the rise of mass culture turned personality into a reproducible—and often female—commodity. Dandyist uniqueness and unreproducibility ceded to the thrill of the new stardom and its mass reproduction of performers' likenesses and biographies.[5] Cabaret stars such as Yvette Guilbert, La Goulue, and Loie Fuller captivated all social classes, even the aristocracy, especially in France. At the newly popular department stores, shoppers could buy clothes modeled after the costumes of their favorite performers. The emergence of cinema only intensified the new lure of celebrity culture.

Media stardom is a complex, multilayered phenomenon that resembles dandyism. "The star phenomenon," writes Richard Dyer, "consists of everything that is publicly available about stars. . . . [A] star's image is also what people say or write about him or her, as critics or commentators. . . . Star images are always extensive, multimedia, intertextual."[6] Unlike mere actors, stars always bring with them an extra layer of personal narrative that supplements whatever role they portray on stage or screen. Personal anecdote merges, in other words, with public, artistic creation. John Wayne, for example, always played "John Wayne," along with his various fictional movie roles. Katharine Hepburn also played a version of her famous, offscreen self while also portraying different characters. Modern fashion or haute couture partakes of the same layering effect, as we shall soon see.

## *Fashion*

Fashion's distinguishing characteristic is its changeability. Unlike simple dress or costume, fashion consists of a sequence of relatively rapid changes in style. Historians find fashion's roots in the late fourteenth or early fifteenth century, when a hitherto unknown realism began to appear in European art. The depiction of more natural, recognizable clothed human forms in early Renaissance painting and sculpture set new visual standards for dress. For perhaps the first time in history, one could find sartorial inspiration in art. In other words, one could try to look like a figure in a picture.[7] Like dandyism, then, fashion results from a curious admixture of the quotidian and the aesthetic realms. Both dandyism and fashion reify the body; both conflate the seduction of the human with the lure of the inanimate world.[8]

But fashion as we know it today, the "haute couture" associated with individual designers' names, did not take shape until the second half of the nineteenth century, when Englishman Charles Frederick Worth opened his Paris studio in 1857. Other famous couturiers from the period include Mme Jeanne Pacquin, who began designing in 1891, and Paul Poiret, who started gaining recognition around 1908.

Haute couture was (and, in a sense, still is) an industry devoted to extremely wealthy women. By the second decade of this century, however, mass production of clothing in factories had become common, allowing secretaries and housemaids to wear copies or "knockoffs" of couture creations.[9] Ironically then, haute couture, an elite art form, wound up creating something of a democracy of style, weakening clear-cut visual distinctions of social class that had long been held in place by sumptuary laws.[10] Like dandyism, then, fashion is both profoundly elitist and oddly democratic.

## Coco Chanel

Richard Klein has astutely noted the connection between dandyism and the work of Coco Chanel, as well as Chanel's status as a transitional figure: "I think the secret of Chanel's genius was that she was the last dandy of the nineteenth century, and in becoming one, destroyed . . . the nineteenth-century woman; she invented the woman of modernity."[11] What created this transition—from dandy to "woman of modernity," in Klein's words—is precisely media celebrity, which both transformed dandyism and made a revolutionary of Chanel.

Gabrielle "Coco" Chanel was not the first famous fashion designer. She was not even the first famous female fashion designer: among those preceding her were the Callot sisters, Madeleine Vionnet, and Madame Palmyre. Chanel was, however, the first *celebrity* fashion designer, the

first couturiere to insert her own personality into her designs so power-
fully that "wearing a Chanel" turned into "wearing Chanel," wearing
the persona constructed a priori by the designer for herself. In this way,
Chanel made use of the layering of extratextual, extra-diagetic narrative characteristic of the media celebrity. While John Wayne and
Katharine Hepburn "wore" their own personae in all their films, the
Chanel customer acquired some of the designer's persona. In this way,
Chanel's clients wound up wearing Chanel's own life story right along
with that little black dress or gold-buttoned bouclé suit.

But in Chanel's case, the layering effect of media celebrity is more
complex and pervasive than it is in the realm of strict performance. The
stage or screen performer gestures only toward his or her own autobiographical—even if fictional—narrative. But as a fashion designer
Chanel did not merely embody her own stardom, she conferred it upon
others. Those who wore her clothes acquired a bit of Coco's narrative
through a process we might call theatrical, contagious celebrity.
Chanel's longtime assistant Lilou Marquand wrote of her employer,
"[M]ore than dresses to sell, she had a message to transmit. Her dream
was to take a woman off the street and transform her."[12] Chanel's close
friend Maurice Sachs wrote of the same phenomenon:

> Chanel . . . created a feminine personage of a sort . . . never before seen.
> Her influence spread far beyond the limits of her work; her name was
> fixed in people's minds. . . . She represented a new being. . . . [S]he exer-
> cised [a reign] over all the women of society. . . . They talked of her in all
> Europe, in all America. Her fame spread over the world.[13]

That "new being," born of the Chanel narrative, finds its roots in the
early years of an orphaned peasant girl from the French provinces.

## Chanel's Self-Invention

Gabrielle Chanel was born in 1883 in Saumur-sur-Loire, the illegiti-
mate daughter of a peasant woman and a peddler. When her mother
died in 1895, Gabrielle's father abandoned the family and left his
daughter to the care of the Sisters of the Congregation of the Sacred
Heart of Mary, at their orphanage in the town of Aubazine. It was the
nuns who would teach Gabrielle to sew.[14]

After leaving the orphanage, Gabrielle had a brief, teen-aged career singing in the local café-concerts. Soon after, Coco, as she came to be known (after a song she sang about a rooster who crows "Ko-ko-ri-ko"), discovered her talent for design and opened a small hat shop. From millinery she moved on to dress design, relying routinely on the financial help of the many wealthy lovers she learned to attract. By the age of thirty-one, Chanel had established herself as a style revolutionary, opening her first boutique in the affluent resort town of Deauville, where she not only dressed the vacationing rich, she became one of them—the first dressmaker to attain the social status of her clients.[15] From the peasant class and an orphanage, Chanel had steered herself into high society, mingling with Europe's moneyed classes. Like the great dandy Beau Brummell, she traded her personality for social advancement and attained a kind of parallel royalty of style. Having received little formal education, she relied on friends and lovers to teach her about art, literature, politics, history. Chanel even made a project of dropping her provincial accent and acquiring more Parisian tones. "She was from a very very simple background," observed Helene de Leusse, who worked as *directrice* of the Chanel boutique in Paris. "[A]t the outset she was completely without culture. She improved herself little by little because she surrounded herself with intelligent people and then of course, she was intelligent herself."[16]

Chanel never married or had children, but continued living publicly with many well-known and often younger lovers well into late middle age. Among her many socially connected and aristocratic lovers were Etienne Balsan, the duke of Westminster (considered at that time the wealthiest man in Europe), the famous playboy and confidant of kings Arthur "Boy" Capel, and Grand Duke Dimitri, cousin to Tsar Nicholas II. Chanel was a celebrity, a trademark personality whose escapades appeared on the society pages of the international press. Her home was photographed for *Vogue* magazine; her parties described in detail. "I developed the habit," she said, "of surrounding myself with people of quality so as to establish a link between myself and society."[17] But whenever Chanel was questioned about her early life, she would offer fictional (and differing) versions of it, with peasant roots, provincial orphanage, and poverty neatly expunged. (In one version, for example, her father was a wealthy businessman who traveled frequently to the United States.) "She began lying very early on," writes Lilou Marquand, "and the lies grew with her until they became her truth. Each event had several versions, and these different stories would contradict one another. You had to forget the earlier version and believe the latest one."[18]

Chanel did not socialize only with the wealthy; she also became a full-fledged member of France's avant-garde, the first dress designer to be taken seriously as an artist. She befriended or collaborated with such artists as Cocteau, Diaghilev, Picasso, Stravinsky (with whom she had an affair), Satie, Blaise Cendrars, Pierre Reverdy, Salvador Dalí, and Colette. "I do not understand literature in couture," said André Gide, "but it's obviously Chanel." Misia Sert said, "Chanel . . . not only destroyed the period of Mucha, Lalique and Tiffany glass, but created an emotional wave in the world of art far more important than clothes."[19] And Cocteau wrote of his friend, "Coco Chanel was to couture what Picasso was to painting."[20]

## *Chanel's Style*

Chanel's transformative power over the way women look, even to this day, cannot be overstated. During her nearly seventy-year career (she remained active until her death in 1971 at the age of eighty-seven) she created an aesthetic sea change that ranks with modernism's other profound transitions—from Petipas to Martha Graham, from Gaudí to LeCorbusier, from Degas to Picasso, from Tchaikovsky to John Cage, from Tolstoy to Beckett.

The Chanel revolution lay in its modernist reduction of the female silhouette, its promotion of an androgynous look, and its underlying conviction that clothes could change one's life. Chanel intended her clothes to encourage the physically unfettered, athletic, and sexually freer life she advocated for women and lived herself. Her designs rejected the old paradigm of woman as immobile art object and eliminated the elaborate layers of fabric and undergarments that women typically wore. Chanel hated what she called the "haut bourgeois" trappings of female fashion. "Women in brocade," she famously declared, "look like old armchairs when they sit down."[21] By casting off the complicated frills of women's clothing and replacing them with solid colors, simple stripes, and straight lines, Chanel added great visual "speed" to the female form, while granting increased actual speed to women, who could now move about more easily than ever before. Unlike the fragmented female body of earlier eras, with its disjointed

*Fig. 1.1.* Chanel outfits, as illustrated in *Vogue*, 1927. Courtesy of the New York Public Library.

parts—exaggerated waist, bosom, hips, and derriere—the Chanel body was boyish and small-breasted, with natural, uncorseted, waist and hips.[22] Chanel clothes hung straight and loosely, skimming rather than exaggerating curves (fig. 1.1).[23] Among the many dramatic innovations for women invented or first popularized by Chanel, we can count pants, ankle-revealing skirts, matching skirt and jacket suits, short hair, the simple black dress (inspired, it has been claimed, by the nuns' plain habits in her orphanage), tortoise-shell eyeglasses—even for those with twenty-twenty vision (both to add panache and to conceal undereye bags in older women), costume jewelry, neutral colors, and suntans (fig. 1.2 ).

Not only did Chanel change the outline of women's figures, she changed the materials women wore as well. Her earliest designs, which

*Fig. 1.2. Left,* a slim-fitting suit by Chanel; *right,* one of her simple, calf-length black evening dresses, both from 1959. Courtesy of the New York Public Library.

she sold in Deauville, were loose-fitting "beach pajamas" and sailor suits, made from knit jersey, a fabric that had previously been used only for men's underwear. Jersey was thin and flexible and could be made by machine. Its light weight and fluid drape enabled Chanel to mold her clothes more closely to the body while at the same time increasing the wearer's range of physical motion. "I wanted," she wrote, "to give a woman comfortable clothes that would flow with her body. A woman is closest to being naked when she is well dressed."[24] With jersey, Chanel could sculpt an elegant yet unencumbered body—a very dandyist ideal.

The sartorial vocabulary of dandyism appears in other aspects of Chanel's work as well. Like Beau Brummell and his disciples, she was much influenced by the casual wardrobe of English aristocratic country life: comfortable, unadorned clothes made for long walks, hunting, golf, and tennis. But Chanel did not find inspiration only among the upper classes. She patterned some of her creations after the simple, inexpensive shirts, pants, and jackets worn by Norman fishermen and sailors. She also admired the clean lines of workers' tucked-in cotton T-shirts, and she especially loved military and school uniforms. "What was so wonderful about Chanel's clothes," wrote Sir Francis Rose in *Vogue*, "was that she made them look like working people's clothing with all the luxury hidden except to the refined eye."[25] This technique came to be known as Chanel's "luxe caché."[26]

By 1925 Chanel had begun designing her own version of school or army uniforms for women: the suit. Chanel's suits consisted of a simple skirt, a pullover, and a jacket, all in wool jersey. She even designed black jersey suits for evening, with equally simple lines that contrasted dramatically with the conventionally elaborate, long evening dresses of the time. To accompany these suits Chanel designed small cloche hats or berets—which reduced and simplified the outline of the head and hair —as well as costume jewelry in the form of long ropes of oversized imitation pearls, emeralds, or rubies. The lavish, colorful (obviously fake) jewelry was all the more striking against the muted beiges and tans and clean lines of the clothes (fig. 1.3).

We can see an interesting mixture of social class elements in Chanel's suits. The simplicity of cut and fabric recalled workers' or soldiers' clothes, the sporty quality (even for evening wear) recalled the outdoor wear of English aristocrats, and the extravagance of the costume jewelry was a parodic turn on the gem-encrusted look of upper-class

*Fig. 1.3.* Chanel tweed suit with costume jewelry, 1959. Courtesy of the New York Public Library.

women. "When costume jewelry is well made," Chanel said, "it is meant to demolish real jewelry. Because I've set out to destroy certain people. . . . Those who make fools of themselves by going out covered with diamonds."[27] In such a remark we hear the orphaned, peasant-born Chanel turning her class resentment into a very modern theory of ironic simulacrum. Her famous predecessor Paul Poiret aptly described Chanel's style as a *"misérabilisme de luxe,"* or "luxurious poverty."[28]

As the first celebrity-couturiere, Chanel served as her own best advertisement. More than just her product, she was selling her entire life. She was frequently photographed and written about in magazines and newspapers, and her good looks, elegant figure, and famous "play-girl" life attracted customers who wanted to emulate her. When Chanel cut her hair, she started an international craze for the short, bobbed, "garçonne" look.[29] When she sported a suntan (formerly scorned as a sign of peasant labor), flaunted her eyeglasses (an accessory women had typically hidden), and wore flat shoes, women copied her. "Unlike male designers," wrote Marquand, "Chanel wore what she made. Her collection was, simply, herself, and she considered imitation an homage."[30] Chanel's zeal to see herself reproduced became particularly apparent at her runway shows, for which she hired models who resembled her both physically and in their movements. The women Chanel used to fit and display her collections were all required to have Chanel's figure, with small breasts, slim hips, straight lines. The models were also instructed to walk, stand, and move like Chanel, one hand in pocket, pelvis slung forward. "The point of reference was always Chanel's own body," wrote Marquand.[31] "Chanel was the first couturière to sell a complete image and show how to create it," writes Anne Hollander. "[Her] success as a designer was inseparable from her personal success."[32]

In his autobiography, *En Habillant l'époque*, the great couturier Paul Poiret makes a remark that illuminates the difference between his understanding of the designer's task and Chanel's later reinterpretation of the art: "Visit the great dressmakers," writes Poiret, "and you will not feel that you are in a shop, but in the studio of an artist who intends to make of your dresses a portrait and a likeness of yourself!"[33] For Poiret, a designer's creation splits and doubles the client's identity, offering her a reflection, perhaps an idealized version, of herself. We see here the importance of the designer as artist, a phenomenon born in the nineteenth century; but we also see the subsuming of that artist's personality within the client's. For Chanel, however (like the dandies before her), only her own personality mattered. She never intended for her clients to buy portraits of themselves. For Coco Chanel, her clients were paying to buy portraits of—Chanel.

In a sense, Chanel transformed fashion in two apparently contradictory ways, both elevating and debasing it. As the first couturiere to attain the status of avant-garde artist, she attracted new respect for her métier. At the same time, by simplifying clothes so dramatically, Chanel made it possible for nearly anyone to acquire a version of the Chanel "look," if not her actual couture creations. Hers was a machine-made aesthetic that she intended to be—and indeed loved to see—reproduced at all levels. Lilou Marquand recalls that "Mademoiselle" loved to see copies of her clothes sold on the street, and considered even a "Prisunic [France's Woolworth's] pullover and a simple straight skirt" to be a Chanel-esque ensemble. In 1926 *Vogue* magazine famously dubbed her new black crêpe de chine sheath "a Ford signed Chanel." The little black dress, that is, would be everywoman's uniform, an assembly line creation that could go anywhere.[34] Chanel, therefore, imbued fashion with reproducible elegance, based in part on the seductiveness of her own highly self-conscious life story. Fashion, in her hands, took on theatrical proportions, with Chanel costuming women as herself—a mass spectacle starring only one character. Those who bought her clothes, even those who bought the knockoffs, entered the theater of society wearing at least two identities; they represented both a new, sleeker version of themselves and that new "garçonne" heroine, "Coco." This additional layer of an external narrative of character was inherent in Chanel's couture, just as it is in all media celebrity. And when Chanel turned her attention to actual theatrical costuming, this layering technique had even more complex results.

## Chanel and a Blue Train

It was Misia Sert who introduced Chanel to the Paris avant-garde. Sert, herself a patron of the arts, encouraged her friend to follow suit. Initially, Chanel provided only financial support to the theater. In 1920, for example, she donated 300,000 francs to Diaghilev in support of a Ballets Russes production of Stravinsky's *Rite of Spring*. Eventually, however, she would come to design costumes for many dance, theatrical, and cinematic productions, working with the Ballets Russes, Balanchine, Cocteau, and numerous French and American film directors. For my purposes here, I will concentrate on Chanel's collaboration with Diaghilev and Cocteau on their "danced operetta," *Le Train bleu*, which premiered on June 20, 1924, at Paris's Théâtre des Champs Elysées.

*Le Train bleu* represents Diaghilev's transition from his prewar, exotic, Oriental ballets, such as *Firebird* or *Scheharazade*, to both a more popular and a more modern form of dance.[35] He wanted, he said, to add "a touch of reality" to the *fantaisiste* spectacles for which he had become known. Consequently, instead of mythology or fairy tales, *Le Train bleu* takes as its subject the life of an actual (though hardly run-of-the-mill) segment of French society: Riviera-vacationing aristocrats and their newly moneyed friends. The "Blue Train" of the title was the nickname of an express that ran from Paris to the Côte d'Azur, frequently taken by the leisure class. The production featured a mix of art forms, including ballet, acrobatics, satire, and pantomime. Bronislava Nijinska (sister of Nijinsky) choreographed the movement; Darius Milhaud composed the music; the cubist sculptor Henri Laurens created the sets; Picasso designed both the stage curtain and the program; and Diaghilev's frequent collaborator Jean Cocteau wrote the libretto. Cocteau then invited Chanel to provide the costumes.

*Le Train bleu*, "the quintessential flapper ballet,"[36] offered a carnivalesque view of France's postwar, more carefree new society. It was a story told in broad strokes, offering a series of scenic tableaux rather than complicated narrative. Accordingly, its characters were not specified by name, only by generic types: "Handsome Kid," "Golf Player," "Tennis Player," and "Bathing Beauty." To underscore the characters' simple, caricaturish identities, Chanel designed outfits that essentially reproduced her already famous Riviera beach and athletic wear. She put the Golf Player in golf clothes, the Tennis Player in tennis clothes, and so on.

In the center photograph of this series (fig. 1.4 ), we can see the recognizable elements that formed Chanel's fashion signature. To the left is the character of the Bathing Beauty, danced by Lydia Sokolova. She wears a swimsuit of Chanel's recognizable striped jersey, rubber bathing shoes, and a head-hugging swim cap, an item that Chanel had actually invented. The rubberized cap is a typical Chanel creation in that it not only enabled women to swim more effectively—offering them physical freedom—it reduced the volume of head and hair to boyish dimensions, in the same way that her cloche hats and short haircuts did. The Bathing Beauty also wears "pearl" stud earrings made of china coated with wax. The earrings' extravagantly large size intentionally telegraphs their status as imitations.

Next to Sokolova is dancer Anton Dolin in character as Handsome Kid. Dolin's striped, two-piece jersey bathing suit is nearly identical to Sokolova's, recalling Chanel's love of unisex clothing. On the other side of the tuxedoed Cocteau (this is opening night) is actor Leon

*Fig. 1.4.* Scenes from *Le Train bleu*, 1924. Courtesy of the New York Public Library.

Woizekhovski, who portrayed the Golf Player. His striped sweater, matching socks, and tweed plus fours were modeled on (and would have instantly evoked) the wardrobe of Edward, Prince of Wales, who, as captain of the Royal and Ancient Golf Club of St. Andrews, Fife, was the era's most-photographed and best-known amateur golfer (and dandy).[37]

Next to Woizekhovski stands Bronislava Nijinska, who herself danced the role of the Tennis Player. She wears a two-piece all-white tennis outfit with short skirt and matching short stockings. For this costume, Chanel had rejected the era's traditional and more encumbering women's tennis outfit of a long skirt, long-sleeved blouse, and tie, as well as the usual garter belt, which she replaced with the simpler knee garters.[38] Nijinska's short haircut and tight-fitting head wrap (which Chanel herself was famous for wearing while horseback riding) echo the reduced dimensions of Sokolova's rubber-capped head and, once again, diminish the usual visual differences between men and women.

None of these costumes differed significantly from Chanel's usual creations. In fact, these were not *costumes* at all, but the everyday clothes of thousands of vacationing French people. For the first time, Ballets Russes dancers were appearing onstage without traditional theatrical costumes. "The costumes by Chanel," writes Lynn Garafola, "might have come from her customers' wardrobes."[39] And since

Chanel's customers were, as we have seen, essentially costumed as Chanel herself, there is a sense in which the different characters in this Ballets Russes production were all performing variations on one role, that of Coco. In this way, Chanel successfully extended to the stage her post-dandyist technique of inserting layers of personal narrative into her couture.

This technique of adding a level of extra-diagetic or extrascenic narrative jibed particularly well with Diaghilev's vision for *Le Train bleu*. Seeking to escape the conventional parameters of ballet, he had turned instead to the French music hall for inspiration, borrowing its easy mixing of dialogue, dance, and song. *Le Train bleu* partook of what Garafola has called "lifestyle modernism," a showcasing of the "sophisticated commonplace," in an adaptation of aristocratic pleasures and modern art.[40] Diaghilev intended to blend an imaginary, highly modern setting with the recognizable patterns of athletic and recreational movement. This becomes clear in his own program notes for the production:

> The first point about *Le Train bleu* is that there is no blue train in it. This being the age of speed, it has already reached its destination and disembarked its passengers. These are to be seen on a beach which does not exist, in front of a casino which exists still less. Overhead passes an aeroplane which you cannot see. And the plot resembles nothing. Yet when it was presented for the first time in Paris, everybody was unaccountably seized with the desire to take the Blue Train . . . and perform refreshing exercises.[41]

That last sentence is revealing. Despite the obviously fanciful and imaginary setting, Diaghilev wanted to create convincing realism. He wanted his Blue Train to evoke the real, historic blue train. And he wanted his dancers to evoke the real, loose-limbed, slightly random movements of actual beachgoers, not the *pas réglés* of traditional ballet. Not surprisingly, this goal of naturalistic movement clashed with the plans of the classically trained Nijinksa. Diaghilev and Cocteau argued repeatedly with her, replacing her balletic steps with pantomimed beach activities and acrobatics.[42] Cocteau counseled her to look for inspiration (and the verisimilitude she despised) at photographs of French tennis champion Suzanne Lenglen on the court and the Prince of Wales on the golf course.[43] For her part, Nijinska rejected this idea of athletic mimeticism and longed, she said, to "negate the libretto" and create "a pure dance form."[44] A look at the stage directions for the first scene suggests who won these dance arguments: "Scene One: Tarts. Gigolos. Sunbathing. The gigolos run (in place) and do gymnastics, while the tarts, in groups, assume the pretty poses of color postcards."[45] This idea of making art of elegant "lifestyle" activities clearly finds its roots in the tenets of nineteenth-century dandyism. In the case of *Le Train bleu*, however, the dandy's drawing room–scale, solipsistic commodification of self exploded outward into a grand, modern spectacle.

It was precisely this inclusion of nontheatrical themes and movement that troubled many critics. Reviews of *Le Train bleu* expressed dissatisfaction with the production's melding of life and theater, of dance and ordinary beach hijinks. After the London premiere, the *Dancing Times* wrote, "It seemed an awful pity . . . that such obviously great artists should spend their efforts on 'cartwheels,' 'handsprings,' and slow-motion running. . . . I cannot call it dancing." The *New Statesman* complained that *Le Train bleu* was "not really a skit or parody . . . [but] an elaborate mannequin parade of bathing and other fashionable seaside costumes by the House of Chanel."[46]

As the *New Statesman*'s remarks make particularly clear, Chanel's costumes did not play a merely supporting role. On the contrary, they gestured away from the internal, fictional world of *Le Train bleu* and announced their provenance in the celebrated couture and famous personal life of Coco Chanel. Her celebrity status infused the whole production, in much the same way that it affected her couture designs. This blending of theatrical and biographical narratives created an arresting disruption, a version of the multiple perspectives and collage technique for which modernism and Cubism in particular were known.

Chanel would continue contributing to modernist drama, costuming many of Cocteau's plays, including *Orpheus*, *La Machine infernale*, *Les Chevaliers de la table ronde*, and *Oedipus rex*. (She had already done *Antigone* in 1922.) In every case, her famous name and life helped attract spectators.[47] And in every case, Chanel would continue her practice of dressing Cocteau's characters in clothes that evoked her own extrascenic, "real-life" couture, whether those characters were queens of Greek mythology or knights of Arthur's court.[48] This anachronistic costuming technique complemented the playwright's own dramatic vision as well as it had Diaghilev's, since Cocteau was famous for allowing the twentieth century to infuse even his most mythological settings. His Orpheus, for example, composes lyric poetry on a typewriter while wearing a Chanel ensemble of tweed slacks and English golf sweater.

## Beyond the French Stage

Chanel's career as a costume designer extended beyond the modernist stage and into work in both French and American cinema. Her clothes were worn onscreen by Romy Schneider, Gloria Swanson, and Ina Claire, among countless others. The films costumed by Chanel, in turn, influenced the fashion sense of millions of female moviegoers, whether or not they could afford a Chanel original. Even today, clothes produced by the House of Chanel (now under the direction of Karl Lagerfeld) signify elite social status and singular elegance, while being endlessly imitated in inexpensive knockoffs.[49] This tension between the necessary elitism of true luxury and the iterability of mass-produced, easily copied designs was always at the heart of Chanel's *oeuvre*. Indeed, the battle between originality and reproducibility drove the entire life of this woman who managed to market and sell not only clothes, jewelry, and perfume, but also the narrative of her very existence, rubberstamping her signature on several continents.

## Fashion and Dandyism: Chanel's Transition

Modern fashion, in general, struggles constantly with the problem of how to maintain an aura of uniqueness in what must, finally, be reproduced endlessly. Despite fashion's will toward instant and self-consuming uniqueness, more than one person must wear a given designer's creation. Chanel took that essential dilemma and turned it into the engine that drove her life and career. Instead of fighting fashion's contradiction, she embodied it, allowing her own carefully created and charismatic image to partake of industrial-scale reproduction. "Anything good ought to be copied and worn by many," she wrote.[50]

This paradox, the task of reproducing what must be unique, recalls the dandyist movement, from which Chanel had inherited so much. But while a number of critics have noticed a striking connection between Chanel and the great dandies, they have all focused on the most obvious similarities, the classic simplicity and ease of the clothes themselves. Of Chanel's "liberating" influence, Gilles Lipovetsky says, "What Brummell's aesthetic claimed for men in the nineteenth century had won over the feminine universe. . . . [F]lamboyant display was eclipsed in favor of the democratic aesthetic of purity, restraint, and comfort."[51] Anne Hollander writes that Chanel's "image was founded on the Beau Brummell principle that clothes while they are being worn must seem not to matter at all."[52]

Yet while Chanel's neutral tones, simple luxury, and clean lines do hark back to Brummell's subdued elegance, far more about her career evokes the great Beau. Chanel created more than a new visual style, she wrote a new narrative for fashion and inserted it into her designs. For her, fashion was theater with millions of players who all portrayed one star. This celebration and perpetuation of a carefully scripted self owed much to the intimate theater of dandies chatting brilliantly in salons. Like the dandies, Chanel ignored class boundaries, reinvented her biography, cavorted with royalty, and lived to see herself imitated in art and in life. But unlike the dandies, Chanel orchestrated the dissemination of her personality on a massive (some might say monomaniacal) scale, conferring glittering bits of her celebrity upon average women, as well as upon characters of ballet, drama, and cinema. Chanel took the dandies' art of commodifying personality and created a narrative of self that flowed far beyond the reaches of aristocratic drawing rooms. Her work and her nearly century-long legacy thus far prove that dandyism never died, it only evolved, merging with modern fashion to enter the twentieth century—the era of mass culture, media celebrity, and, of course, cheap designer knockoffs.

NOTES

1. Roland Barthes, "Le Dandysme et la mode," in *Le Mythe du dandy*, ed. Emilien Carassus (Paris: Armond Colin, 1971), 312–15.

2. For an explanation, see Rhonda Garelick, *Rising Star: Dandyism, Gender, and Performance in the Fin de Siècle* (Princeton: Princeton University Press, 1998), passim.

3. See Barbey d'Aurevilly's famous essay of 1843, "Du dandysme et de George Brummell," in *Oeuvres romanesques complètes* (Paris: Gallimard, 1966), 2:667–733.

4. See Honoré de Balzac, "Traité de la vie élégante," in *Oeuvres complètes* (Paris: Louis Conard, 1938), 2:152–85, esp. 165–68.

5. Oscar Wilde's career offers an excellent early example of the transition from dandyism to modern celebrity. While he produced very dandyist literary texts (such as *The Picture of Dorian Gray* and *The Importance of Being Earnest*), he also made a career of being an extratextual, public celebrity. Wilde turned himself into a trademark personality through his persona, his outrageous witticisms, the sunflower he carried, and his cultivation of what we now call a gay sensibility. It was in America, the eventual headquarters of the culture industry, that Wilde really began his career as a modern celebrity. His 1882 tour of the United States taught him much about the machinery of stardom. It was here, after all, that the "Oscar Wilde" brands of soap and clothing were launched, and here where the "Oscar Wilde Waltz" became a popular tune.

6. Richard Dyer, *Heavenly Bodies: Film Stars and Society* (New York: St. Martin's, 1986), 3–4.

7. See Valerie Steele, *Fashion and Eroticism: Ideals of Feminine Beauty from the Victorian Era to the Jazz Age* (New York: Oxford University Press, 1985), passim, for an excellent discussion of the beginnings of fashion.

8. In his elegant impassivity, the dandy defies and transcends human mutability; he is more *objet d'art* than man. The dandy, wrote Balzac, "becomes a piece of boudoir furniture, an extremely ingenious mannequin, who can sit upon a horse or a sofa . . . but a thinking being . . . never." See "Traité de la vie élégante," 177. Dorian Gray, for example, owed his success as a forever-youthful dandy, a *puer eternis*, directly to his relationship to an inanimate object—his aging portrait—that remains hidden. Fashion works in much the same way. Adorning the body, it also denatures it, inscribing it into a cultural narrative of constant change. As Benjamin said, "Fashion prostitutes the living body to the inorganic world." See Walter Benjamin, "Paris, the Capital of the Nineteenth Century," in *Charles Baudelaire: A Lyric Poet in the Era of High Capitalism,* trans. Quintin Hoare (London: Verso, 1983), 155–76, 166.

9. Steele tells us that it was World War I army uniforms that were first mass produced, followed by men's suits, and then women's and children's clothing. *Fashion and Eroticism*, 236 ff.

10. This inherent contradiction of fashion remains apparent in the phenomenon of modern fashion magazines—publications available to and read by women of every social class, featuring clothes unaffordable (as couture originals) to nearly everyone but the wealthiest, worn by models who represent an unattainable aristocracy of youth and beauty. Fashion is for everyone and for no one.

11. See Richard Klein, "Chanel's Cosmos," *Sites: The Journal of Twentieth-Century Contemporary French Studies* 1, no. 1 (ca. 1998): 251–62, 254.

12. Lilou Marquand, *Chanel m'a dit* (Paris: Editions Jean-Claude Lattès, 1990), 103.

13. Maurice Sachs, *The Decade of Illusions: Paris, 1918–1928*, trans. Gwladys Matthews Sachs (New York: Knopf, 1933), 153–54.

14. See Frances Kennett, *Coco: The Life and Loves of Gabrielle Chanel* (London: Victor Gollancz, 1989), 9 ff. See also Axel Madsen, *Chanel: A Woman of Her Own* (New York: Henry Holt, 1990); Alice Mackrell, *Coco Chanel* (New York: Holmes and Meier, 1992); and Iris Ashley, "Coco," in *Paris Fashion: The Great Designers and Their Creations*, ed. Ruth Lynam (London: Michael Joseph, 1972), 113–37.

15. While other great designers, such as Poiret or Worth, had indeed attained the status of artists, they did not socialize with their clients. For discussion of Chanel's social rise, see particularly Mackrell, *Coco Chanel*.

16. Quoted in Kennett, *Coco: The Life and Loves of Gabrielle Chanel*, 50.

17. Quoted in Edmonde Charles-Roux, *Chanel and Her World*, trans. Daniel Wheeler (Paris: Vendôme Press, 1981), 191.

18. Marquand, *Chanel m'a dit*, 62.

19. Quoted in Sir Francis Rose, "Chanel Always Now," *Vogue* 154, no. 10 (December 1969): 120–22.

20. Quoted in Madsen, *Chanel: A Woman of Her Own*, 108.

21. Quoted in Anne Hollander, "The Great Emancipator, Chanel," *Connoisseur* 213 (February 1983): 84.

22. While it was her predecessor Paul Poiret who first dispensed with corsets, his designs continued to be curvilinear. Chanel was the first to promote a female body of largely straight lines.

23. Of course it should be noted that, while liberating to many women, for others, Chanel's spare look required an unattainably lithe figure.

24. Quoted in Rose, "Chanel Always Now," 116.

25. Ibid., 116.

26. Gilles Lipovetsky writes in *The Empire of Fashion*, trans. Catherine Porter (Princeton: Princeton University Press, 1991), 60, "Chanel managed to dress society women in tailored jersey suits and grey, black, or beige pullovers. . . . From that point on it was chic not to appear rich."

27. Quoted in Rhonda Lieberman, "The Chanel Super-Ego," *Artforum* 31 (November 1992): 6.

28. Quoted in Charles-Roux, *Chanel and Her World*, 157.

29. The term *garçonne* (usually translated as "flapper") had been introduced by the 1922 novel *La Garçonne*, by Victor Margueritte.

30. Marquand, *Chanel m'a dit*, 91.

31. Ibid., 72.

32. Hollander, "The Great Emancipator," 83.

33. Paul Poiret, *En habillant l'époque* (Paris: Bernard Grasset, 1930), 43.

34. Quoted in Charles-Roux, *Chanel and Her World*, 156.

35. See Dale Harris, "Legends: Chanel and Diaghilev," *Architectural Digest* 46 (September 1989): 42–50.

36. This is Lynn Garafola's term for the production. See Lynn Garafola, "Reconstructing the Past: Tracking Down *Le Train bleu*," *Dance Magazine*, April 1990, 40.

37. For more on these costumes, see Mackrell, *Coco Chanel*; Lynn Garafola, *Diaghilev's Ballets Russes* (New York: Da Capo, 1989); and Harris, "Legends: Chanel and Diaghilev."

38. See Mackrell, *Coco Chanel*, 62 ff.

39. Garafola, *Diaghilev's Ballets Russes*, 108.

40. Ibid., chap. 4.

41. Quoted in Kennett, *Coco: The Life and Loves of Gabrielle Chanel*, 61.

42. For discussions of artistic differences on the set of *Le Train bleu*, see Erik Aschengreen, *Jean Cocteau and the Dance*, trans. Patricia McAndrew and Per Avsum (Copenhagen: Institute for Nordic Philology, Copenhagen University, 1986); Garafola, "Reconstructing the Past: Tracking Down *Le Train bleu*"; and Frank W. D. Ries, *The Dance Theatre of Jean Cocteau* (Ann Arbor: UMI Research Press, 1986).

43. See Charles-Roux, *Chanel and Her World*; Ries, *The Dance Theatre of Jean Cocteau*; Aschengreen, *Jean Cocteau and the Dance*; and Garafola, *Diaghilev's Ballets Russes*.

44. Quoted in Garafola, "Reconstructing the Past: Tracking Down *Le Train bleu*," 42.

45. Ibid.

46. Reviews quoted in Ries, *The Dance Theatre of Jean Cocteau*, 99–100.

47. Charles Dullin, actor and owner of Montmartre's Théâtre de l'Atelier (where *Antigone* premiered), commented on the box office lure of Cocteau's celebrated collaborators: "many society people came to the performances because of Chanel . . . [and] Picasso." Quoted in Francis Steegmuller, *Cocteau: A Biography* (Boston: Little, Brown, 1970), 298.

48. Cocteau suggests his fascination with anachronistic dramatic play when he writes, "To costume my princesses I wanted Mlle Chanel, because she is our leading couturière and I cannot imagine Oedipus's daughters patronizing a 'little dressmaker.'" Quoted in Steegmuller, *Cocteau: A Biography*, 297.

49. Lagerfeld, truly Chanel's disciple in style, has begun "copying backwards" in his designs for the Chanel label. In past years he has found inspiration in the inner-city culture of hip-hop, imitating street kids' outsized fourteen-karat gold chain necklaces with pendant initials. Lagerfeld has draped his own, imitation gold versions of these heavy, exaggerated—and strangely Chanel-esque—accessories (complete with interlocking double Cs) over the necklines and around the waists of classic bouclé suits. The curious result is Manhattan society matrons lunching at Mortimer's while wearing copies of the

adornments worn by ghetto teenagers—a twist one feels sure "Mademoiselle" would have loved.

50. Quoted in Lieberman, "The Chanel Super-Ego," 6.
51. Lipovetsky, *The Empire of Fashion*, 60.
52. Hollander, "The Great Emancipator," 86.

BIBLIOGRAPHY

Aschengreen, Erik. *Jean Cocteau and the Dance*. Translated by Patricia McAndrew and Per Avsum. Copenhagen: Institute for Nordic Philology, Copenhagen University, 1986.

Ashley, Iris. "Coco." In *Paris Fashion: The Great Designers and Their Creations*, edited by Ruth Lynam, 113–37. London: Michael Joseph, 1972.

Balzac, Honoré de. "Traité de la vie élégante." In *Oeuvres complètes*, 2:152–85. Paris: Louis Conard, 1938.

Barbey d'Aurevilly, Jules. "Du Dandysme et de George Brummell." In *Oeuvres romanesques complètes*, 2:667–733. Paris: Gallimard, 1966.

Barthes, Roland. "Le Dandysme et la mode." In *Le Mythe du dandy*, edited by Emilien Carassus, 312–15. Paris: Armand Colin, 1971.

Benjamin, Walter. "Paris, the Capital of the Nineteenth Century." In *Charles Baudelaire: A Lyric Poet in the Era of High Capitalism*, 155–76. Translated by Quintin Hoare. London: Verso, 1983.

Charles-Roux, Edmonde. *Chanel and Her World*. Translated by Daniel Wheeler. Paris: Vendôme Press, 1981.

Dyer, Richard. *Heavenly Bodies: Film Stars and Society*. New York: St. Martin's, 1986.

Garafola, Lynn. *Diaghilev's Ballets Russes*. New York: Da Capo, 1989.

———. "Reconstructing the Past: Tracking Down *Le Train bleu*." *Dance Magazine*, April 1990, 40–44.

Garelick, Rhonda. *Rising Star: Dandyism, Gender and Performance in the Fin de Siècle*. Princeton: Princeton University Press, 1998.

Harris, Dale. "Legends: Chanel and Diaghilev." *Architectural Digest* 46 (September 1989): 42–50.

Hollander, Anne. "The Great Emancipator, Chanel." *Connoisseur* 213 (February 1983): 82–90.

Kennett, Frances. *Coco: The Life and Loves of Gabrielle Chanel*. London: Victor Gollancz, 1989.

Klein, Richard. "Chanel's Cosmos." *Sites: The Journal of Twentieth-Century Contemporary French Studies* 1, no. 1 (ca. 1998): 251–62.

Lieberman, Rhonda. "The Chanel Super-Ego." *Artforum* 31 (November 1992): 5–7.

Lipovetsky, Gilles. *The Empire of Fashion*. Translated by Catherine Porter. Princeton: Princeton University Press, 1991.

Mackrell, Alice. *Coco Chanel*. New York: Holmes and Meier, 1992.

Madsen, Axel. *Chanel: A Woman of Her Own*. New York: Henry Holt, 1990.

Marquand, Lilou. *Chanel m'a dit*. Paris: Editions Jean-Claude Lattès, 1990.

Poiret, Paul. *En habillant l'epoque*. Paris: Bernard Grasset, 1930.

Ries, Frank W. D. *The Dance Theatre of Jean Cocteau*. Ann Arbor: UMI Research Press, 1986.

Rose, Sir Francis. "Chanel Always Now." *Vogue* 154, no. 10 (December 1969): 116–22.

Sachs, Maurice. *The Decade of Illusions: Paris, 1918–1928*. Translated by Gwladys Matthews Sachs. New York: Knopf, 1933.

Steegmuller, Francis. *Cocteau: A Biography*. New York: Little, Brown, 1970.

Steele, Valerie. "Chanel in Context." In *Chic Thrills: A Fashion Reader*, edited by Juliet Ash and Elizabeth Wilson, 121–26. Berkeley: University of California Press, 1992.

———. *Fashion and Eroticism: Ideals of Feminine Beauty from the Victorian Era to the Jazz Age*. New York: Oxford University Press, 1985.

## Chapter 2

# "Indian Dandies"
## *Sartorial Finesse and Self-Presentation along the Columbia River, 1790–1855*

## *Robert E. Moore*

### *Introduction*

Dandyism as a cultural phenomenon has always been closely associated with certain special qualities of metropolitan life in Europe: the sidewalks, arcades, and commercial displays of major urban centers like Paris that served as a kind of proscenium for the flaneurs, dandies, and other memorable characters who enlivened the public scene during the nineteenth century. This chapter's setting is rather far removed from such sites. Indeed, the phenomena discussed here unfolded on the far western frontier of North America, along the Columbia River in what is now Oregon and Washington, during the early decades of the nineteenth century.

When Lewis and Clark first reached the Dalles area of the Columbia River in the Pacific Northwest in 1805, they encountered American Indian people who already owned—and knew the English names for—muskets, brass teakettles, and various other items of European manufacture. Between 1805 and 1855 (when treaties were signed establishing Indian reservations in the area) it became clear that the Whites had entered into a preexisting network of transcultural exchange and trade, fueled by the participation of people from a wide variety of places and cultural backgrounds (heretofore all Native, of course), and involving the movement of goods brought to the Dalles area from all over the western section of the continent.

The "managers," middlemen, and facilitators of this mercantile empire were Chinookan Indians, residents of permanent winter villages along both banks of the Columbia from the Dalles area west about two hundred miles to the Pacific Ocean.

With the arrival of Europeans, the lower Columbia region became embroiled in a global network of trade and exchange. New items and new media for exchange were developed, and sumptuary goods, items of linguistic and material culture, and people all began to circulate in ever widening spheres that connected the already "cosmopolitan" Columbia River region with Polynesia, China, the trans-Canadian fur trade, and the East Coast of the United States. In the process, some local Indian people became wealthy beyond anyone's expectations.

Out of this welter of intense intercultural contact emerged a new class of Native *nouveaux riches,* Chinookans (mainly males) who enriched themselves by "brokering" and monopolizing business contacts with this new group of important outsiders—for this is how the Euro-Americans, at least initially, were understood. This chapter focuses on these mediating figures, analyzing their often flamboyant sartorial practices in the context of the cultural "contact zone" where they emerged—seemingly in the 1820s and 1830s—and then just as quickly disappeared, for the phenomenon had run its course by the 1850s, when Native populations who had survived decimation by epidemic diseases were being dispossessed and resettled onto reservations.

Indian dandyism along the Columbia, then, was a brief, almost fugitive cultural phenomenon, though its traces remain in the writings of fur traders, missionaries, explorers, and other Europeans who visited this remote area in the first years after European contact. Partly because of the inherent limitations of the source material, and partly because of one's sense that these sartorial displays might best be understood as inherently "fugitive" and aleatory forms of expressive behavior, no systematic attempt is made here to reconstruct, out of these early sources, an ethnographically valid account of the actual activities and intentions of these Native "dandies." The account presented here is perhaps better understood as a study of European anxiety in the face of such exquisitely attired "Others," insofar as such anxiety manifests itself in the literary style of the texts where these "Indian dandies" appear at center stage.

The essay begins by laying out the rhetorical framework and literary style of narrative and other descriptive vignettes featuring Indian forms of "dandyism," moves on to describe the sociocultural and historical context for Indian dandyism's emergence in this region at this time, and concludes by discussing the range of interpretative strategies that these sartorial displays seem to make available—to the Indian people, to their European observers at the time, and to us, as students and historians of dandiacal phenomena in the broadest sense.

### Irresistible "Savages"

In the late spring of 1841 the black-robed Oblate priest F. N. Blanchet arrived at a Klallam (Coast Salish) village on the Straits of Juan de Fuca, not far from the present-day site of Seattle, Washington. Blanchet noted with approval that the Indians who greeted him not only "took hold of my baggage, and carried it over to the camp," but actually "vied with each other as to who would have a part of the burden."[1] The seeming solicitude and courtesy of the Indian people and the apparently high level of their general interest in his activities led the priest to think of himself "in heaven rather than in a wild and barbarous land."[2]

Almost immediately, Blanchet and his small group of coreligionists began to train Native catechists. Two of the most important of these went by names that Blanchet transcribed as Tsalakom and Witskalatche; both were identified by these Europeans as "chiefs."[3] In a journal entry dated 31 May 1841, Blanchet described how "Witskalatche, arrayed in French style with trousers, shirt, jacket, *sous-veste*, topcoat ornamented with a star fashioned from porcupine quills, hat, cravat, everything complete, appeared at the head of his people accompanied by several underchiefs."[4]

The image is a striking one: a Native personage of some consequence, apparently, "arrayed in French style," with "everything complete"—*more* than complete, actually, since he wore a "topcoat ornamented with a star fashioned from porcupine quills."

This vignette from the journals of an important early Catholic missionary is only one example of many in the early literature of contact in the Pacific Northwest. Peppered through the journals, reminiscences, and other kinds of firsthand reportage produced by the early explorers, fur traders, missionaries, and emigrants to the Northwest are brief descriptive passages, almost set pieces, in which the narrator describes an encounter with one or another Native person arrayed in what is usually described as a "fantastic" ensemble of European and indigenous clothing.

These passages are noticeable, even memorable, to anyone perusing this large literature of contact in the Pacific Northwest, for several reasons. They seem intended by their European authors to function as light, comical interludes leavening the narration of other, weightier material of historic significance. Their authors frequently attempt, and sometimes achieve, significant heights of rhetoric to create a kind of descriptive texture, to infuse their texts with the sense of place and character that is so convincingly redolent of the picturesque—something that the best of them knew their readers, then and now, would be looking for. Finally, it is in passages like these that readers encounter individual Indians (often identified by name) as full-blown characters in their own right, even if (or, more likely, because) they are reduced, in the same descriptive moment, to grotesques.

Many of the main points of my discussion are illustrated in a brief passage from Washington Irving's *Astoria*, an early "authorized biography" of a multinational corporation, the Astor Fur Company (and based on then-unpublished company documents to which Irving was given exclusive access by John Jacob Astor). *Astoria* appeared and became an instant best-seller in 1836, several years before many of the accounts written by the "Astorians" (fur company employees) themselves had appeared in print.[5] Its influence on subsequent writing about frontier life in the Northwest was enormous. The following passage comes immediately after Irving's description of the "traditional," presumably pre-European-contact, clothing of the Lower Chinooks:

> An intercourse with the white traders, however, soon effected a change in the toilets of both sexes. They became fond of arraying themselves in any article of civilized dress which they could procure, and often made a most grotesque appearance. . . . Both sexes were fond of adorning themselves with bracelets of iron, brass, or copper. They were delighted, also, with blue and white beads, particularly the former, and wore tight bands of them round the waist and ancles [*sic*]; large rolls of them round the neck, and pendants of them in the ears. The men, especially, who, in savage life carry a passion for personal decoration farther than the females, did not think their gala equipments complete, unless they had a jewel of *haiqua*, or wampum, dangling at the nose. Thus arrayed, their hair besmirched with fish oil, and their bodies bedaubed with red clay, they considered themselves irresistible.[6]

In this passage from Washington Irving several themes of importance are sounded, themes that one can follow through the whole corpus of literature of early contact in the Pacific Northwest. First, one notices the patronizing tone, sustained throughout: the Indians' acquisitive behavior, their "fondness" for "any article of civilized dress which they could procure," becomes the basis for assuming that their motivation or intent in wanting and wearing European clothes is to imitate the Whites. This is an assumption that holds, unquestioned, through the whole large literature of contact in the Northwest.

The Indians fail, of course, for no matter what items of European clothing they contrive to "array themselves" in, they persist in "besmirching" their hair with fish oil, "bedaubing" themselves with red clay, and so on.[7] In a kind of reversed version of the 1960s-era Native American stereotype of the Apple, here it's White on the outside (i.e., the clothes), but Red on the inside (the bodies).

There is, then, the particular quality of the "grotesque appearance" that Indians are portrayed as achieving, in a sense despite themselves. With the rather arch humor of the superiorly knowing observer (perhaps with eyebrows literally arched), these texts present ostensibly unintended sartorial achievements, effects quite unimagined by the wearer and visible in fact only to the "civilized" observer (your reporter on the scene and by extension you, the civilized reader). This seems partly to involve the unconventional ways that items of "civilized dress" were put to use, or worn, or combined in this early period of contact, but it is partly also a matter of the wearer's personal bearing or style in performance, creating a "grotesque appearance" and yet persisting in "considering themselves irresistible" (to whom? one might ask), apparently carrying off the whole performance with a certain hauteur that is, again, "grotesque" because it is incongruous. The perspective from which the incongruity becomes visible is only, and exclusively, that of a "civilized" observer.

It is interesting to see how important what we today would call the "gendered" qualities of the performance were to authors like Washington Irving (and no less to the various other observers—missionaries, explorers, fur company employees, etc.—who were actually on the scene). Irving points out that "both sexes" were fond of bracelets, beads, and the like, adorning their necks, wrists, and ankles with an abundance of such things. Only later does he declare that among these Indians the men "carry a passion for personal decoration farther than the females." This theme is well established, of course, in (perhaps especially northern) European literature of this period and before. A whole range of male Others, in the first instance perhaps southern Europeans (Italians, Spaniards, Portuguese), have been stereotyped as "colorful," silken, high-dressers of a foppish sort. Similarly, in the literature of European exploration, authors often tried "placing" the peoples they encountered in terms of a relative "balance" between the sexes, often declaring them ignorant or deluded in matters of ostensibly "natural" gendering.

There is, finally, the notion that the Indians had a sense of the "completeness" (or lack thereof) of an ensemble of clothing and accessories, a sense that being fully turned out or dressed to the nines involved attention to a number of components of one's total appearance, a sense, in other words, of what it was, in sartorial terms, to construct a coordinated whole of various parts. This theme is expressed somewhat subtly in this passage from Washington Irving. We're told that these Indian dandies, for example, "did not think their gala equipments complete, unless they had a jewel of *haiqua*, or wampum, dangling at the nose." But it will surface again, quite explicitly and in some surprising ways, in literature produced by the actual "Astorians," among others. Irving's description is typical, too, in turning this observation, once again, to the purpose of constructing a vignette of "grotesque" incongruity in the comical (tragic?) gap between the effects that were intended and those that were actually achieved. The vignette's final purpose, perhaps, is to illustrate—really, to offer proof of—the basic and intractable "savagery" of the Indians. And it is a "savagery" that remains invisible to themselves, for apparently they considered themselves quite up-to-date, "in style," even "irresistible."

It is important to see what is achieved in and by the deployment of this rhetoric in the texts produced by men like Blanchet, Washington Irving, and others, and to see the real value of these vignettes as light interludes, for they must have served purposes that we—in the light, or darkness, of subsequent history—can be justified in calling deadly serious. These exercises in prose description were themselves exercises of political and cultural power. For power to manifest itself so openly and observably—and hence, unavoidably, to render itself vulnerable, for it is vulnerable to the degree that it is visible, to the degree that its lineaments can be traced from the text to the (likely) context of its reception—the phenomenon being described in this fashion must have been felt as a threat of some sort.

Indeed, the social acts and actual encounters that remain behind these passages of descriptive prose, serving as their purported object, must have had a double-edged quality. Were these "grotesque" Indian dandies merely "imitating" the Whites in an earnest but ultimately misguided attempt to "improve" and/or ingratiate themselves? If so, their sartorial productions can in effect be laughed off, even seen as endearing, in the manner suggested by the texts themselves. But the problem, the vulnerability, resides in the fact that these descriptions, by their very nature, raise other, more troubling interpretive possibilities. Were these performances of sartorial hybridity and cross-cultural dandyism something more aggressive and ultimately more "civilized" than any of the European parties to these encounters could possibly afford to admit?

Perhaps, as interactional performances, they represented something on the order of "imitating" someone *to his face*: an act almost never sincere and even more rarely flattering. Perhaps they were like the Western Apache performances that Keith Basso describes in his book *Portraits of "The Whiteman,"* those hilarious interactional set pieces in which various late-twentieth-century Euro-American behavioral clichés get reperformed with a kind of droll intensity by (and among) groups of young Apache men—only this time, perhaps, the "portraits" are being held up and shown to the very Whitemen who originally "sat for them."[8]

In any case, the patronizing tone seems instantly and for all time to have become the only tone for these European observers to adopt, the presentation of intractable, oil-besmirched savages trying ridiculously to pass themselves off as civilized became the only image that could be countenanced (or the only countenance that could be imaged), and the interpretation as endearingly grotesque (or grotesquely endearing) became the only form of rhetorical generosity that could possibly be afforded.

But beneath the surface, beneath the calm assurance, the arched eyebrows, and the patronizing tone, there is an edge of nervousness, a nervous energy—the anxiety, perhaps, of an observer who wonders if he is being led along, or even lampooned, right to his face, and who adopts the patronizing stance in order to insulate himself, if not in the event, then retrospectively and ever after in his textual account of it, achieving thereby that *ne plus ultra* of interactional anxiety, "the last laugh." It is this nervous energy that my own account here will essay.

Of course, since we have no access to the performances of these "Indian dandies" except through the texts produced by Europeans, and so far as I know no early pictorial record of what these remarkable Native people actually looked like has survived, there is a great deal that we cannot know. But perhaps by attending to the edge of nervous energy, the abiding sense of interpretive instability that is in these texts, we can reconstruct something of what stimulated that instability in the first place.

## In the "Contact Zone"

Ethnographic, ethnohistorical, and archaeological studies of the Columbia River region all indicate the presence here, prior to European contact, of a number of features not generally associated in most people's minds with the lifeways of indigenous peoples, features that certainly do not accord with the popular image of Native Americans.[9] Far from being egalitarian, the Indian societies of the "greater lower Columbia," like those of the more northerly Northwest Coast, were rank-conscious, slaveholding societies with considerable emphasis on the display of inherited wealth.[10] Residence was stable in permanent winter villages, and the aristocratic families who formed the central core of each village resided in large multifamily houses crafted from massive cedar planks. (The houses around the Dalles area were constructed with cedar planks imported from miles west of the Cascades for this purpose.)

Fantastically productive salmon fisheries along the major waterways—the best fishing sites along which remained in the control of these same "upper-class" families—produced a massive amount of surplus wealth, the basis for a brisk and far-reaching sphere of mercantile exchange and trade. This mercantile sphere was managed mainly by Chinookan-speaking Indians, sedentary traders locally famous as much for their multilingualism as for their shrewdness.[11]

"Commodities" in the form of dried salmon and berries, often pounded and mixed together and sold in containers whose size and price were standardized, circulated within and beyond the region. Commercial transactions utilized a number of fixed media and rates of exchange; certain goods that were valuable in themselves could also serve as currency (dried pounded salmon as well as blue beads, and eventually blankets, assumed this "monetary" function). Moreover, shells of Dentalium (*háikwa* in Chinook Jargon, the regional lingua franca), a bivalve native to a restricted area off the coast of Vancouver Island, simultaneously served as a form of money and as an item of personal adornment. On special occasions, young women of marriageable age would in effect wear their dowries on their persons, securing in their pierced ears strings of dentalium shells that extended all the way to the ground, in an impressive, if ostentatious, display of wealth. The Native society was highly stratified, with "class" distinctions between "nobles," "commoners," and "poor people," and a distinction of caste separating free people from slaves, who were taken by capture from Indian groups to the south, and identifiable instantly by the fact that their heads had not been flattened in infancy.

The period under consideration encompasses the first actual "contact" between Native peoples in this area and Europeans (usually reckoned to begin with Broughton in 1791),[12] for indeed, various items of European material culture obtained through trade had already reached the Indian people of this region, and had already been appropriated to a variety of practical/technical, commercial, and aesthetic (including sartorial) purposes by the time of Lewis and Clark's arrival in 1805–6. By the mid-nineteenth century, "emigrants" began arriving in large numbers in the "Oregon country," eventually displacing the Indian populations. Treaties establishing Indian reservations in the area were signed in 1855; settlement took place over the next thirty years.

At various times, but especially in the 1830s, the indigenous populations suffered catastrophic losses due to disease epidemics. Indian groups west of the Cascade mountains were especially hard-hit by smallpox, malaria, and influenza during 1832–38, in some cases losing upwards of 90 percent of their populations in a period of two or three years.[13]

But despite these cataclysms, and despite what may seem in retrospect as a determined (and ultimately "successful") European effort to control, convert, and dominate the Indian peoples in the region, it is important to realize that there was a period (say, 1805–45) when Indian people, despite everything, were numerically, politically, economically, and culturally dominant in this area and the few Europeans living permanently in the region were in fact dependent on the Indians for their very survival, a fact that some authors acknowledged.

This was a period, then, when local Indian groups were enriched by the introduction of European goods and empowered by the participation of European people in the area, especially insofar as they were able to manage the influx of new kinds of goods and to oversee, mediate, and monopolize the participation of Europeans in this regional system of exchange and trade—to set the terms, in other words, on which Europeans could participate. This early period of enrichment and expansion of local indigenous exchange networks has been described by Marshall Sahlins for the Polynesian region of what he terms "the Trans-Pacific sector of the World System"; here, then, is the corresponding development in the Northwest Coast segment of this same world system.[14]

This zone of cultural "contact" and trade was centered at the lower Columbia River, from the Pacific Ocean inland about two hundred miles to its epicenter around the Dalles area.[15] Cole and Darling's overview of the early contact period in the Pacific Northwest as a whole corroborates this, and gives a sense of the economic seriousness of all parties to the cultural encounter:

> Indians were quick to exploit the opportunities that the establishment of forts presented. . . . The Chinook were able to control commerce northward to Puget Sound as well as to the west and south. . . . In 1824 Gov. George Simpson of the Hudson's Bay Company found that nearly all the furs at Fort George passed through Chinook hands. To other tribes "they represent us as Cannibals and every thing that is bad" and were "so tenacious" of their monopoly as to pillage and even murder to protect it. The Chinook did little trapping themselves. "In short," wrote Simpson, "they are quite a Nation of Traders and not of Hunters."[16]

It is interesting to note in Simpson's comments here the notion that one of the ways the Chinooks may have tried to consolidate their position in the region as the preeminent "culture brokers" was to spread tales to other tribes about the "savagery" (e.g., cannibalism) of the Europeans.

The confidence and acuity of the Chinookans were evidently still paying off years after the maritime fur trade had been replaced by the land-based trade. Captain Charles Wilkes of the United States Exploring Expedition, which arrived in the area in 1841, offers something akin to grudging praise for the "business" acumen of these Indians:

> An Indian is not slow in perceiving your wants, and views the dilemmas in which you may be placed with a becoming sang-froid. . . . [I]t was impossible to proceed without the Indians, who were always prone to recede from their bargains, under a feeling that they had not received enough. After a bargain was completed, and the price agreed upon, under the form of "potlatch" or "gift," the equivalent was always to be

again treated for, and thus the price of the article or service was always very much enhanced. In dealing with these Indians it was always necessary to feign much indifference of manner, in order to obtain the article, and also in closing the bargain after the preliminaries are settled. They readily close when they think their customers indifferent, for fear of a competitor among themselves, and are not in the habit of forming a combination, as they show little or no confidence in each other, and are rather disposed to rivalry.[17]

The Methodist missionary Gustavus Hines, who traveled throughout the area and well into the interior in the early 1840s, noted the same traits in the Upper Chinookan Wascos and Wishrams he encountered in the vicinity of the Dalles, at the opposite (eastern) end of Chinookan territory from the site of Fort George/Fort Clatsop, though his moral tone was clearer. Note that Hines here explicitly acknowledges the fact of European dependence on Indians:

> these Indians . . . seem instinctively to overreach those who, in any measure, are dependent upon them. I was particularly struck, while we were negotiating with them, with their astonishing tact in cheating. As a matter of course, lying has much to do with their system of trade, and he is the biggest fellow who can tell the biggest lie, make men believe it, and practice the greatest deception.[18]

What is most notable about the social context of the sartorial and related expressive practices that I want to discuss is the frequency and intensity of so-called economic behavior in this area—trade and exchange, involving all sorts of goods and services—as well as the particular form it took in the Columbia River area: "haggling and arguing between individuals."[19] Here, in general, we find individuals bargaining in a relatively unconstrained setting against the background of a constantly shifting field of short-lived and ad hoc alliances and "partnerships."

Using the rate of such a "face"-intensive form of economic activity as an index of the intensity of cultural "contact" and exchange more broadly in this area during this period, one can begin to see how rich a field this would be for various productions of cultural hybridity. Daily life along the Columbia in this period must have offered a wealth of opportunities and occasions on which to display, to good effect, one's knowledge of a wide variety of identities, languages, and customs, including (but by no means limited to) those of Europeans.

One of the consequences of the fur trade, in the Columbia River area as elsewhere in the Northwest, was the emergence of a new set of leaders from within the indigenous communities, a group of mostly male economic and political "operators" whose newfound wealth was based on their astute self-positioning as "culture brokers" and as brokers of commercial transactions in this rapidly developing situation of contact, trade, and intercultural exchange. The seemingly "cultivated" self-presentation of these Native *nouveaux riches* (often identified by the early Europeans as "chiefs" or "principal men of the village") and indeed some aspects of their attire invite comparisons to the more familiar European "dandies" who emerged in the nineteenth century. But for all the vaunted "cosmopolitanism" of the polyglot Chinookans,[20] were not these North American Indian communities profoundly different from the industrialized, urban settings that produced European modernism, and out of which dandyism of the familiar sort emerged?

My purpose here, in the broadest sense, is to suggest that despite the very great difficulties inherent in making analogies between events on the far frontier of North America and developments in the rapidly growing cities of Europe, such a comparison might actually help us to conceptualize in a more precise fashion the social and cultural conditions in which dandyism and other such vividly personalistic imaginings of transitional social spaces actually develop.

### Indians as Objects of Ambivalence

It is important to notice in this literature of contact the tension, ambivalence, and strikingly dissonant characterizations that emerge, especially when the Chinookans are being described. According to the rather homespun account of "mountain man" Thomas Jefferson Farnham, "the Chinooks flatten their heads more, and are more stupid, than any other tribe on the Columbia."[21] The explorer and ornithologist John Kirk Townsend, in the area in 1832–33, however, pointed out that head flattening did not appear materially to affect the intellect, for

> I have never seen . . . a race of people who appeared more shrewd and intelligent. I had a conversation on this subject, a few days since, with a chief who speaks the English language. He said that he had exerted himself to abolish the practice [of head flattening] in his own tribe, but . . . their ears were firmly closed on the subject.[22]

The Astorian Robert Stuart, who passed through the Dalles area in 1812, observed that "They pass a great portion of their lives in revelry and amusement, music, dancing, and play from their customary diversions."[23] Anastasio additionally notes that the carnivalesque atmosphere of the Dalles area during peak fishing and trading season posed difficulties for the early Euro-Americans who tried to gain control over matters:

> from the viewpoint of White traders and missionaries, there were a number of adventurers, outcasts, gamblers, and other potential trouble-makers who came because life was easy and the chances for gain were good. The intensity of trading and other intergroup activities varied rapidly from site to site, and the burden of supervising intergroup relations fell on the local chiefs, who were not always able to cope with the situation.[24]

The opinions of the mountain man and former fur trapper Thomas Farnham might well be typical of the White views Anastasio is alluding to: "This band of Indians have been notorious thieves ever since they have been known to the whites. Their meanness has been equally notorious. Destitute of every moral virtue, they and their fathers have hung around the Dalles, eaten salmon, and rotted in idleness and vice."[25] In *Astoria*, paraphrasing an entry from the (then unpublished) diary of Wilson Price Hunt, Washington Irving writes of the Chinookans around the trading center at the Dalles that "Trade had sharpened their wits, though it had not improved their honesty; for they were a community of rogues and freebooters."[26]

"A community of rogues and freebooters," perhaps, but sophisticated and well-informed—a point about which these early authors seem in virtually unanimous agreement, however uneasily. In any case it is quite clear that these Chinookan-speaking peoples never lived a stereotypically "primitive" existence of the locally bounded cultural universe.

"The trading operations of the inhabitants" at the Dalles, wrote Irving, "had given them a wider scope of information, and rendered their village a kind of head-quarters of intelligence."[27] The Astorian Wilson Price Hunt—in the diary entry paraphrased by Irving above—saw fit to compare the large Indian settlement at the Dalles to a fishing port on the eastern seaboard of the United States:

This is the site of the great fishery of the Columbia. It resembles one of the small fishing ports on the eastern coast of the United States. . . . The Indians of this place are the most intelligent I have yet seen. One of them knew several words of English; he told me that Mr Stuart had gone on one of the northerly tributaries of the Columbia to spend the winter there. . . . He recounted to me the catastrophe of Mr McKay and of the ship *Tonquin*.[28]

James G. Swan, writing about life around the mouth of the Columbia in the 1850s, likewise notes how rapidly and how accurately "news" was transmitted over a wide region:

What newspapers are to us, these traveling Indians are with each other, and it is astonishing with what dispatch and correctness information is transmitted from one part of the country to another. I have frequently, by this means, obtained correct intelligence of matters transpiring in other portions of the territory weeks before the regular mail communication.[29]

This was a period, then, when Europeans were being incorporated into an already long-established indigenous network of trade and exchange. The ethnohistoric data clearly point to the existence of a "world system" that in all likelihood had been functioning for a very long time, a system of transcultural exchange and trade that was fueled by the participation of people from a wide range of places and cultural backgrounds, people from all over Native North America. Over the course of the nineteenth century it came to include Europeans, African Americans, Polynesians, Asians, and others.[30]

## Nakedness, Civilization, and Slavery

In order to understand the sartorial preferences and performances of these newly rich "Indian dandies," one must always bear in mind the single fact that accords to clothing an entirely different status in these Native societies than it had in those of the European invaders—or, for that matter, in ours. In these indigenous societies, wearing clothing itself was optional rather than required. Indeed, older Indians are reported as persisting at least occasionally in the practice of going without clothes well into the 1850s, both at the mouth of the Columbia and in the vicinity of the Dalles, though this was "rationalized" by the Europeans (and seemingly also by some Indians) as a consequence of their "poverty."[31]

The anthropologist Wayne Suttles, in his introduction to the *Northwest Coast* volume of the Smithsonian Institution's *Handbook of North American Indians*, points to the social value of various modes of bodily alteration and adornment.[32] Drawing on the work of Hajda, he shows how the "Greater Lower Columbia" must have functioned in pre-contact times as a "regional social system," and he indicates the importance of forms of bodily adornment as signifiers of the shared understandings (about the rules governing marriage, food exchanges, and so on) that seem to have been in place among the linguistically diverse and in some respects culturally different Native groups living in the area:

> Although such networks of intermarriage included tribes who were linguistically and to some extent culturally different, they presumably required some shared understandings about social status and the interfamilial obligations that marriage involved. It should be possible to identify indicators of such shared understandings. Permanent modifications of the human body may be seen as markers of actual or potential participation in regional social systems. On the Northwest Coast there were three such modifications—pierced lips for labrets, modified head shape, and facial tattooing.[33]

Persons, in fact, must be included in any consideration of the system of valuable objects in circulation in the Columbia River region, because human beings of various sorts were in fact in circulation, and sometimes for retail sale, in this area. Aristocratic marriages were formalized through an elaborate series of exchanges between the kin groups that the bride and groom represented. The Dalles area, meanwhile, was a central marketplace for slaves, most of them captured in the first instance from northern California Indian groups, and sold to the Chinookans at the Dalles for immediate resale and transshipment to the north, or for purchase by local families. James G. Swan, a long-term resident of the area around the mouth of the Columbia, puts it rather bluntly:

> What they consider as property is any thing they can exchange or barter away for articles they desire to possess. This consists of Chinese chests, blue beads, blankets, calico, brass kettles, and other culinary articles, guns, fishing apparatus, canoes, and slaves or horses. . . . The price [for one slave] is from one hundred to five hundred dollars, or from twenty

to one hundred blankets, valued at five dollars each. Some are even higher than that, and not unfrequently a valuable canoe is added to the bargain.[34]

Among the perceived "deficiencies" and signs of "savagery" of these people that were most salient to these early authors were three that come up again and again: lack of (adequate) clothing, lack of agriculture, and the practice of head flattening. The Europeans attempted to intervene in all three, as will become clear.

### Acquiring an Ensemble of Clothing

It was not only missionaries, as it turned out, who were concerned with persuading the Indians to wear clothes on a regular basis. Indeed, the "civilizing" project of persuading local Indians to refrain from going without clothes on a daily basis took most of the first half of the nineteenth century and required the combined (though almost never coordinated) efforts of missionaries, fur traders, and others.

Lewis and Clark, presumably the first White people seen by the Chinookans and other Indian people along the Columbia, distributed a number of items during their 1805–6 stay in the area. The major items were, first, "Chief's Suits," a precise description of which I have been unable thus far to locate; and second, a "Friendship Medal," a silver medallion bearing a motif stamped on its face depicting hands clasped in a gesture of greeting: on one of them the sleeve of a tailored European jacket is clearly visible, and underneath it the cuff of a shirt sleeve; the other arm is clad in fringed buckskin.

In the early period, when most of the reports were written by men connected to the fur trade in some capacity, two patterns emerge. First, these writers describe events in the course of which Indians acquire ensembles of clothing or individual pieces (a shirt, a pair of breeches, etc.) from the Europeans they encounter in the course of commercial transactions, and/or as "gifts" that are intended, perhaps, to establish or maintain friendly relations. Second—far more commonly found in the literature—the writers describe incidents that show the "thievery and pilfering proclivities" of the Indians.

The fur trader Gabriel Franchère, in his journal of the winter of 1811–12, describes how he and his fur-trading colleagues would keep a pile of old pairs of pants outside their tent, requiring that the Indians who came to trade with them put the pants on before entering their tent to do business; but these pants were not gifts, rather they were "rented" to the Indians for the duration of the transaction, and the Indians were expected to put them back in the pile outside the door of the tent as they left: "These western Indians would adopt European manners quite early and rather liked wearing clothes if they were given them; this we encouraged by not allowing the chiefs to enter our houses without breeches, which we lent them."[35] Far more prominent in this literature are incidents in which Indians are depicted as wheedling, cajoling, bargaining, coaxing, coercing, extorting, "begging," or stealing items of European-style clothing. The following passage from Alexander Ross is representative in its tone of many in the literature produced by the Astorians. Note the quasi-"dandyism" that is (sarcastically, to be sure) imputed to the Indians in this passage, who are addressed superciliously here as "gentlemen":

> Their pilfering propensities had no bounds. The more we gave them the more they expected, and of course the more trouble they gave us; and notwithstanding all our care and kindness to them, they stole our canoe, axe and a whole suit of clothes, excepting the hat, belonging to Mr M'Lennan, which we were unable to recover. We had no sooner embarked, than Mr M'Lennan in his usual good-humor, standing up in the canoe, and throwing his hat amongst them, said, "Gentlemen, there's the hat, you have got the rest, the suit is now complete," and we pushed off and left them.[36]

Another "classic" passage that could serve as a representative sample of the pervasive tone of complaint in early Europeans' narratives of contact with Chinookans also comes from Alexander Ross. Here we can see how the Chinookans made it clear to the Europeans that *they* would be setting the terms of the encounter and that Europeans would simply have to become "acculturated" and learn that they had to *pay for services* like portaging of canoes while in Chinookan territory. The vignette opens as Ross is helping to get the cargo over the rocky portage at Cascades:

> Not being accustomed myself to carry, I had of course, as well as some others, to stand sentinel; but seeing the rest almost wearied to death, I took hold of a roll of tobacco, and after adjusting it on my shoulder, and holding it fast with one hand, I moved on to ascend the first bank; at the

top of which, however, I stood breathless, and could proceed no farther. In this awkward plight, I met an Indian, and made signs to him to convey the tobacco across, and that I would give him all the buttons on my coat; but he shook his head, and refused. Thinking the fellow did not understand me, I threw the tobacco down, and pointing to the buttons one by one, at last he consented, and off he set at a full trot, and I after him; but just as we had reached his camp at the other end, he pitched it down a precipice of two hundred feet in height, and left me to recover it the best way I could. Off I started after my tobacco; and if I was out of breath after getting up the first bank, I was ten times more so now. During my scrambling among the rocks to recover my tobacco, not only the wag that played the trick, but fifty others, indulged in a hearty laugh at my expense; but the best of it was, the fellow came for his payment, and wished to get not only the buttons but the coat along with them. I was for giving him—which he richly deserved—buttons of another mould; but peace, in our present situation, was deemed the better policy; so the rogue got the buttons, and we saw him no more.[37]

Passages like these, in which the European narrator depicts himself as the victim of Indian treachery and the target of Indian laughter, occur throughout this literature of early contact.

The missionary Samuel Parker offers an anecdote of an Upper Chinookan "chief" boarding the ship that brought Parker to Oregon and extracting an ensemble of clothing piece by piece from the ship's captain:

A chief of the Skilloots with a few of his people came on board. He was very talkative and sportive. When he was about to leave, he told Capt. L[ambert] that as they had been good friends, and were now about to separate, he wished a present. Capt. L. told his steward to give him a shirt. The chief took it and put it on, and then said, "how much better would a new pair of pantaloons look with this shirt." The Captain ordered him the article asked for. Now, said the chief, "a vest would become me, and increase my influence with my people." This was also given. Then he added, "well, Tie [sic; Chinook Jargon tayi, "chief"], I suppose we shall not see each other again, can you see me go away without a clean blanket, which would make me a full dress." The captain answered, "go about your business; for there is no end to your asking so long as I continue to give."[38]

In the course of their March 1838 trip upriver from the Walamet Mission settlement, traveling heavily burdened with the supplies and provisions needed to establish a new mission settlement at Wascopam in the Dalles area, the Methodist missionaries Henry Perkins and Daniel Lee met a "chief" of the "Wascopam" (i.e., Wasco Chinookan) Indians, "Wamcutta," whom Perkins in his diary describes as "dressed in the French style."

It is also interesting to note that Wamcutta and his compatriots were evidently pleased at the prospect of having a European settlement in their immediate environs, making magnanimous offers of help. Again, in being favorably disposed to the establishment of such settlements in their midst, Wamcutta and people like him were probably typical of many Indians in the Northwest who "considered the rewards to be gained as agents and dealers, rather than as hunters and trappers, so beneficial that they favored the establishment of posts among them."[39]

> We met at the portages three loads of our Dalles or Wascopam Indians, going with dry salmon and acorns to the fort to trade, and among them their chief, Wamcutta. Wamcutta [and his people] was very glad to see us, having heard we were coming, and offered to accompany us, and build houses [for us], if we desired it. He was dressed in the French style, and over all a large buffalo skin. We made him a small present, and passed on.[40]

Wamcutta (who apparently also went by the name Wamcutsul) was apparently a person of some influence, with ties to (probably Clackamas Chinook) villages near Willamette Falls, and other places west of the Cascade Mountains.[41] "Within a year," Boyd notes, Wamcutta's "relations with the missionaries had soured," and he quotes a Perkins letter of 24 February 1839 mentioning how "a report spread that Wamcutsul and his people were going to tie me up today and whip me, because I would not sell them an axe for six dozen salmon. Wamcutsul insisted that he threatened no such thing. God only knows."[42]

He is mentioned once more in documents associated with the Wascopam Mission, in a ledger entry of 31 July 1841 written by Henry Brewer, which indicates that items of Euro-American attire were indeed serving more or less as items of currency in and around Wascopam: "Bought Wamcuttas claim on a small piece of land west of the spring. We pay 1 blanket, 1 pair pants, 1 vest, 1 common shirt"—yet another "complete outfit," perhaps.[43]

Reciprocity is also the theme of the next extract, taken from Gustavus

Hines's report of his brief visit to Wascopam, passing through on his way to see Whitman and Spaulding in the spring of 1843, a particularly tense time in "Indian–White relations," as will become clear. Here we can see how the intervention of people like Dr. Elijah White created new categories of political leadership within the indigenous social groups, even as it exacerbated (perhaps preexisting) divisions of other sorts. In this remarkable passage, the group of newly appointed "chiefs" agrees to comply with White's program of meting out punishment with "the lash" (promulgated by White under the inspiration of similar practices established by Whitman and Spaulding among the nearby Nez Perce about this time). A second group of "leaders" operating without official "portfolio," as it were, was less pleased, apparently willing to agree to let White's system continue in place provided that they were compensated, *in blankets, shirts, and pants of European manufacture*, for receiving these whippings:

> Soon after we arrived, about twenty Indians came to the house of Mr Brewer, where we stopped, to have a talk with Dr White. When he was up the winter before, he prevailed on these Indians to organize themselves into a kind of government. One high chief, and three subordinates, were elected; laws were enacted, and penalties annexed were whippings more or less severe, according to the nature of the crime. The chiefs had found much difficulty in enforcing the laws. . . . But the other influential men who were not in office, desired to know of Dr White, of what benefit this whipping system was going to be to them. They said they were willing it should continue, provided they were to receive blankets, shirts and pants, as a reward for being whipped. They had been whipped a good many times, and had got nothing for it, and it had done them no good. If this state of things was to continue, it was all (*cultus*) good for nothing, and they would throw it all away. In reply they were told by the Doctor that . . . they need not expect pay for being flogged, when they deserved it. They laughed heartily at the idea, and dispersed, giving us an opportunity to make arrangements for the continuance of our journey.[44]

Again, Indian laughter. Just as Alexander Ross describes how the Indians at the portage at Cascades "indulged in a hearty laugh" at his expense as he scrambled to retrieve his roll of tobacco, here the Indians "laughed heartily" at the suggestion that they *not* receive payment in blankets, shirts, and pants to compensate them for the inconvenience of receiving whippings.

## Encounters with *"Indian Dandies"* along the Columbia

In the spring of 1841, just as Father Blanchet was arriving in the Klal-lam village and encountering a Coast Salish Indian "arrayed in French style," the Wilkes expedition's ships were temporarily retreating north-ward from the treacherous seas about the mouth of the Columbia; here they were boarded by a group of Indians, probably also Coast Salish speakers. There are two accounts, one from Lieutenant George Colvo-coresses, an officer, and one from Captain Charles Wilkes himself.[45] The officer's account makes it clear that the one Indian of the party who was "dressed in corduroy pantaloons, and a jacket made of scarlet cloth" was the same person who "could speak a little English," while the second account, Wilkes's, identifies him as "the principal man of the party" and describes his coat as being equipped with "the Hudson's Bay Company buttons." Wilkes also reports that the first question put to his group was whether their ship was of "King George" or "Boston" provenance, noting that the Indians of the area used these terms to dif-ferentiate English from American vessels.

Gustavus Hines, one of the missionary "reinforcements" to the Ore-gon Methodist mission who arrived on the *Lausanne* in 1839, de-scribed how his ship, traveling upriver on the Columbia toward the Willamette, was boarded by first one and then another group of Lower Chinooks.[46] In this case, the putative "chief" is not the one who is dressed to the nines, but apparently his wife, or one of his wives (iden-tified here, obviously superciliously, as "the queen"), who is wearing "a calico dress, a neckerchief, and a red woolen shawl."[47] The rest of the party—which included, Hines tells us, "some of the *nobility*" (ital-ics in original)—was not so well dressed. "Most of them were very small in size," he writes, "and very poorly clad, some of them not hav-ing sufficient clothing to cover their nakedness."[48]

The following vignette from the Oregon journal of the naturalist John Kirk Townsend was obviously intended by its author as a comical interlude, and its overall flavor and tone suggest that by the early 1830s at least some of these explorers were already keeping careful di-aries of their experiences with an eye to the prospects for eventual pub-lication upon their return to "civilization."

> *March 1st* [1836].—There is an amusing little Indian living in this neigh-borhood, who calls himself *"tenas tie,"* [Chinook Jargon *tunus tayi*]

(little chief,) and he is so probably in every sense of the term. In person, he stands about four feet six, in his moccasins; but no exquisite in the fashion world, no tinselled dandy in high life, can strut and stamp, and fume with more dignity and self consequence. . . . If you answer hi[s many questions], he attempts the pronunciation [of English words and phrases] after you, and it is often not a little ludicrous. He is evidently proud of the name the white people have given him, not understanding its import, but supposing it to be a title of great honor and dignity. If he is asked his Indian name, he answers very modestly, Qualaskin (muddy river,) but if his *pasiooks yahhalle* is required, he puffs up his little person to its utmost dimensions, and tells you with a simper of pride and self complacency, that it is *"mizzy moddy."* [49]

Gustavus Hines, the Methodist missionary who had arrived with the other "reinforcements" to the Oregon Indian mission on the *Lausanne* in 1839, accompanied the territorial Indian agent Elijah White on his "corrective" trip into the interior in May 1843 and provides an account of his encounter, while en route there, with a Cayuse "chief" whom he identifies with the evocative name of Feathercap. The passage from which this extract is taken seems intended to serve in Hines's narrative as a light interlude in a longer and more detailed description of the serious tensions in relations between Indians and Europeans in the eastern part of the region at this time. While at Umatilla, they were invited to inspect the "Indian plantations" being cultivated by Feathercap's people. A party was assembled, and on 8 May 1843 set out on a "pleasure tour," with Feathercap serving as a kind of tour guide:

The captain of the party was a Kayuse chief, by the name of Feathercap: and of all the Indians I have seen he has a countenance the most savage. But, with this, there is a dignity and decision manifested in his movements, which might put a white man to the blush. He is about five feet ten inches high; has a voice of the stentorian order, and possesses all the native characteristics of an orator. His dress was quite fantastical, being composed of skin breeches, a striped scarlet coat, gilted off very much in the fashion of the regimentals of a British general. His head-dress was composed, first of a cotton handkerchief thrown loosely over his head, then a cap made of otter skin over the handkerchief, and on top of the cap, fastened with a savage taste, the long hair of a white horse's tail, which hung in ringlets down the back side of his neck. Thus rigged, he was prepared to guide us on a tour of pleasure.[50]

The "pleasure tour" that Feathercap conducted that day was to show Hines and his guests the agricultural achievements of the group under his control: small, carefully tended parcels of land, "well fenced and well cultivated," about the size of garden plots, on which Feathercap's people had sown and raised wheat, corn, peas, and other crops.[51] This ostensibly recreational excursion was gotten together in the midst of serious political conflict between Europeans and Indians in the area, tensions that were to flare into open violence four years later in the regionally famous "Whitman massacre" of 1847.[52] Hines, White, and their colleagues had sent word that they wanted to meet with the Nez Perce and Cayuse chiefs, though the Indians said this would not be convenient, because many of the chiefs were off elk hunting in the mountains—"a mere pretence," in Hines's view.[53] The Indians were stalling, Hines thought, awaiting the arrival of a Nez Perce chief and several hundred warriors.

It was at this precise moment that Feathercap appeared in all his finery, and proposed to take the visitors on the "pleasure tour." This, then, is the context for the description we began with, of Feathercap's "fantastical" attire:

> We came to the conclusion that the meeting of the two tribes [Cayuse and Nez Perce] should, if possible, be prevented. While considering this subject, we were solicited by the chiefs to take a ride among the Indian plantations. Accordingly, a party was made out which would have made all the sacerdotal order laugh to contemplate. The captain of the party was a Kayuse chief, by the name of Feathercap: and of all the Indians I have seen.[54]

Once again, conjoined to a description of Indian dandyism, one finds laughter in the midst of real tension—in this missionary's memoir, sacerdotal laughter.

## Regiments of Value

The notion that Indian uses of Euro-American items of clothing were motivated by a desire to "imitate" Europeans has all the shortcomings of mere "motivational" accounts of any social or cultural process, to say nothing of the fact that it is patronizing and empirically inadequate. Indeed, it is clear that these "Indian dandies," once arrayed in all their "astonishing" finery—finery that blended European and indigenous forms of personal adornment and decoration—did not, in fact, resemble Europeans very closely at all. Perhaps they were in sartorial terms a *third* category, neither simply "Indian" nor simply "White," but rather, in a complex fashion, something that comprehended both in a demonstrably "knowing" way.

If individuals' motivations must enter the discussion at some point, then it would seem at least as likely that rather than "imitating" the Europeans, these "Indian dandies" might have been wanting to demonstrate—to Europeans and to other Indians alike—their knowledge of a range of sartorial forms and practices, including, but not limited to, those of the Europeans. In this context, the Indian preference for and focus on ornamental (including regimental) elements of European clothing—for example, the kinds of clothes, like military and other uniforms, whose mode of ornamentation is an exact index of the wearer's position in a hierarchical social order of some sort—begin to make cultural sense. Indeed, what could better explain the otherwise unremarked-upon Indian preference for *regimental* clothing that one notices again and again in these vignettes, over the whole period and throughout the whole region (from Astoria to the Dalles), to say nothing of the "fantastical" combinations of indigenous forms of personal adornment with European regimental elements, colors, and styles, and regimental details of the cut, embroidery, or assemblage of clothing items?

If this were the case, moreover, then these demonstrations of knowledge about and familiarity with certain Euro-American "fashions" in clothing would be perfectly parallel to these same personages' demonstrations of their knowledge of European fashions in speaking that we have seen in so many of these vignettes (perhaps most vividly in Townsend's vignette of "Mizzy Moddy").[55]

Buttons, especially brass buttons, seem to have been assimilated to the same category with medals, medallions, and (Chinese and other) coins. In fact, there is evidence of this in James G. Swan's account: he describes the narrative of an old Chinook woman named Carcumcum, who seems to have recounted to him her memories of the Indians' first experiences with liquor in the area. In this passage it is important to note the details of Lieutenant Broughton's clothing that the woman remembers and the terms she uses to describe them (in Chinook Jargon):

old Carcumcum . . . remember[ed] the first time that any liquor was given to the Chenook Indians, and, from her description, I should think it was when Broughton went into the Columbia on the brig Chatham [in 1791], for she said the *tyee*, or chief of the vessel, had *gold dollar* things, meaning epaulets, on his shoulders, and was in a man-of-war. They drank some rum out of a wine-glass—how much she did not recollect; but she *did* recollect that they got drunk, and were so scared at the strange feeling that they ran into the woods and hid till they were sober.[56]

The focus especially upon the "decorative" elements—brass buttons, epaulets, and the like—that serve as sartorial signifiers indicating the wearer's rank in a hierarchical social order would seem to be consistent both with aboriginal practices of personal adornment and with the apparent tendency on the part of Indians to treat European clothing of whatever sort as primarily "ornamental" in value.

It is hard not to connect the preference for regimental blue military uniforms and parts thereof with the earlier passion for blue beads. Moreover, blue and red were regimental colors, and red had long been important in the indigenous groups, as the preferred color for face and body paint. Indeed, these color preferences seem to have remained constant throughout the early to mid-nineteenth century. Lewis and Clark noted the strong preference for blue beads over any other kind in 1805–6, and at the end of the period under consideration, James G. Swan notes a preference for blue calicoes on the part of Indian women, who by the 1850s were routinely producing dresses after European models for their own use:

[Indians of the area] are very fond of dress, and are apt and excellent imitators. The women are expert with the needle, and fashion and make their dresses with great rapidity, imitating as near as they can the dresses of the white women they may have seen. They prefer calicoes with small figures on them; and a blue ground, with little white dots or sprigs, seem to be most in demand. . . . They are excellent judges of such articles as they want and are accustomed to. The women try the calicoes, to ascertain if the colors are fast, by chewing the cloth in their mouths.[57]

## *Work and the Arts of "Reproduction" in the Contact zone*

As Swan's description suggests, the Indians were not wholly dependent on buying, "trading," or "stealing" finished items of European clothing.

There is, moreover, clear evidence that the Indians of this region became adept at making high-quality "reproductions" of Euro-American items of clothing quite rapidly following European contact, some of them even filling orders from Whites who wished to procure items of this sort. The British naturalist David Douglas, who was near the Dalles on 20 June 1825, noted that

> the natives are inquisitive in the extreme, treacherous, and will pillage or murder when they can do it with impunity. Most of the tribes on the coast (the Chenooks, Cladsaps, Clikitats, and Killimucks) from the association they have had with the Europeans are anxious to imitate them and are on the whole not unfriendly. Some of them are by no means deficient of ability. Some will *converse in English tolerably well, make articles after the European models*, &c.[58]

In fact, it seems that at about this time, one enterprising twelve-year-old girl in one of the villages farther west was able to fill Douglas's order for four custom-made hats in the English fashion he desired:

> Last night my Indian friend Cockqua arrived here from his tribe on the coast, and brought me three of the hats made on the English fashion, which I ordered when there in July; the fourth, which will have some initials wrought in it, is not finished, but will be sent by the other ship. I think them a good specimen of the ingenuity of the natives and particularly also being made by the little girl, twelve years old, spoken of when at the village. I paid one blanket (value 7s.) for them, the fourth included. We smoked; I gave him a dram and a few needles, beeds, pins, and rings as a present for the little girl.[59]

Drawing on documentation relevant to the more northerly section of the Northwest Coast, Cole and Darling show that even as Indian people were learning to fashion European-style clothing and accessories of a quality and style suitable for retail sale to Whites, Europeans were learning—under duress, at times—how to manufacture items of clothing and accessories to suit indigenous tastes:

> The pattern in trade exchange indicates that the Indians, like any set of consumers, exercised a strong discrimination in their selection of items. If traders could not offer the type or quality of articles Indians demanded, there could be no trade. The records of early traders are replete with complaints at Indian refusals to trade. . . . Capt. James Cook had already noted that the Nootka were selective even in what they

stole. Maquinna was interested only in window panes, firearms, and blue cloth.[60]

Cole and Darling discuss how European traders, operating with such disadvantages, sought to fashion the kinds of objects Indians wanted, in the styles they wanted, doing their best with materials that they had *in situ,* and technologies that they brought with them. One also notices that the kinds of objects the Indians wanted were almost always, it seems, objects that could be used for personal adornment— clothing, items of jewelry, and other accessories:

> Traders were sometimes able to adapt to altered tastes. When Joseph Ingraham found his goods difficult to sell, he put a smith to work forging necklaces in twisted iron rods made in imitation of the copper ones he observed being worn by a woman alongside the *Hope* in Parry Passage in 1791. . . . Rings and bracelets were similarly made. Such inventiveness was often of temporary duration and still subject to the whims of local taste. Following Ingraham by two years, Josiah Roberts found that iron neck pieces were out of fashion among the Haida. . . . The demand was now for elkskins to be fashioned into tunics or cuirasses. He met this new demand by acquiring the hides from Chinooks, who wanted copper.[61]

## *"Style," Fashion, and History in Costume*

Several of the more careful European observers describe generational contrasts in the sartorial practices of Indians, noting how older men and women alike tended to adhere to traditional forms of dress and personal adornment, including continuing to go without clothes of any sort, while suggesting that it was the members of a younger generation who were the rapacious consumers of European goods and ostentatious users (displayers) of European items of clothing and personal adornment.

James G. Swan, for example, provides a colorful and closely observed account of life around the mouth of the Columbia in the 1850s, a period when the remnant Lower Chinook (Clatsop and Shoalwater) populations who had survived the disease epidemics of the 1830s were beginning to be "assimilated" culturally and linguistically into the larger neighboring group of Salishan-speaking Chehalis Indians. Swan noted many generational differences in the "consumption patterns" and clothing preferences of the Indians in the area:

> Before the introduction of blankets and calicoes among them, they used the dressed skins of the deer, bear, and sea-otter. The women wore a sort of skirt or tunic, made from the inner bark of young cedar. . . . This garment is still used by old women, and by all the females when they are at work in the water, and is called by them their *siwash coat*, or Indian gown. The young men dress in clothes procured from the whites, and some of them, when dressed up, look well enough to appear in almost any company. The old men, like old Toke and his brother Colote, seldom wear any clothing but a shirt and a blanket.[62]

The cultural landscape at the other end of Chinookan territory, around the Dalles area, in the 1840s and 1850s was different in a number of respects, as the richly detailed observations of the Methodist missionaries at Wascopam and visitors like the Methodist missionary Gustavus Hines make clear, although it appears that parallel processes of ethnic transformation were beginning to develop within the indigenous populations here, too.[63]

At this eastern "frontier" of the Chinookan-controlled "contact zone," the influence of Sahaptian-speaking groups like the Nez Perce and their congeners like the Sahaptin-speaking Umatilla and the Cayuse (speakers of an unrelated language, but fluently bilingual in Sahaptin) was growing rapidly, and many of the Chinookan-speaking Wascos and Wishrams, who continued to intermarry with Sahaptins under reservation conditions (beginning in the 1870s), increasingly became "assimilated" to the culture and emergent "ethnicity" of the numerically dominant Sahaptin groups.

Meanwhile, the Nez Perce, Cayuse, Umatilla, and neighboring smaller Sahaptin groups were all themselves being heavily influenced by Plains Indian cultural traits and "fashions," including especially the whole "complex" of cultural practices associated with horses and horsemanship. Feathercap's ensemble, with its ringlets of white horsetail falling down his back, represents a (perhaps "fantastical") admixture of British regimental and Plains Indian sartorial elements.

Here, too, we find indications of generational contrasts—even conflicts—within the Indian groups, not only in "styles" of clothing, but in the general orientation toward the increasingly intrusive Euro-American settler population, which by the 1840s and 1850s was clearly fomenting a cultural episode of a new and heretofore unprecedented order. At the eastern boundary of the Columbia River "contact zone," it was the younger generation of male *arrivistes* and "chiefs" who sought European and Plains Indian items of clothing, even as they favored direct and violent responses to European incursions (so much for the "imitation" theory of Indian use of European clothing). Plains Indian elements of costume and Plains material culture generally were coming to stand for a self-consciously "recalcitrant" and markedly "Indian" cultural and ethnic identity, evoking as they do the image of a Plains Indian buffalo-hunting "warrior" on horseback.

## Coda

"Martin!" exclaimed the late Mrs. Celia Ashue of White Swan, Washington, when I showed her a photograph of the Wasco "chief" Martin Spedis on a blazing hot afternoon in July 1989 (fig. 2.1). I had found a stack of these photographs for sale at a price of fifty cents each in a nearby used-furniture store, and bought several, thinking they might make good gifts. Indeed, at least three or four of my Chinookan linguistic consultants at Warm Springs and Yakima reservations were related to Martin Spedis in one way or another; he was one of the last functioning "chiefs" at the Wishram-Wasco village at the Dalles (later also called Spearfish, and sometimes Spedis, after him). A few families, including Martin Spedis's, continued to live at the site into the 1930s. By 1957 it was underwater, inundated along with the Sahaptin village of Wayam a few miles upriver at Celilo Falls when the Dalles Dam, a U.S. Army Corps of Engineers hydroelectric project, was completed.

Celia Ashue had been described to me by relatives of hers at Warm Springs as a fluent speaker of Chinookan, someone who "knew a lot about old things," the kind of person I should make a point of seeking out. She was about ninety years old when I visited her, unable to move from the large, state-of-the-art hospital bed that now took up almost all of her large bedroom on the first floor of the large clapboard house that itself took up almost all of the small dusty lot where it sat, hard by a newly built convenience store on a side street in the small town of White Swan, Washington, on the Yakima Reservation.

*Fig. 2.1.* Martin Spedis, Wishram-Wasco Chinookan chief at the (now submerged) village of Nixliudix, across the Columbia River from the present-day city of The Dalles, Oregon. Cabinet photograph by Rutter, North Yakima, WA, circa 1890. Photograph courtesy of Robert E. Moore. Reproduced by permission.

The most recent in a series of strokes had left Mrs. Ashue unable to take care of herself, barely able to speak. A granddaughter, who welcomed me cordially when I knocked at the front door—a complete stranger—was there to take care of her. Celia Ashue, like Martin Spedis, was related to most of my Wasco consultants at Warm Springs in one way or another; one Warm Springs friend in particular told me how Celia used to come from Yakima to visit her mother, and she—a young woman herself at the time—would sit in the next room, listening as Celia and her mother visited in Wasco, using "old, old words that nobody knows anymore."

Celia Ashue beamed at the photograph, and her granddaughter had appeared in the doorway to her bedroom, smiling too, as I carefully leaned the photograph in a place of honor on top of a tall chest of drawers next to her hospital bed, where it could be easily seen.

Martin Spedis wears two rows of large dentalia across his chest. Beneath his hat, displayed (perhaps on an easel?) beside him, is a several-fathoms-long string of very large dentalia, and he wears more of this shell-money around his neck, in the form of a "choker." Beneath the dentalia on his chest is a beaded vest, worn over what must have been a colorful polka-dotted tunic or shirt, perhaps made of silk; there is also a beaded apron, as well as leggings and moccasins, decorated with beadwork, and he wears on each wrist a wide bracelet, probably of copper or brass. In his right ear there appears to be a Chinese coin, though it looks unusually large, and may be a medallion of some sort; any earring that might be in his left ear is obscured by his carefully combed hair. As one of my other Wasco friends noted, marveling at this photograph and his attire, "he was a fine man."

## Conclusion

On the Columbia, the phenomenon of "Indian dandyism" was remarkably short-lived. By the time the Indians were being resettled on reservation lands and forming communities there (around the 1870s), the wearing of clothes was no longer a "choice," it was compulsory, and it had become routinized (and starting in this later period, incidentally, one can validly speak of attempts to imitate White styles, along with the development of new, self-consciously "Indian" styles). When he posed for his formal photograph at the studio of "Rutter" in North Yakima, Washington, Martin Spedis wore his finest, but it was the formal wear of a bygone age. By the 1870s, the era of these vividly transcultural sartorial statements had passed, and with it the indigenous dandies who "fashioned" them.

## *Afterword*

Even though I know of no discussion of this rather fleeting phenomenon of "Indian dandyism" in all of the historical and anthropological literature on the Pacific Northwest, it should be remembered that seeking and finding dandyism on the western frontier of America rather than (or in addition to) the European metropole are far from unprecedented. No less central a figure than Baudelaire himself pointed out that "Dandyism is a mysterious institution. . . . it is of great antiquity, Caesar, Catiline, and Alcibiades providing us with dazzling examples; and very widespread, Chateaubriand having found it in the forests and by the lakes of the New World."[64]

Walter Benjamin, likewise, notes the popularity of Alexandre Dumas's *Mohicans de Paris* in the Paris of the 1840s, noting that "the most interesting thing" about the influence of James Fenimore Cooper's (at least in retrospect, somewhat kitschy) novelistic representations of American Indians is that "it is not concealed but displayed."[65] Benjamin quotes a florid promotional blurb for Dumas's novel, taken from the publisher's leaflet: "Paris—the Mohicans . . . these two names clash like the *qui vive* of two gigantic unknowns. An abyss separates the two; through it flashes a spark of that electric light which has its source in Alexandre Dumas."[66]

Like Dumas, Balzac "never tired of referring to Cooper as his model."[67] For Balzac, the

> poetry which stood Cooper in such good stead attaches in the same way to the smallest details of Parisian life. The pedestrians, the shops, the hired coaches, or a man leaning against a window—all this was of the same burning interest . . . as a tree stump, a beaver's den, a rock, a buffalo skin, an immobile canoe, or a floating leaf was to a reader of a novel by Cooper.[68]

Balzac's enthusiasm was perhaps less than universal, since Benjamin notes that "at an early date there were objections to his 'Mohicans in spencer jackets' and 'Hurons in frock coats.'"[69]

Baudelaire himself helped to construct just this sort of portrayal of American Indians as objects deserving of the most refined and dandyistic sort of imagistic delectation—an image and a stance that are strikingly at odds with the unfavorable or at least ambivalent ones found in the early contact literature sampled here: "Dandyism is the last spark of heroism and decadence; and the type of discussion by our traveller in

North America does nothing to invalidate this idea; for how can we be sure that these tribes that we call 'savage' may not in fact be the *disjecta membra* of great extinct civilizations?"[70]

NOTES

This chapter is based on a paper presented at the College Art Association's eighty-sixth annual conference, in a session on "Dandies: Sartorial Finesse and Cultural Identity," organized by Susan Fillin-Yeh, in Toronto, 26–28 February 1998. I am grateful to a number of my New York University colleagues, notably Thomas Abercrombie, Karen I. Blu, Paul Chevigny, Barbara Kirshenblatt-Gimblett, and Fred R. Myers, for their encouragement and support. Valuable suggestions and important help with the writing and/or research came from a variety of sources, notably Brian A. Blanchfield, David W. Dinwoodie, John Gallahue, Gary M. Johnson, Paul D. Kroeber, Michael Silverstein, and Susan Fillin-Yeh. Anthropological and linguistic fieldwork at Warm Springs and Yakima Reservations and environs (1982–present) has been supported at various times by the Jacobs Research Funds (Whatcom Museum Foundation), the Phillips Fund of the Library of the American Philosophical Society, the Center for Psychosocial Studies (Chicago), and the Dean's Development Fund of Reed College. None of these individuals or institutions, needless to say, can be held responsible for the many defects of the presentation.

1. Francis Norbert Blanchet et al., *Historical Sketches of the Catholic Church in Oregon during the Past Forty Years* (Portland, OR: n.p., 1956), 63.

2. Ibid., 64.

3. In their survey of early contact history in the Northwest, Cole and Darling probably represent the dominant view among ethnohistorians about how to understand the emergence of "chiefs" among indigenous groups, seeing the very institution of "chiefdom" itself as a complicated outgrowth of the dynamics of cultural encounter in the area. See Douglas Cole and David Darling, "History of the Early Period," in *Handbook of North American Indians*, vol. 7, *Northwest Coast*, ed. Wayne Suttles (Washington, DC: Smithsonian Institution, 1990), 128–29:

> Scholars are in agreement that the effect of contact and trade was to strengthen social stratification and the role of the leader. . . . European explorers and traders needed to deal with some form of authority who might act as spokesman for all the Indians in a particular area, someone who might authorize the use of local resources and who might mediate points of conflict. Indians, too, could benefit from leaders who could negotiate with the visitors, bringing trade benefits to their own group.

Native leaders competed for this position, offering—and often magnify-ing—their abilities, influence, and power. . . . The European presence seems to have increased competition among Indian leaders for preemi-nence at the same time as it decreased their number. From formerly being simply a kind of "first among equals," the village chief often came to occupy a distinct position. While European preferment was an element in the elevation of some to recognized preeminence, that posi-tion seems not to have been attained by any who had no indigenous claims to leadership status.

4. Blanchet et al., *Historical Sketches of the Catholic Church in Oregon*, 66.

5. Washington Irving, *Astoria, or Anecdotes of an Enterprise beyond the Rocky Mountains* (1836; Philadelphia: J. B. Lippincott, 1961).

6. Ibid., vol. 2, 294–95.

7. Of course, the idea that these Indian people actually "besmirched" their hair with fish oil and "bedaubed" themselves with red clay is only one of many of the egregious falsehoods promulgated in Washington Irving's best-seller. Far more trustworthy is the testimony of James G. Swan, who may very well have had *Astoria* in mind when he disputed the reports of earlier writers. See James G. Swan, *The Northwest Coast* (1857; Seattle: University of Washington Press, 1972), 112–13. According to Swan, other writers claimed that the Chinooks

are a filthy, greasy set, . . . [and] that they regularly anoint their bodies with fish-oil and red ochre. Such, however, is not the fact. As soon as their work is done, they wash themselves, and generally bathe two or three times a day. All the painting or oiling I have ever seen them do is to rub a little grease and vermillion, or red ochre, between their hands, and then smear it over their faces. The women will also paint the head, in the line of the parting of the hair, with dry vermillion, and give an extra touch to their eyebrows; but I have never seen either men or women put oil or grease of any kind on their bodies. . . . Whatever may have been the former practice among the Chinook Indians relative to personal dec-oration, they certainly have at present relinquished the custom [of tattoo-ing], and are only anxious at present to get white people's garments to clothe themselves with, wearing, as their only ornament, a sort of band of black ostrich feathers round their caps, which they purchase of the Hudson's Bay Company.

8. Keith Basso, *Portraits of "The Whiteman": Linguistic Play and Cultural Symbols among the Western Apache* (Cambridge: Cambridge University Press, 1979).

9. For archaeology, standard sources include William Duncan Strong, W. Egbert Schenck, and Julian H. Steward, "Archaeology of the Dalles-Deschutes

Region," *University of California Publications in American Archaeology and Ethnology* 29, no. 1 (1930): 1–154; for Chinookan contact history, see David French, "Wasco-Wishram," in *Perspectives in American Indian Culture Change*, ed. E. Spicer (Chicago: University of Chicago Press, 1961), 337–430; and Yvonne Hajda, "Regional Social Organization in the Greater Lower Columbia, 1792–1830" (Ph.D. diss., University of Washington, Seattle, 1984); for a reconstruction of Chinookan pre-contact life (by the method of "memory ethnography"), see Leslie Spier and Edward Sapir, "Wishram Ethnography," *University of Washington Publications in Anthropology* 3, no. 3 (1930): 151–300.

10. See Hajda, "Regional Social Organization in the Greater Lower Columbia"; Michael Silverstein, "Chinookans of the Lower Columbia," in Suttles, *Handbook of North American Indians*, vol. 7, *Northwest Coast*, 533–46; David French and Kathrine S. French, "Wasco, Wishram, Cascades," in *Handbook of North American Indians*, vol. 12, *Plateau*, ed. Deward E. Walker (Washington, DC: Smithsonian Institution, 1999), and references therein.

11. The Chinookan languages were once spoken in and around villages on both banks of the Columbia River in present-day Washington and Oregon, from the mouth of the river (present-day Astoria, Oregon, Willapa Bay and Shoalwater Bay in Washington, and environs) eastward for a distance of about two hundred miles, to the area around the present-day city of The Dalles, Oregon. All but the easternmost dialects of Kiksht—Wasco, Wishram, and Cascades—have been extinct for some time: the Lower Chinookan dialects and Kathlamet since about 1900, Clackamas since about World War II. Remaining speakers and semispeakers of Wasco-Wishram continue to reside at the Warm Springs Reservation in Oregon and the Yakima Reservation in Washington state.

12. Silverstein, "Chinookans of the Lower Columbia."

13. See Robert T. Boyd, "The Introduction of Infectious Diseases among the Indians of the Pacific Northwest, 1774–1874" (Ph.D. diss., University of Washington, Seattle, 1985); also see Robert T. Boyd, "Demographic History, 1774–1874," in Suttles, *Handbook of North American Indians*, vol. 7, *Northwest Coast*, 135–48.

14. See Marshall Sahlins, "Cosmologies of Capitalism: The Trans-Pacific Sector of the World System," *Proceedings of the British Academy* 74 (1988): 1–51.

15. See Hajda, "Regional Social Organization in the Greater Lower Columbia"; also see Angelo Anastasio, "The Southern Plateau: An Ecological Analysis of Intergroup Relations," 1955; *Northwest Anthropological Research Notes* 6, no. 2 (1972 [1955]): 109–229; and French, "Wasco-Wishram."

16. Cole and Darling, "History of the Early Period," 124–25.

17. Charles Wilkes, *Narrative of the United States Exploring Expedition*

*during the Years 1838, 1839, 1840, 1841, 1842* (Philadelphia: Lea and Blanchard, 1845), 4:310–11.

18. Gustavus Hines, *Life on the Plains of the Pacific. Oregon: Its History, Condition, and Prospects. . . .* (Buffalo: Geo. H. Derby and Co., 1851): 158.

19. Anastasio, "The Southern Plateau," 161.

20. Claude Lévi-Strauss, "Comopolitanism and Schizophrenia," in *The View from Afar* (New York: Harper and Row, 1985), 177–85.

21. Thomas Jefferson Farnham, *Travels in the Great Western Prairies, the Anahuac and Rocky Mountains, and in the Oregon Territory* (Poughkeepsie: Killey and Lossing, 1849), 161.

22. John Kirk Townsend, *Narrative of a Journey across the Rocky Mountains to the Columbia River*, 1839; reprinted in *Early Western Travels, 1748–1846: A Series of Annotated Reprints*, ed. Reuben Gold Thwaites (Cleveland: A. H. Clark, 1905), 21:303.

23. Robert Stuart, *The Discovery of the Oregon Trail: Robert Stuart's Narrative of His Overland Trip Eastward from Astoria, 1812–1813,* ed. Phillip A. Rollins (1812; New York: Scribner's, 1935), 54.

24. Anastasio, "The Southern Plateau," 163.

25. Farnham, *Travels in the Great Western Prairies,* 163.

26. Irving, *Astoria*, vol. 2:280.

27. Ibid., 281.

28. Stuart, *The Discovery of the Oregon Trail,* 305 (Hunt's entry for 31 January 1812).

29. Swan, *The Northwest Coast,* 170.

30. Anastasio, "The Southern Plateau"; French, "Wasco-Wishram"; French and French, "Wasco, Wishram, Cascades"; Hajda, "Regional Social Organization in the Greater Lower Columbia."

31. See, e.g., Swan, *The Northwest Coast,* passim; also see Daniel Lee and Joseph H. Frost, *Ten Years in Oregon* (1844; Fairfield, WA: Ye Galleon Press, 1967), 101–3 and passim. Consider, for example, the following passage from the "Autobiography," of the Methodist missionary H. K. W. Perkins; the bracketed passages in this extract represent parts of the original manuscript of Perkins's "Autobiography," restored by Boyd to the version that was published in the *Christian Advocate and Journal.*

> We went into some houses today at the Dalles, and seeing the children naked, and the adults not much better, we asked them why they did not clothe themselves. "Oh," they said, "we are very poor. We have no skins, and no clothes. If you will come and trade with us, we will give you salmon, and you will give us clothes, and we will clothe ourselves." We saw their predicament and ours, too. [The Lord have mercy on those who are hoarding their thousands in the land of plenty.] Yesterday Tum-

sowit showed me his ragged pants, and begged a little piece of cloth and
some thread to mend them. I had not a patch [to give him], but I gave
him one of the little bags you had made us and told him to cut it up and
mend his clothes, which he did. My heart is pained from day to day on
account of our poverty. Our brethren have sent us here to behold
wretchedness, without the means to relieve it. [A few days ago I went to
the house of one of the men who has been at work for us, and is a good
wood chopper, to take him with me into the woods, and seeing him come
with me without any clothes, I told him to go and put on his trousers. He
said "One of my men has gone after a horse and I have lent him my
trousers and have nothing else to wear." You may imagine my feelings. I
told him to return to his house and I would see him again, for I did not
want him to work in the hot sun naked. The next morning I carried him
a shirt and set him to work. His name is Hanecunewitt.]

Robert T. Boyd, *The Wascopam Mission Papers of Henry Perkins, 1838–1844*
(ms. dated 1990), 97–98. The events described took place in April 1838.

32. Wayne Suttles, introduction to Suttles, *Handbook of North American
Indians*, vol. 7, *Northwest Coast*, 12 ff.; cf. Hajda, "Regional Social Organization in the Greater Lower Columbia."

33. Suttles, introduction, 12–13.

34. Swan, *The Northwest Coast,* 166–67.

35. Gabriel Franchère, *A Voyage to the Northwest Coast of America*, ed.
Milo Milton Quaife (1820; New York, Citadel Press, 1969), 107 (entry dated
December 1811).

36. Alexander Ross, *Adventures of the First Settlers on the Oregon, or Columbia, River, 1810–1813*, in *Early Western Travels, 1748–1846; a Series of
Annotated Reprints*, ed. Reuben Gold Thwaites (Cleveland: A. H. Clark,
1904–7, 7: 124–25.

37. Ibid., 122–23.

38. Samuel Parker, *Journal of an Exploring Tour beyond the Rocky Mountains* (Ithaca, NY: Andrus, Woodruff, and Gauntlett, 1844), 153–54. The putative Indian group of whom this personage was "a chief" represents one of the
more amusing ethnographic fictions to arise out of Indian-White contact along
the Columbia. First identified by Lewis and Clark, "the Skilloot nation" and
this man are, as a separate group, a mirage: "they" were first seen by Lewis and
Clark near the Cascades—also the locale for this observation of Samuel Parker,
which is probably the explanation for his perpetuation of the term. "Skilloot,"
it turns out, is nothing more or less than an imperative verb form (probably
Upper Chinookan, perhaps in the dialect of Kiksht known in the literature as
Cascades), *sik'lútkt!* meaning "look at him!" It is not, and has never been, the
name of any Chinookan people or village. Lewis and Clark were surprised

when they encountered members of this mythical "group" at various places up
and down the Columbia, a fact that is less surprising when one knows the actual meaning of the term. See Silverstein, "Chinookans of the Lower Columbia," for further information regarding ethnonymy.

39. Cole and Darling, "History of the Early Period," 125.

40. Boyd, *The Wascopam Mission Papers of Henry Perkins*, ms. p. 81
(Henry Perkins, "Diary," entry for Monday, 19 March 1838).

41. See the "Biographical Sketch" in Boyd, *The Wascopam Mission Papers
of Henry Perkins*, at ms. pp. 914–15. Wamcutta volunteered to act as a guide
for Daniel Lee's trip over the Cascades to Willamette Falls in the late summer
of 1838, but was unable at the last minute to do so, ostensibly because he was
in the mountains hunting elk; cf. Lee and Frost, *Ten Years in Oregon,* 158, 161.

42. Quoted in Boyd, *The Wascopam Mission Papers of Henry Perkins*, ms.
p. 915.

43. Ibid.

44. Hines, *Life on the Plains of the Pacific,* 156–57. The italicized word in
parentheses (*cultus*) is in the regional lingua franca, Chinook Jargon, and
means "foolish, ludicrous, pointless, silly."

45. Lieut. Geo. M. Colvocoresses, *Four Years in the Government Exploring
Expedition; Commanded by Captain Charles Wilkes . . . in One Volume,* 2d ed.
(New York: R. T. Young, 1853), 227. Wilkes's eyewitness account can be found
in Wilkes, *Narrative of the United States Exploring Expedition,* vol. 4:297.

46. See Cornelius J. Brosnan, *Jason Lee, Prophet of the New Oregon*
(1932; Rutland, VT: Academy Books, 1985), passim.

47. Hines, *Life on the Plains of the Pacific,* 88.

48. Ibid.

49. Townsend, *Narrative of a Journey across the Rocky Mountains,* in
Thwaites, *Early Western Travels,* 21:341.

50. Hines, *Life on the Plains of the Pacific,* 166.

51. Ibid.

52. For additional details on the background of these events, see ibid., 147,
164–65.

53. Ibid., 166.

54. Ibid.

55. Again, Keith Basso's *Portraits of "The Whiteman"* comes to mind.

56. Swan, *The Northwest Coast,* 156; emphasis in original.

57. Ibid., 154.

58. John Davies, *Douglas of the Forests: The North American Journals of
David Douglas* (Seattle: University of Washington Press, 1980), 42 (Douglas
diary entry for 20 June 1825); emphasis added.

59. Ibid., 55 (Douglas diary entry for 19 August 1825).

60. Cole and Darling, "History of the Early Period," 122–23.

61. Ibid., 123.

62. Swan, *The Northwest Coast,* 154–55.

63. Robert T. Boyd, *People of The Dalles: The Indians of Wascopam Mission* (Lincoln: University of Nebraska Press, 1995), passim. Hines, *Life on the Plains of the Pacific,* passim.

64. Charles Baudelaire, "The Painter of Modern Life," in *The Painter of Modern Life and Other Essays,* trans. and ed. Jonathan Mayne (London: Phaidon, 1965), 26. I am indebted to Susan Fillin-Yeh for pointing out this passage.

65. Walter Benjamin, "The Flâneur," in *Charles Baudelaire: A Lyric Poet in the Era of High Capitalism* (1938; London, New York: Verso, 1997), 41.

66. Ibid.

67. Ibid., 42.

68. Balzac, quoted in ibid., 42.

69. Ibid.

70. Baudelaire, "The Painter of Modern Life," 29.

BIBLIOGRAPHY

Anastasio, Angelo. "The Southern Plateau: An Ecological Analysis of Intergroup Relations." 1955. *Northwest Anthropological Research Notes* 6, no. 2 (1972): 109–229.

Basso, Kieth. *Portraits of "The Whiteman": Linguistic Play and Cultural Symbols among the Western Apache.* Cambridge: Cambridge University Press, 1979.

Blanchet, Francis Norbert et al. *Historical Sketches of the Catholic Church in Oregon during the Past Forty Years (1838–1878).* Portland, OR: n.p., 1956.

Boyd, Robert T. "Another Look at the Fever and Ague of Western Oregon." *Ethnohistory* 22, no. 2 (1975): 135–54.

———. "Demographic History, 1774–1874." In *Handbook of North American Indians.* Vol. 7, *Northwest Coast,* edited by Wayne Suttles, 135–48. Washington, DC: Smithsonian Institution, 1990.

———. "The Introduction of Infectious Diseases among the Indians of the Pacific Northwest, 1774–1874." Ph.D. diss., University of Washington, Seattle, 1985.

———. *People of the Dalles: The Indians of Wascopam Mission.* Lincoln: University of Nebraska Press, 1995.

———. *The Wascopam Mission Papers of Henry Perkins, 1838–1844.* Unpublished manuscript in author's possession, 1990.

Boyd, Robert T., and Yvonne P. Hajda. "Seasonal Population Movement along the Lower Columbia: The Social and Ecological Context." *American Ethnologist* 14, no. 2 (1987): 309–26.

Brosnan, Cornelius J. *Jason Lee, Prophet of the New Oregon.* 1932. Rutland, VT: Academy Books, 1985.

Caldwell, Warren W. "The Archaeology of Wakemap: A Stratified Site near the Dalles of the Columbia." Ph.D. diss., University of Washington, Seattle, 1956.

Cole, Douglas, and David Darling. "History of the Early Period." In *Handbook of North American Indians.* Vol. 7, *Northwest Coast,* edited by Wayne Suttles, 119–34. Washington, DC: Smithsonian Institution, 1990.

Colvocoresses, Lieut. Geo. M. *Four Years in the Government Exploring Expedition; Commanded by Captain Charles Wilkes . . . in One Volume.* 2d ed. New York: R. T. Young, 1853.

Davies, John. *Douglas of the Forests: The North American Journals of David Douglas.* Seattle: University of Washington Press, 1980.

Dobyns, Henry. "Estimating Aboriginal American Population, 1: An Appraisal of Techniques with a New Hemispheric Estimate." *Current Anthropology* 7, no. 4 (1966): 395–416.

Drucker, Philip. "Rank Wealth and Kinship in a Northwest Coast Society." *American Anthropologist* 41, no. 1 (1939): 55–65.

———. "Some Variations on the Potlatch." In *Indians of the North Pacific Coast,* edited by T. McFeat, 105–12. Seattle: University of Washington Press, 1980.

Farnham, Thomas J. *Travels in the Great Western Prairies, the Anahuac and Rocky Mountains, and in the Oregon Territory.* Poughkeepsie: Killey and Lossing, 1841.

Franchère, Gabriel. *A Voyage to the Northwest Coast of America.* Edited by Milo Milton Quaife. 1820. Reprint, New York: Citadel Press, 1969.

French, David. "Wasco-Wishram." In *Perspectives in American Indian Culture Change,* edited by E. Spicer, 337–430. Chicago: University of Chicago Press, 1961.

French, David H., and Kathrine S. French. "Wasco, Wishram, Cascades." In *Handbook of North American Indians.* Vol. 12, *Plateau,* ed. Deward E. Walker. Washington, DC: Smithsonian Institution, 1999.

Hajda, Yvonne P. "Regional Social Organization in the Great Lower Columbia, 1792–1830." Ph.D. diss, University of Washington, Seattle, 1984.

Hajda, Yvonne P., Henry Zank, and Robert Boyd. "The Early Historiography of Chinook Jargon." Paper presented at the eighty-seventh annual meeting of the American Anthropological Association, Phoenix, Arizona, November 16–20, 1988.

Hines, Rev. Gustavus. *Life on the Plains of the Pacific. Oregon: Its History, Conditions and Prospects.* Buffalo: Geo. H. Derby, 1851.

Irving, Washington. *Astoria, or Anecdotes of an Enterprise beyond the Rocky Mountains.* Vols. 1 and 2. 1836. Reprint, Philadelphia: J. B. Lippincott, 1961.

Lee, Daniel, and Joseph H. Frost. *Ten Years in Oregon.* 1844. Reprint, Fairfield, WA: Ye Galleon Press, 1967.

Lévi-Strauss, Claude. "Cosmopolitanism and Schizophrenia." In *The View from Afar.* Translated by Joachim Neugroschel and Phoebe Hoss. New York: Harper and Row, 1985.

———. "The Social Organization of the Kwakiutl." In *The Way of the Masks.* Translated by Sylvia Modelski. Seattle: University of Washington Press, 1982.

Lewis, Meriweather, and George R. Clark. *The Journals of the Lewis and Clark Expedition.* Vol. 5, 28 July–1 November 1805. Edited by Gary Moulton. Lincoln: University of Nebraska Press, 1988.

Parker, Samuel. *Journal of an Exploring Tour beyond the Rocky Mountains.* Ithaca, NY: Andrus, Woodruff, and Gauntlett, 1844.

Pratt, Mary-Louise. "Linguistic Utopias." In *The Linguistics of Writing*, edited by Nigel Fabb et al., 48–66. New York: Methuen, 1987.

Ross, Alexander. *Adventures of the First Settlers on the Oregon, or Columbia, River, 1810–1813.* In *Early Western Travels*, edited by Reuben Gold Thwaites. Vol. 7. Cleveland: A. H. Clark, 1905.

Sahlins, Marshall. "Cosmologies of Capitalism: The Trans-Pacific Sector of the World System," *Proceedings of the British Academy* 74 (1988): 1–51.

Sapir, Edward. "Fashion." In *Selected Writings of Edward Sapir.* Berkeley: University of California Press, 1949.

———. "Preliminary Report on the Language and Mythology of the Upper Chinook." *American Anthropologist* 9 (1907):533–41.

———. *Wishram Texts.* Publication of the American Ethnological Society, 2. Leyden: E. J. Brill, 1909.

Silverstein, Michael. "Chinookans of the Lower Columbia." In *Handbook of North American Indians.* Vol. 7, *Northwest Coast*, edited by Wayne Suttles, 533–46. Washington, DC: Smithsonian Institution, 1990.

———. "The 'Value' of Objectual Language." Paper presented at the eighty-third annual meeting of the American Anthropological Association, Denver, 14–18 November 1984.

Spier, Leslie, and Edward Sapir. "Wishram Ethnography." *University of Washington Publications in Anthropology* 3, no. 3 (1930): 151–300.

Strong, William Duncan, and W. Egbert Schenck. "Petroglyphs Near the Dalles of the Columbia River." *American Anthropologist* 27, no. 1 (1925): 76–90.

Strong, William Duncan, W. Egbert Schenck, and Julian H. Steward. "Archaeology of the Dalles-Deschutes Region." *University of California Publications in American Archaeology and Ethnology* 29, no. 1 (1930): 1–154.

Stuart, Robert. *The Discovery of the Oregon Trail: Robert Stuart's Narrative of His Overland Trip Eastward from Astoria, 1812–1813.* Edited by Philip A. Rollins. 1812. New York: Scribner's, 1935.

Suttles, Wayne. Introduction to *Handbook of North American Indians*. Vol. 7, *Northwest Coast*, edited by Wayne Suttles, 1–15. Washington, DC: Smithsonian Institution, 1990.

Swan, James G. *The Northwest Coast*. 1857. Reprint, Seattle: University of Washington Press, 1972.

Townsend, John Kirk. *Narrative of a Journey across the Rocky Mountains to the Columbia River*. 1839. Reprinted in *Early Western Travels, 1748–1846*, edited by Reuben Gold Thwaites. Cleveland: A. H. Clark. 1905.

Wilkes, Charles. *Narrative of the United States Exploring Expedition during the Years 1838, 1839, 1840, 1841, 1842*. Vols. 4 and 5. Philadelphia: Lea and Blanchard, 1845, 1850.

Wyeth, John B. *Oregon; or A Short History of a Long Journey*. 1840. Reprint, Fairfield, WA: Ye Galleon Press, 1970.

Zenk, Henry. "Chinook Jargon and Native Cultural Persistence in the Grand Ronde Indian Community, 1857–1907: A Special Case of Creolization." Ph.D. diss., University of Oregon, 1984.

## Chapter 3

# Dandyism and Abstraction in a Universe Defined by Newton

## *Carter Ratcliff*

"The dandy," wrote the English belletrist Cyril Connolly, "is but the larval form of a bore." He registered this opinion in 1960, after England had weathered two world wars and, four years earlier, watched its last grand imperial gesture end in fiasco at Suez. Connolly concluded that an England bereft of empire must now make itself felt in the world chiefly as a civilizing example. A new sort of authority would have to be claimed, a gracious prestige that excessive affectation would undermine. In the political circumstances of 1960, to charge the dandy with incipient tediousness was to lodge a moral judgment.[1]

Morality's objections to dandyism took a different shape in Thomas Carlyle's *Sartor Resartus*, published in 1836, when England was still assembling its empire. Shaking with Calvinist fervor, Carlyle pointed to a world of work in need of being done, then at the dandy: "a Clothes-wearing Man, a Man whose trade, office, and existence consists in the wearing of Clothes." Carlyle believed that the god the dandy worships—himself—is not only false but patently empty. The poor are gathering their strength, warned Carlyle. Revolution threatens, but the dandy is concerned, above all, that his trousers "be exceedingly tight across the hips." Carlyle didn't mention the responsibilities of empire that agitated later moralists, from Alfred Lord Tennyson to Rudyard Kipling, yet his attack on dandyism helped form the Victorian belief—the prejudice, if you like—that simple decency requires one to shoulder one's allotted portion of the world's work, whether at home or abroad.

Carlyle saw moral failure in the dandy's wish to be no more than "a visual object, or a thing that will reflect rays of light. Your silver or your gold . . . he solicits not; simply the glance of your eyes. . . . [D]o but look at him, and he is contented."[2] The dandy is entrepreneurial, but not in the right market. Accepting only the admiring glance as a token of exchange, he does no business of the proper bourgeois sort. The dandy's refusal to bother with mundane varieties of exchange recommended him to Charles Baudelaire, who saw dandified hauteur as the mark of "a new kind of aristocracy, all the more difficult to break down because established on the most precious, the most indestructible faculties, on the divine gifts that neither work nor money can give"—among them, taste so refined that its judgments cannot be exploited for moral or utilitarian purposes. "An institution outside the law," dandyism challenges received standards with new ones calculated to discomfit, even to disrupt.[3] The Baudelairean dandy is a recent ancestor of the avant-gardist.

This observation supplies the dandy with a salient place in modern life, but it has the unfortunate effect of locking him into static opposition to his enemies. Exclusive stress on the dandy's antimoralism engages this votary of disengagement with ethical questions that would have bored him thoroughly. It reduces him to a historical artifact as outdated as the moralizers and utilitarians he opposed. The dandy feels, as Baudelaire noted, "an unshakable determination to remain unmoved." Yet, despite Baudelaire's talk of a new aristocracy with a new "code of laws," the dandy's stillness is not the rigidity of one who strains against the weight of a monolithic bourgeoisie. The dandy is not a revolutionary, nor, despite his legacy, an incipient avant-gardist. He seeks no new order. He seeks nothing, and does next to nothing. He makes jokes, dresses with intimidating correctness, and hands down judgments of taste calculated to fill the uninitiated with trepidation, permitting none of this behavior to serve any purpose save the maintenance of his frozen equipoise.

The dandy looks immobile because he knows how to give the impression that, having eluded the world's chains of cause and effect, he stands above its clash of energies. The dandy's frivolity, his inconsequentiality, is a precisely modulated indifference to consequences. Carlyle deplored fashionable Londoners' determination to be "so *very* unsubstantial in their whole proceedings. . . . From day to day and year to year the problem is not how to use time, but how to waste it least painfully."[4] Jules Barbey d'Aurevilly saw heroism in the dandy who "may spend ten hours a day dressing, if he likes, but once dressed . . . thinks no more about it."[5] Beau Brummell and other dandies of the Regency spent time as if there were no question of spending it well. Their affectations included the fiction that money is like air: necessary to life but available for no effort. Cultivating an insolence more phlegmatic than cheeky, they were disinclined to acknowledge events, those products of causes and effects whose patterns they preferred not to notice.

Though Brummell is remembered as a wit, little that he said caused people to laugh. Interviewing Brummell's friends in the expectation of collecting armfuls of rarefied quips, Barbey found none worth translating into French. "We omit the witticisms of Brummell," Barbey wrote, explaining that wit, like wine, often doesn't travel well.[6] William Hazlitt, who now and then met Brummell at dinner, understood that his wit was not so much untranslatably English as unfunny. He wrote that the Beau's jokes "are of a meaning so attenuated that 'nothing lives 'twixt them and nonsense': they hover on the brink of vacancy, and are in their shadowy composition next of kin to nonentities." Elsewhere, Hazlitt is an advocate of "gusto." In the company of Brummell, he lets himself be entranced by

> our hero's answers to a lady, who asked him if he never tasted vegetables—"Madam, I once ate a pea!" This was reducing the quantity of offensive grossness to the smallest assignable fraction: anything beyond *that* his imagination was oppressed with; and even this he seemed to confess to with a kind of remorse, and to hasten from the subject with a certain monosyllabic brevity of style.

All is to revert to a nothingness tinged by the dandy's will. "Had his head been fastened in a vise," Hazlitt wrote of Brummell, "it could not have been more immovably fixed than by the 'great idea in his mind,' of how a coxcomb should sit. . . . [T]he Beau preserved the perfection of an attitude—like a piece of incomprehensible *still life*—the whole of dinner-time." Under Hazlitt's gaze, Brummell turns so statuesque that he loses a dimension; he becomes pictorial, a still life. But of what subject? As a still life painting, Hazlitt's Brummell cannot be made out; he is "incomprehensible."[7]

I don't think Hazlitt confesses a weakness of understanding here. He means that Brummell willfully chose to make no sense, or to make only the inhuman sense of a perfected image. Brummell was a heavy drinker, a gambler, and a social climber who managed to scramble up to the plateau occupied by the Prince Regent. For a time, he stood high enough to look down on his royal patron, at least in matters of taste. Accepted into society, he was nonetheless not a social presence of the usual sort. He presented a patch of inexplicability. The dandy is illegible and, in a way, invisible. An unfunny wit, he is also a fashion plate who dresses so that he can go almost, but not quite, unseen. Brummell's "chief aim," recalled his biographer William Jesse, "was to avoid anything marked, one of his aphorisms being that the severest mortification which a gentleman could incur, was to attract observation in the street by his outward appearance."[8] Yet the dandy's image of absence from the world is only an image, a deliberate pose. He intends the initiated to see his invisibility, so to speak, and in moments of acute perception they do.

George Moore, the Anglo-Irish novelist and art critic, records such a moment in his autobiographical novel, *Confessions of a Young Man* (1888). As Moore sat in a Paris cafe, "Manet entered," undeniably French, yet to Moore's eye and ear "there was something in his appearance and manner of speaking that often suggested an Englishman." Like Barbey and Manet's colleague Baudelaire, the painter affected a degree of Brummellesque austerity. The hyperalert Moore remembers him as a "clean-cut" presence, shoulders square and waist thin. He decorates him with a flurry of avant-garde virtues: passion, frankness, honesty, and so on. Yet there is an instant when all questions of morality give way before a description of a "visual object" (Carlyle's phrase) converted to an abstraction: Manet embodied "an idea of beauty of line."[9]

When Moore examined Manet's works he usually found what Emile Zola and Theodore Duret did: images of contemporary life made vivid by the abandonment of much that was traditionally considered essential to the art of painting. For Zola, Duret, Moore, and many later critics, that is the point: dispensing with inherited means, Manet invented fresh, more pertinent ones that allowed him to make an idiosyncratically persuasive record of his times. "'Reality' is the fixed element," Zola said, and Manet is great because he "gives us a new and personal vision" of the real.[10] This praise qualifies Manet as a Baudelairean dandy, the "aristocratic" individual, outside the law, who invents a law for himself, but it overlooks what is most disturbing about dandyism: its knack for inconsequence.

Usually Zola's most faithful English-speaking follower, Moore occasionally strayed, and in straying he noticed that knack in Manet. Having applauded the painter for seeing Paris "truly, frankly, and more beautifully than any of his contemporaries," he adds that Manet sometimes draws forms that look "hollow within"; a head may seem "a sort of convulsive abridgement, the hand void, and the fingers too, if we seek their articulations."[11] Moore judged Manet the best artist of his period, so this is not an instance of the backward complaint that avant-gardists never learn to draw. Nor did Moore praise Manet's paintings for their hollow places, their unarticulated voids. Still, he did transfer from the dandy's person to dandified painting the indifference to cause and effect that Hazlitt saw in Brummell.

Representation wants to bring about certain effects, among them the viewer's recognition of a subject. When Moore talks of voids and hollows, he points to those passages where Manet begins to thwart representation's causal ambitions. Though Moore's Manet lets one make out the forms of fingers, hands, and heads, his rendering is a kind of emptying. Occasionally, the painter's brushwork covers his canvas in a manner so calmly, so arrogantly acausal that it produces a complete blank. Depicting no subject, not even insubstantial hands or fingers, these patches are easiest to see in backgrounds—as in the Metropolitan Museum's *Woman with a Parrot* (1866). They do not serve as foils for faces or gestures, like featureless backgrounds in earlier portraiture, nor do they perform any compositional function. They neither brood, as dark passages in Courbet's paintings often do, nor offer variants on the emotional agitation in the depths of Delacroix's Baroque revival style. They define no space and evoke no atmosphere, nor do they assert the picture plane with any vigor. Our habits of viewing often lead us to feel pictorial effects like these when there is no cause, but if we elude the authority of habit for a moment, we might glimpse an unrelenting acausality in Manet's painting.

Not all these tense vacuities are in backgrounds. Sometimes his brush imposes a touch of inconsequentiality, a subtle but defiant pointlessness, on a plane that defines a face, even the face of a personage like Zola, who sat for Manet in 1868 (fig. 3.1). At crucial points in the definition of his sitter's face—at the joining of two planes, for instance, or at the start of a tonal shift that shapes a volume—the painter made certain marks that insist on being understood as nothing more or less than marks of his brush, an image we have been taught to understand as the sort of cause that produces the effect known as a good likeness. I'm not saying that the *Portrait of Emile Zola* is a bad likeness; rather, that

*Fig. 3.1.* Edouard Manet, *Portrait of Emile Zola*, oil on canvas, 1868, 57 1/2 × 44 7/8 in. Lauros-Giraudon Musée d'Orsay. Reproduced by permission.

once we sense the dandyism at the hollow core of Manet's art, we'll see that his *Zola* mocks the very idea of likeness—mocks it without bothering to dispense with it.

In the modern marketplace, a cause in its simplest form is called a demand; supply is the effect. (Only when advertising becomes sophisticated in manipulating images do supplies of goods appear to create demands as well as fill them.) Resenting subjugation to causal imperatives in any form, the dandified artist ignores the marketplace or, if that is not feasible (and usually it is not), he deploys a pretense of ignoring it. Forced to acknowledge economic pressures, he often responds in a peremptory style, as if one high-handed gesture could still the shifting patterns of hungry demand and reluctant but eventually acquiescent supply.

In 1877 James McNeill Whistler sent a painting called *Nocturne in Black and Gold: The Falling Rocket* and six others to a group show at the Grosvenor Gallery in London. John Ruskin, the great reformer who provided a model for William Morris and, through him, for many of our century's utopians, attended the exhibition and complained afterward of "eccentricities . . . almost always in some degree forced; and . . . imperfections gratuitously, if not impertinently, indulged." Enraged by the price set on *The Falling Rocket*, Ruskin wrote that he had "seen, and heard, much of cockney impudence before now; but never expected to hear a coxcomb ask two hundred guineas for flinging a pot of paint in the public's face."[12] Whistler sued him for libel.

The issue at trial was whether the painter had given his picture a sufficient measure of what the nineteenth century called "finish." In short, had he worked hard enough to justify a price of two hundred guineas? Asked how long it had taken him to "knock off that nocturne," Whistler replied that it had taken him a day. Allowing that he may have added a few touches the following morning, he prompted an attorney to inquire, "The labor of two days, then, is that for which you ask two hundred guineas!" "No," said Whistler, "I ask it for the knowledge of a lifetime." The painter claimed value not for what he did but for what he was, for the refinement of perception and feeling that he had come to embody and could, with a few gestures, indicate on canvas.

By defending in court this dandified definition of value, Whistler hoped to reinforce the illusion, accepted by his admirers, that he was superior to the need to act in ordinary ways.[13] Whistler won his libel suit and received a farthing's damages. This was a legal victory canceled by financial defeat. In sum, the result was static and therefore satisfactory to the fictive, dandified Whistler that the artist presented to his public. Privately, though, his bankruptcy after the Ruskin trial forced him to take the desperately practical measure of hiding assets from creditors, even as he made peace with them. Throughout his life Whistler was too active on his own account, too flashily dressed, too floridly pugnacious to count as a dandy of the most exquisitely inert kind. But his art shows abundant signs of inertia, modulations of tone and texture that make sense only as evidence of perceptions frozen into permanence by an implacable refinement of taste.

Before the end of the 1870s the textures of Manet's and Whistler's and possibly Henri Fantin-Latour's brushwork had, in their far from insistent way, pushed nearly to completion the argument that the canvas, the visual object, should be valued not only for its connections to external things but for its independence from them—that is, for its deepening indifference to the task of representation. To perform this task is to forge links between a painting, its audience, and the world. This linkage is causal; near the end of the chain of effects it sets in motion is the viewer's delight in recognizing the painting's subject matter. As a dandy's witticism often neglected to cause laughter, so the acausal blanks in Manet's brushwork show that he now and then neglected to generate the pleasure in recognition that, even today, many find reassuring. Acausal blanks also occur in Degas's late paintings. Van Gogh did not tolerate them. Gauguin and his followers did, especially Maurice Denis.

Noting that painters' images were fading to blankness, Denis made a comment that implies abstract painting: "a picture—before being a battle horse, a nude, or some anecdote—is essentially a plane surface covered with colors assembled in a certain order."[14] Small gestures of resistance to the anecdotal flickered with increasing strength through Cézanne's late work. Then, in the Cubism of Braque and Picasso, this resistance became militant indifference and settled into the image unapologetically. Analytical Cubism, in particular, displays surprisingly large stretches of *terrain vague*, passages that are representationally weak but make no strong argument for abstraction.

Looking back in 1917 to steps taken almost a decade earlier, Braque said that "the goal is not to be concerned with the *reconstitution* of an anecdotal fact, but with the *constitution* of a pictorial fact."[15] The abstract canvas's claim to independence is familiar; three-quarters of a century ago, it was just as usual in avant-garde circles to suppose that a canvas representing an object could be so focused on pictorial matters that it, no less than an abstraction, counted as autonomous. It had become legitimate to argue that elaborating the pictorial traits of, say, a still life painting was an end in itself—as in certain of Braque's and Picasso's canvases from 1909 to 1911, which attain something equivalent to the dandy's disengagement. Soon avant-gardists of programmatic bent defined this disengagement as a goal to be achieved. Moreover, they wanted the audience to recognize their achievement as a necessary step toward an aesthetically improved future.

The Cubist theorist and painter Jean Metzinger argued in 1910 that, by "rejecting every ornamental, anecdotal or symbolic intention," Picasso "achieves a painterly purity hitherto unknown."[16] A few years later, the Dadaist Man Ray claimed that an artist advances by "uncover[ing] the pure plane of expression that has so long been hidden by the glazings of nature imitation, anecdote, and the other popular subjects."[17] Defining pictorial purity as a principle to be advanced, a cause to be served, these artists made it a cause in another sense: a force that produces an effect, changing both the audience's responses and the future of art. It became increasingly incumbent on painters capable of dandified impulses to neglect these revamped causes and effects. They needed to find a new acausality.

Among the passages in Braque and Picasso's Cubism that refuse to depict a thing or to signal an emotion are some that refrain as well from all effort to effect a recognition of the painting's independence. Making no attempt to assert the picture plane, maintain the integrity of the edge, or insist on the materiality of pigment, these passages do nothing to advance the logic of autonomy that critics and historians of modern art dedicate so much effort to explicating. The institutions of art criticism and art history clash at many points, yet they share a dedication to the fallacy that a good painting is a mechanism whose every part functions perfectly, giving the apparatus of explication an opportunity to display its verbal command of pictorial cause and effect. But critics and curators have accounted for only the grossest features of Cubism.

Their dedication to a causal view of painting and to their institutional missions prevents them from describing or even noticing passages where Braque or Picasso indulge in pointless reiteration or leave gaps that neither deprive their images of clarity nor supply them with the benefits of well-managed ellipsis. As the dandy's ineffably unfunny joke opens a void in a social pattern and fills it with the force of his baffling will, so a nonfunctioning interlude of Cubist brushwork disrupts the smooth, ingratiating argument for pictorial autonomy. Offhandedly exquisite, these disruptions give the Cubist canvas—the visual object—an air of obdurate pride, for it was in their works, not in their persons, that the Cubist painters showed their dandyism.

The twentieth-century art world's only authentic dandy appeared in the person of Marcel Duchamp after he rejected painting as too "retinal," too implicated in patterns of cause and effect.[18] Duchamp was bored by the predictability of such patterns, especially in Impressionist painting, which received his most intensely dismissive scorn. He also sneered in an arch and listless way at the Cubists, though they pointed him along the antiretinal path with their occasional refusals to cause thoroughly pictorial effects. These refusals looked inadequate to Duchamp, who believed, rightly, that Cubism's sporadic blank spots are not enough to protect the style from a retinal response. He designed his readymades to correct that vulnerability.

*Bicycle Wheel* (1913) is elegant but vacuous. The wheel revolves, yet it is as inert as the "still life" that Hazlitt saw in the exquisitely arranged figure of Beau Brummell. *Bicycle Wheel* is a blank. No blankness can protect itself from interpreters, and a variety of meanings have been projected onto Duchamp's readymades. These may be the twentieth century's most vigorously analyzed objects. I don't say that the commentaries offered by Duchamp's supporters or the questions raised by the most thoughtful of his detractors are useless. I say only that no reading of the readymades has taken into account their indifference to the task of offering a coherent meaning.

In 1967 Duchamp told Pierre Cabanne that *Bicycle Wheel* "was just a distraction. I didn't have any special reason to do it."[19] Though we may doubt that Duchamp is entirely forthcoming here, *Bicycle Wheel*'s motion does have a distracting quality. "I enjoyed looking at it," said the artist two years later, "just as I enjoy looking at the flames dancing in a fireplace."[20] Duchamp liked the sort of motion that calms the desire to move, to act (see his hypnotic *Rotary Glass Plates* of the 1920s), and he liked chess, which requires the devotee to learn gambits almost as rigid as the game's basic rules. The spinning bicycle wheel, flames on the hearth, chessmen tracing and retracing their familiar paths—all move constantly and none makes any sort of progress. Some interpretations of the readymades are surely legitimate, but not one of them accounts for Duchamp's enchantment with pointless motion, with inconsequentiality.

He became a dandy by permitting his indifference to cause and effect to reach from his art to his person and render him elegantly nondescript.[21] Like Jules Laforgue's Frenchified Hamlet, the public Duchamp was a variation on Pierrot, the *commedia dell'arte*'s pale and melancholy introvert. I don't mean that he dressed the part. A dandy's outfit is never a costume, never a matter of looking bohemian or rebellious, of wearing overalls to dinner or a monocle on Fifty-seventh Street. Like every Pierrot, Duchamp's offered a contrast to particolored Harlequin, Picasso's favorite alter ago, who is the allegorical figure of activism on the fronts of style and sensibility (though I suppose the Picassoid Harlequin is hyperactive, for this figure's antics included an occasional impersonation of Pierrot, master of inconsequence). The mid-nineteenth-century dandy dressed chiefly in black. All in white, Pierrot is the figure of the self as the palest of monochromes: abstemious, idle, resistant to interpretation and to the causal forces that interpretation tries so busily to control—a dandy in a state of exhaustion, probably feigned, to give greater weight to the rhetoric of distaste.

Laforgue said that Baudelaire's poems are "as vague and inconsequential as the flutter of a fan, as equivocal as make-up, so that the bourgeois who reads them asks: 'So what?'"[22] This comment does not make common cause with obtuse sensibilities. Rather, it points beneath the lush surface of Baudelaire's verse to a dandified refusal to engage any topic in a way that the general reader recognizes as effective. Duchamp's readymades are similarly incompetent and similarly defiant in their refusal to perform. His *Large Glass* (1915–23) doesn't so much deny relations of cause and effect as elaborate them to the point of absurdity and beyond. This work is so complex a machine for the production of meaning that it destroys meaning, and thus defeats interpretation. One could argue that *The Large Glass* is too richly significant for any commentary to be exhaustive, but I think it would be truer to say that it is a meaning-machine designed not to work.

When members of the public run across such machinery, they tend to assume that they are faced with a hoax. I have no wish to be cruel, but I ought to point out that dandies and their present-day descendants do not respect the public enough to hoax it. They are too fastidious to want to be noticed by the uninitiated, or to make a mark in history as it is popularly understood. Their inertia disinclines them even to acknowledge the passage of time. When Duchamp said that he didn't "think that the work that I've done can have any social importance whatsoever in the future," he was stating not a hypothesis he could defend but a hope he treasured.[23] Dandified emptiness and immobility are means to freedom from institutions—means ironically deployed, for, as the dandy knows, only the image of such freedom is possible. The most ordinary facts of time and space, as ordinarily understood, imprison us.

The dandy objects to Isaac Newton, or, since one can imagine Duchamp but not Brummell pondering Newton's axioms of motion, it is better to say that the dandy objects to the utilitarian view of the world that appeared as Newtonian physics engendered John Locke's cause-and-effect psychology. In the art world and in literary circles, many claim to believe that we live in a post-Newtonian universe, built by quantum mechanics and haunted by the terrifying ambiguities of Heisenberg's principle of indeterminacy. Because few who profess this faith have even a weak grasp of modern physics, it counts as a pretension too coarse, too transparent to interest a dandy.

In 1972 a pair of interviewers asked John Ashbery, whose poems sit on the page like fragments of refined but no longer functioning prose, if he had ever been "specifically influenced in terms of a certain sense of indirectness, randomness, sense of time, by relativity, quantum physics or thermodynamics?" The poet replied, "No, not at all, I know absolutely nothing about physics."[24] Brusque in tone but elegant in effect, this response dismisses in a single gesture the notion that a modern writer need pay attention to developments in modern thought. Yet it is not enough for Ashbery to deny any knowledge of physicists' recently devised theories. With what I think is a degree of untruth, he also professes ignorance of the old-fashioned, Newtonian science that describes a familiar universe shaped by intuitively obvious forces and counterforces. Ashbery pretends to believe that, by refusing to understand about actions and the equal and opposite reactions they precipitate, he can protect his sensibility from disturbance. His image, his ideal, of dandified inertia is hard to distinguish from the inertia defined by the Newtonian science of cause and effect that he so fastidiously abhors. Thus it would be difficult for him to deny the charge that he employs a modern notion in arranging his abstention from modern life. This is an irony the dandy may perceive but will never acknowledge.

He finds it sufficient to be put off by the developments in science that historians call "the mechanization of the world picture."[25] Far beyond the reach of physicists' theories, this mechanization gave its tone to the institutions—academic, economic, political—that try to reduce us to definable, therefore manageable bits of data. We are to become functions of whatever causal forces an institution wants to put into play. The dandy takes only the most careless note of this institutional image of the self. Yet he understands it and he intends his inertia to remove him from all the demeaningly manipulated patterns of causality that shape his moment. Nonetheless, the dandy never complains about the aspects of modern life that he finds so tedious. A complaint would be too obviously an effect generated by some cause. Others are not so inhibited.

William Blake's *Jerusalem* (1804–20) presents this vision of the modern, mechanized universe:

> I turn my eyes to the Schools & Universities of Europe
> And there behold the Loom of Locke whose Woof rages dire
> Washd by the Water-wheels of Newton. black the cloth
> In heavy wreathes folds over every Nation; cruel Works
> Of many Wheels I view, wheel without wheel, with cogs tyrannic
> Moving by compulsion each other: not as those in Eden: which
> Wheel within Wheel in freedom revolve in harmony & peace.[26]

Like Blake, the dandy refuses to be merely a cog "moving by compulsion," but unlike Blake he does not believe that the mechanisms of modern life can be redesigned to produce "harmony & peace." So he affects stillness, the image of one who neither acts nor is acted on, unengaged by any machinery whatsoever.

Most who object to modernity would rather be utopians than ironists of the excruciating, dandified kind. It is a choice between wild hope and no hope at all—alternatives not as clear as they might seem, for there are moments when certain utopians display something like the dandy's pose of blank defiance. Not Blake, I think. He immersed himself too deeply in sensual particulars to assume, even for an ironic instant, the pose of an inanimate object. Dandified episodes are more likely in the careers of utopians who move from particulars to abstraction. I'm thinking of Piet Mondrian, though I don't deny the usual understanding that he was driven to his utopian visions by a Calvinist sense of good and evil (fig. 3.2).

Mondrian hoped that a universal style would release painting from the snares of individual ego. Purified of the painter's self, canvases would become sculpture, sculpture would attain the scale of architecture, and architecture would generate urban planning so transcendently rational that society would evolve into a state of harmony. Nothing like the First World War would again occur. Art was to be the cause and the effect would be a heavenly city on earth. Yet one sees equivalents to the dandy's self-centered inertia in Mondrian's nonobjective paintings: lines doubled without advancing the clarity of a

*Fig. 3.2.* Piet Mondrian, *Opposition of Lines: Red and Yellow*, oil on canvas, 1937, 17 × 13 in. Philadelphia Museum of Art: The A. E. Gallatin Collection. Reproduced by permission.

composition; rectangles counterpoised with a tense precision that neither guides a painting to harmonious closure nor opens it up; chalky, torpid passages of white. I take none of these nuances to be faults. Moreover, I intend no adverse criticism when I point out that the shape of Mondrian's career sent much of his energy in a circle around an immobile center. From the early 1920s until he launched *Broadway Boogie-Woogie* in 1942, Mondrian repeated himself with a doggedness that baffles those who understand him as a straightforwardly progressive utopian. Little energy remained for pushing his art forward.

Mondrian could envision his grandiose and radical program of change only because, like a dandy, he resisted the ordinary standards of taste and morality that prescribe for artists and everyone else the purposes they ought to pursue. The rules of banal good taste and proper morals form intangible institutions. By disobeying their dictates, Mondrian put himself at odds with institutions of another sort—the art market, museums, and so on. Granted, his purpose was to create new institutions, first de Stijl, then the bureaucracies of the utopian world he expected de Stijl to engender. When he left de Stijl in 1924, it was because the group's more practical members showed too little interest in rebuilding society. Other, more visionary groups were more to his liking, so he joined them, yet he did nothing tangible to launch the new future. Conservative taste asks for propriety; the avant-garde wants progress. In Mondrian's dismissal of both demands, his arrogance proclaimed itself. He was intransigent, and when intransigence allies itself with taste as austerely elegant as Mondrian's or Brummell's, it produces the static postures of the dandy.

Beau Brummell designed himself as a visual object to assert an intractable independence. The visual object called an abstract painting does the same for its maker's self, opening a blank space in the texture of institutionally approved meaning. Few artists leave that void empty for long. Even when the object is a monochrome painting that seems not to picture but to embody blankness, the artist assigns meanings to it. But before the artist can feel the confidence necessary for the deployment of this rhetorical machinery, there needs to have been a moment when the work was empty and, in its emptiness, resistant to the demand that images be interpretable. Having blanked out that demand, the self can make demands of its own, and blankness is blanked out in its turn: meanings are imposed.

In 1915 Kasimir Malevich proclaimed a new art movement, Suprematism, and installed himself as its commissar. A Suprematist canvas might display three colors or two or only one, he said, and the viewer is to understand it as a "'desert,' where nothing is real except feeling." His manifestos argue that "pure feeling" constitutes authentic reality. So, to Malevich's eyes, his abstractions looked far from void: they contain everything that truly exists. Or they emanate everything in pure form, a purposeful characteristic, for Suprematist emanations were to purify ordinary life.[27] Malevich delivered his theories pantingly, at the top of his lungs. His public self couldn't have shown less of the icy refinement that Barbey admired in the dandy.[28] Yet Malevich's abstractions suggest that he too was capable of the dandy's inert arrogance.

Commandeering Romanticism's clichés about the "creative will" of the artist and "the creative forms" of nature, he turned them into Suprematist axioms.[29] To carry out this imperious maneuver, he needed to assert himself, at least fleetingly, as absolutely self-enclosed and therefore impervious to meanings sanctioned by institutional authority. Unreachable in those instants, he could not be reduced to an effect by any external cause. And he needed to be certain that he could abstract himself from the patterns of causality whenever he felt himself being drawn into them—whenever he felt that a Romantic cliché or a standard avant-garde notion was pushing him toward a banal intelligibility. Always, he fought against his tendency to give pleasure by making lively and obvious sense. The earnest sputter of his Suprematist polemics obscures this stubbornness, but one can see it plainly in the blankest of his canvases.

Finally, though, Malevich was too obstreperous to qualify as a descendant of Beau Brummell. Ad Reinhardt disqualified himself by setting up shop as a nag. Reproachfully, repetitiously, he insisted that art must display "no object, no subject, no matter. No symbols, images or signs. Neither pleasure nor pain. No mindless working or mindless no-working. No chess playing."[30] Reinhardt's monochromes look to me like logos accompanying his moral strictures, but they are not that for a sympathetic critic, Lucy Lippard, who argues that his black canvases in particular gain their significance by acknowledging what the theologian Paul Tillich called "the unconditional and infinite character of the Ultimate."[31] Reinhardt appears to have believed that there are realms where concepts like "the Ultimate" make sense.

Evidently, he intended his art to have purposes, both in transcendent regions and on earth, amid the art world institutions he liked to scold. Yet I don't think his sense of mission would have been so strong, his grappling with institutions so vigorous, if he had never seen himself as a presence utterly disengaged and self-sufficient: the imaginary source of all authority. That image devised, Reinhardt could discard it and get on with the moralist's and the mystic's neglect of selfhood. Nonetheless, to see his black paintings fully, one must look through the dark glow of their spiritual ambitions to a darkness that is merely dull and inert: an emblem of intractable self-involvement.

Max Kozloff, who also has shown a dandified impulse to push nuance to pointless extremes, argued that "Reinhardt's excessive craftsmanship dissolved into a puzzling darkening of image and variation." By contrast, Andy Warhol's art signals "an ostentatious lack of effort." Further, "Warhol refuses to be understood by accepting everything; Reinhardt rejects interpretation by despising everything"—everything worldly, that is. These differences reveal similarities: "both artists . . . thwarted all expectations of what art looks like."[32] Interpretation refused to be thwarted, and by 1971, when Kozloff published these remarks, commentators had defined Reinhardt's and Warhol's careers as effects of formal, historical, and cultural causes. Yet even now the work of both artists preserves a degree of unaccountability, a willful resistance to explanation. With his silverish wig, Warhol was obviously a fop. Less obviously, he shared with Reinhardt the dandy's reluctance to be entirely at the world's disposal. He gave in to his culture so thoroughly that it could only sweep over him and through his art, leaving both unmoved. Warhol's inertia showed itself in his despotic lack of affect. It is still visible in his gridded pictures, those graphic displays of immobility.

Warhol and the Minimalists learned the stillness of tautology from Jasper Johns, who sometimes rendered the word "BLUE" in blue paint. That he has rendered the same word in orange paint shows that he is capable of flat-footed inanity—illogic too deliberately inert to be seen as an offer to transport the imagination. Frank Stella showed how to put Johnsian inertia in motion, aiming it at the future. Stella's development has been a single, sustained exhibition of purpose: to respond to the aesthetic demands of postwar American painting, as defined by formalist criticism. I find those demands no more compelling than Reinhardt's faith in absolutes and ultimates, yet I acknowledge what is obvious: Stella's version of history has institutional authority. He has done much (but not everything) to define the history his career exemplifies. Institutions like the Museum of Modern Art have done the rest. Working hand in hand with the Modern and with museological and corporate entities that take their cues from it, Stella himself has become something of an institution. To put it another way: offering no resistance to institutional imperatives, he merges his interests with those of curators and collectors so thoroughly that his public persona is not quite that of a self. It is more that of an agency for the development of historically correct images.

Yet Stella's persona has a few scraps of selfhood, or it did for a season in the 1960s, when the impersonal logic of his progress faltered. According to the artist's historical scheme, his aluminum paintings made a necessary step beyond the black ones, the copper paintings advanced beyond the aluminum, and so forth. But the concentric "portraits" of 1963 defied this forward momentum. Circling around their empty cores, they suspended the artist's progress. Inert, they hinted at the possibility that a dandified Stella had come into conflict with Stella the developing institution. The hint was not taken up. Since then, even Stella's most overproduced series have looked all too legibly purposeful. Artists like Peter Halley mimic that legibility. Because they are so careful to offer no impediment to interpretation, their works look like quizzes administered in a crash course on how to assimilate oneself to shifts in institutional fashion.

Though his early work registers occasional doubts about the art world's specialized patterns of cause and effect—the "dialectic" of formal development, the mechanics of reputation—Stella was in command of those patterns when he appeared on the scene.[33] Other abstract painters are veterans of roughly equal tenure, yet because they do not engage the art world's "cogs & wheels" with Stella's determination, they seem less thoroughly present. Look, for instance, at Brice Marden, whose work is admired but, like the artist himself, is only obliquely in attendance. Institutions approve of his painting, yet they can't entirely enclose it. Robert Ryman and his art stand similarly askew, like the several generations of monochrome painters who have followed Ryman and Marden in New York (fig. 3.3).

Neither accommodating nor resisting institutions, they remain in odd, half-assimilated positions. Reluctant to acknowledge the gratuitous blankness in their art, they cultivate the modest, utilitarian morality of artists with proper purposes. Nonetheless, as the nuances of their pigments grow more delicate and their expanses of color more blank, their aims remain undefined. The dandyism of their art is a secret they keep from themselves. I'm thinking of monochromists like Marcia Hafif and Jo Baer, though these remarks apply as well to "conceptualist" painters like Robert Huot or to a geometric revivalist like Harvey Quaytman. They too display refinement and blankness. They too offer at least a shadow of resistance to the demand that a painting be a cause whose effect is a meaning that an institution can use.

*Fig. 3.3.* Robert Ryman, *Untitled*, 1959, oil on cotton canvas, 43 1/2 × 43 1/2 in. © Robert Ryman. Photograph courtesy of Pace Wildenstein. Reproduced by permission.

George Moore's introduction to *An Anthology of Pure Poetry*, which he edited in 1924, speaks of Tennyson "and many other poets . . . that have been devoured one by one by one by the needs of empire." Empire required its poets to moralize and to sustain morale, to buttress the great imperial institutions by shaping attitudes to their demands. Moore asks, "Which shall it be, art or empire?"[34] He believed that artists could choose one or the other. The artist who rejected empire would be pure. Yet modern life admits of no purity in the sense that a fin-de-siècle aesthete like Moore used the word. Dandyism and abstraction are easily exploited for institutional purposes. The most re-calcitrant of the dandified abstractionists are sometimes given blue-chip status as compensation.

The postwar American art world has produced few sharply resistant figures—Pollock, Johns, Warhol, perhaps several others. Thus the unassimilable core of their art is difficult to see for it is buried by many layers of official interpretation at its most reassuringly bland. These are the ultra-blue-chip-super-gilt-edge figures whose work receives the full weight of institutional anxiety. Aside from connoisseurs of entropy and ungraspable nuance like Robert Smithson and Max Kozloff, members of the American art world make a particular effort to exaggerate the legibility of defiantly illegible artists. But I think there is another reason that illegibility is so rarely seen. It is scarce. Most American artists are still so convinced by myths of unencumbered individuality that it is dif-ficult for them to believe that institutions exert powers deserving to be resisted, by dandyism or any other method.

Taking their independence for granted, as an automatic benefit of being American, they feel no conscious need to defy the standards and expectations held out to them by postwar institutions. Consequently, much American art of the last four decades has been staunch and proper in its optimism; in its programmatic clarity; in its reliance on a mechanistic notion of form as a cause that produces the effect of inter-pretable meaning. In short, obedience to institutional assumptions about the nature of art is widespread, and that is why one sees in this era so few sharply focused moments of arrogant, dandified resistance.

This is an essay about blankness, so it may seem odd that I have not mentioned Stéphane Mallarmé and his devotion to "le vide papier que la blancheur defend"—the empty page defended by its own white-ness.[35] It is possible to define Mallarmé as a dandy, and to interpret his striving toward perfect emptiness as an attempt to establish an ab-solutely inert void. But the image of a dandified Mallarmé requires one to ignore the immense scale of his art. The dandy confines himself to the small scale of the self. Under Mallarmé's gaze, the empty page ex-pands to contain the universe—or, rather, all the meaning it is able to generate. "Everything," he said, "exists for the sake of ending up in a book."[36] Having imagined the possibility of writing the great, all-inclu-sive Book that would subsume every previously written book, he tried to show, in his poetry, what transformations things must undergo if they are to find a place on the pages of this ultimate work.

There, nothing remains its ordinary self. Converted to Mallarmean nuance, everything loses its specificity. In return for this sacrifice, it is gathered into a system of absolute truths. Mallarmé's imaginary Book reduces all things of whatever kind to a single, transcendent essence, a subtle cog in an infinitely vast play of metaphysical machinery. With their absorptive whiteness, the pages of his Book show us an image of the modern institution in its most abstract, most thoroughly aesthetized form. Like that book, each real institution is driven by an ideal, some absolutist notion of efficiency, profit, or power. These notions are voids designed to absorb and transform all that lies outside the institution, all that is not yet institutionalized, especially the self, which is to be turned into data, the better to snare it in patterns of cause and effect or supply and demand or fact and explication. Like an inert passage in a painting, the dandy's blankness resists this process. Modern culture pits institutions against selves. At its cruelest, this is a struggle between two kinds of emptiness.

NOTES

1. Cyril Connolly, "The Dandy: II," in *The Evening Colonnade* (New York: Harcourt Brace Jovanovich, 1975), 134.

2. Thomas Carlyle, *Sartor Resartus: The Life and Opinions of Herr Teufelsdroch*, ed. Kerry McSweeny and Peter Sabor (1836; Oxford: Oxford University Press, 1987), 207, 212–15.

3. Charles Baudelaire, "Le Peintre de la vie moderne" (1868), in *Oeuvres complètes*, ed. Claude Pichois (Paris: Gallimard, 1976), 2:709. Author's translation.

4. Carlyle, quoted in Ellen Moers, *The Dandy: Brummell to Beerbohm* (Lincoln: University of Nebraska Press, 1978), 179.

5. Jules Barbey d'Aurevilly, "Du Dandysme et de George Brummell" (1843), in *Oeuvres romanesques complètes*, ed. Jacques Petit (Paris: Gallimard, 1966), 2:692. Author's translation.

6. Ibid., 697.

7. William Hazlitt, "Brummelliana" (1828), in *The Complete Works of William Hazlitt*, ed. P. P. Howe (London: J. M. Dent, 1934), 20:152–53.

8. William Jesse, *Beau Brummell* (1844; London: Grolier Society, n.d.), 1:55.

9. George Moore, *Confessions of a Young Man*, ed. Susan Dick (1888; Montreal: McGill-Queen's University Press, 1972), 104. In an autobiographer's rather than a novelist's voice, Moore retells the story of meeting Manet and remarks on the painter's "simple, scrupulous clothes, and yet with a touch of the

dandy about them." This passage appears in George Moore, "Chavannes, Millet, and Manet," in *Modern Painters*, rev. ed. (London: Walter Scott, 1900), 31.

10. Emile Zola, "Edouard Manet" (1867), in *Portrait of Manet by Himself and His Contemporaries*, ed. P. Courthion and P. Cailler, trans. M. Ross (Cassell, 1960); reprinted in *Modern Art and Modernism: A Critical Anthology*, ed. Francis Frascina and Charles Harrison (New York: Harper and Row, 1982), 30. For Zola's belief that "A work of art is a corner of the universe viewed through a temperament," see Elizabeth Holt, *The Art of All Nations, 1850–1873: The Emerging Role of Exhibitions and Critics* (Garden City, NY: Anchor Books, 1981), 457. This is only half the program of the Baudelairean dandy, who inherited from Barbey and Brummell the notion that one accepts society to resist it.

11. Moore, *Modern Painters*, 41–42.

12. John Ruskin, "Letter the Seventy-ninth," *Flors Clavigera*, July 2, 1877, 201; quoted in Andrew McLaren Young, *The Paintings of James McNeill Whistler* (New Haven: Yale University Press, 1980), Text volume, 98.

13. James Abbott McNeill Whistler, "The Action," in *The Gentle Art of Making Enemies* (1892; New York: Dover, 1967), 2–18. For one of several other accounts of the trial, see E. R. Pennell and J. Pennell, *The Life of James McNeill Whistler* (Philadelphia: J. B. Lippincott, 1909), 1:229–45. All full accounts record the painter Edward Burne-Jones's reluctant admission that he didn't believe that his friend Whistler had worked hard enough on *The Falling Rocket* to justify the asking price. For an account of Ruskin's method of arriving at a fair price for a painter's labor, see E. R. Pennell and J. Pennell, *The Whistler Journal* (Philadelphia: J. B. Lippincott, 1921), 322–24. Briefly, Ruskin claimed he could determine a proper price or exchange value of a picture by assessing, with his practiced eye, not merely the amount but the quality of labor, mental and physical, required for the object's production. This is a labor theory of value of the sort expounded by many theorists, among them Adam Smith, David Ricardo, and Karl Marx. Like theirs, Ruskin's theory attempted to base prices on the strength of the worker's effort, rather than the importunity of the customer's demand, which he thought had a distorting influence on the prices for pictures in a time when so many conceived "the object of Art to be ornament rather than edification." By pointing to the several purposes of art, some lofty and some less so, he tinged questions of exchange value—that is, price— with those of use value, and thus obliquely referred to John Locke's notion that the good "effects of labor" are to create "the Products of the Earth useful to the Life of Man." See John Locke, *Two Treatises of Government*, ed. Peter Laslett (1690; Cambridge: Cambridge University Press, 1988), 296. For a nineteenth-century British writer to invoke Lockean economics, however indirectly, was to conjure up an atmosphere of primordial truth and justice. In that air, thought Ruskin, art could breathe and thrive. He believed that in the dust of

the modern marketplace, where he saw in Whistler one of many charlatans, art could only be demeaned to the condition of a commodity sold at prices set by vulgar whim. Whistler, too, invokes ideas with Lockean origins. By basing his legal claim on "the knowledge of a lifetime," he put an extreme construction on an idea common since the seventeenth century: personal experience is in some way a form of capital. Whistler dandified the idea by insisting that one gains the most valuable kind of experience by being a superior sort of person rather than by doing the sorts of painstaking work, whether with a brush or some other tool, that are commonly considered useful. The elements that combine to form the idea of experience as capital appear, disconnected, in Locke's theories of property (created by mixing labor with natural things) and of the psyche (which labors to construct ideas from the perception of things). See Carter Ratcliff, "Dramatis Personae, parts 4 and 5," *Art in America* 74, no. 2 (February 1986): 9, 11, 13; no. 5 (May 1986): 9, 11, 13, 15, 170–71, 173.

14. Maurice Denis, "Definition of Neotraditionalism" (1890), in *Théories; 1890–1910*, 4th ed. (Paris: Rouart and Watelin, 1920), reprinted in *Theories of Modern Art*, ed. Herschel B. Chipp (Berkeley: University of California Press, 1969), 94.

15. Georges Braque, "Thoughts and Reflections on Art" (1917), in *Nord-Sud* (Paris), ed. Pierre Reverdy, reprinted in Chipp, *Theories of Modern Art*, 260.

16. Jean Metzinger, "Note on Painting" (1910), in *Cubism*, ed. Edward F. Fry (New York: McGraw-Hill, 1966), 59.

17. Man Ray, "Statement" (1916), in *Dadas on Art*, ed. Lucy Lippard (Englewood Cliffs, NJ: Prentice-Hall, 1971), 156.

18. Pierre Cabanne, *Dialogues with Marcel Duchamp*, trans. Ron Padgett (New York: Viking, 1971), 43.

19. Ibid., 47.

20. Arturo Schwarz, ed., *The Complete Works of Marcel Duchamp* (New York: Abrams, 1969), 442.

21. When Pierre Cabanne asks Duchamp if it true that, as some say, he "arrived in the United States as a missionary of insolence," the artist says that he did, adding, "Still, I wasn't all that insolent." Duchamp's stance is typical of a dandy, for what he means is that he was dreadfully insolent but in an oblique, phlegmatic way that only the most refined could appreciate or even notice. See Cabanne, *Dialogues with Marcel Duchamp*, 49–50.

22. Cited in Martin Green and John Swan, *The Triumph of Pierrot: The Commedia dell'Arte and the Modern Imagination* (New York: Macmillan, 1986), 28.

23. Cabanne, *Dialogues with Marcel Duchamp*, 72.

24. Janet Bloom and Robert Losada, "Interview with John Ashbery," *New York Quarterly* 9 (winter 1972): 21.

25. Discussed by E. J. Dijksherhuis, "Isaac Newton: The Axiomatization of

Classical Mechanics," in *The Mechanization of the World Picture*, trans. C. Dikshoorn (1950; Oxford: Oxford University Press, 1961), 464–77.

26. William Blake, *Jerusalem: The Emanation of the Giant Albion* (1804), in *The Complete Poetry and Prose of William Blake*, rev. ed., ed. David V. Erdman (Garden City, NY: Anchor Press, 1982), 159.

27. Kasimir Malevich, "Suprematism," in *The Non-Objective World*, trans. Howard Dearstyne (1927; Chicago: Theobald, 1959), reprinted in Chipp, *Theories of Modern Art*, 341–46.

28. Barbey d'Aurevilly, "Du Dandysme et de George Brummell," 681, 690, 692, 693.

29. Kasimir Malevich, "From Cubism and Futurism to Suprematism: The New Painterly Realism" (1916), in *Russian Art of the Avant-Garde*, rev. ed., ed. and trans. John E. Bowlt (New York: Thames and Hudson, 1988), 119, 121, 123.

30. Ad Reinhardt, "Twelve Rules for a New Academy," *Artnews* (New York), May 1957. Reprinted in Ad Reinhardt, *Art as Art: The Selected Writings of Ad Reinhardt*, ed. Barbara Rose (Berkeley: University of California Press, 1991), 206.

31. Lucy Lippard, *Ad Reinhardt* (New York: Abrams, 1981), 184.

32. Max Kozloff, "Andy Warhol and Ad Reinhardt: The Great Accepter and the Great Demurrer," *Studio International* 181, no. 931 (March 1971): 113–17.

33. Michael Fried, "Shape as Form: Frank Stella's Irregular Polygons" (1966), in *Art and Objecthood: Essays and Reviews* (Chicago: University of Chicago Press, 1998), 78–81. In this passage one sees at work the "dialectic" of formalist criticism that meshes so smoothly with the machinery of art world reputation. The cogs and wheels of formalism meet those of the art institution in, for example, William Rubin's art-historical rewriting of Fried's art-critical analysis. See William Rubin, *Frank Stella* (exhibition catalog) (New York: Museum of Modern Art, 1970).

34. George Moore, ed., *An Anthology of Pure Poetry*, ed. and intro. George Moore (1927; New York: Liveright, 1973), 1819.

35. Stéphane Mallarmé, "Brise Marine" (1887), in *Mallarmé*, ed. Anthony Hartley (Baltimore: Penguin, 1965), 29.

36. Quoted in Hartley, *Mallarmé*, ix.

### BIBLIOGRAPHY

Barbey d'Aurevilly, Jules. "Du dandysme et de George Brummell." In *Oeuvres romanesques complètes*, ed. Jacques Petit, 2:667–733. Paris: Gallimard, 1966.

Baudelaire, Charles. "Le Peintre de la vie moderne." 1868. In *Oeuvres Complètes*, edited by Claude Pichois. Paris: Gallimard, 1976.

Blake, William. *Jerusalem: The Emanation of the Giant Albion.* 1804. In *The Complete Poetry and Prose of William Blake.* Rev. ed. Edited by David Erdman. Garden City, NY: Anchor Press, 1982.

Bloom, Janet, and Robert Losada. "Interview with John Ashbery." *New York Quarterly* 9 (winter 1972): 21.

Braque, Georges. "Thoughts and Reflections on Art." 1917. In *Theories of Modern Art,* edited by Herschel B. Chipp. Berkeley: University of California Press, 1969.

Cabanne, Pierre. *Dialogues with Marcel Duchamp.* Translated by Ron Padgett. New York: Viking, 1971.

Carlyle, Thomas. *Sartor Resartus: The Life and Opinions of Herr Teufelsdroch.* 1836. Reprint, edited by Kerry McSweeny and Peter Sabor. Oxford: Oxford University Press, 1987.

Connolly, Cyril. "The Dandy: II." In *The Evening Colonnade.* New York: Harcourt Brace Jovanovich, 1975.

Denis, Maurice. "Definition of Neotraditionalism." 1890. In *Theories of Modern Art,* edited by Herschel B. Chipp. Berkeley: University of California Press, 1969.

Dijksherhuis, E. J. *The Mechanization of the World Picture.* Translated by C. Dikshoorn. 1950. Reprint, Oxford: Oxford University Press, 1961.

Fry, Edward, ed. *Cubism.* New York: McGraw-Hill, 1966.

Green, Martin, and John Swan. *The Triumph of Pierrot: The Commedia dell'Arte and the Modern Imagination.* New York: Macmillan, 1986.

Hazlitt, William. "Brummelliana." In *The Complete Works of William Hazlitt.* Edited by P. P. Howe. London: J. M. Dent, 1934.

Jesse, William. *Beau Brummell.* 1844. London: Grolier Society, n.d.

Kozloff, Max. "Andy Warhol and Ad Reinhardt: The Great Accepter and the Great Demurrer." *Studio International* 181, no. 931 (March 1971): 113–17.

Lippard, Lucy. *Ad Reinhardt.* New York: Abrams, 1981.

Malevich, Kasimir. "Suprematism." In *The Non-Objective World.* 1927. In *Theories of Modern Art,* edited by Herschel B. Chipp. Berkeley: University of California Press, 1969.

Mallarmé, Stéphane. "Brise Marine." 1887. In *Mallarmé,* edited by Anthony Hartley. Baltimore: Penguin, 1965.

Moers, Ellen. *The Dandy: Brummell to Beerbohm.* Lincoln: University of Nebraska Press, 1978.

Moore, George. "Chavannes, Millet, and Manet." In *Modern Painters.* Rev. ed. London: Walter Scott, 1900.

———. *Confessions of a Young Man.* 1888. Reprint, edited by Susan Dick. Montreal: McGill-Queen's University Press, 1972.

———, ed. *An Anthology of Pure Poetry.* 1927. Reprint, edited and with an introduction by George Moore. New York: Liveright, 1973.

Pennell, E. R., and J. Pennell. *The Whistler Journal*. Philadelphia: J. B. Lippincott, 1921.

Ratcliff, Carter. "Dramatis Personae." Parts 4 and 5. *Art in America* 74, no. 2 (February 1986): 9, 11, 13; no. 5 (May 1986): 9, 11, 13, 15, 170–71, 173.

Ray, Man. "Statement." 1916. In *Dadas on Art*, edited by Lucy Lippard. Englewood Cliffs, NJ: Prentice-Hall, 1971.

Whistler, James Abbott McNeill. "The Action." In *The Gentle Art of Making Enemies*. 1892. Reprint, New York: Dover, 1967.

Young, Andrew McLaren. *The Paintings of James McNeill Whistler*. New Haven: Yale University Press, 1980.

Zola, Emile. "Edouard Manet." In *Modern Art and Modernism: A Critical Anthology*, edited by Francis Frascina and Charles Harrison. New York: Harper and Row, 1982.

*Chapter 4*

# Dandies, Marginality, and Modernism
## *Georgia O'Keeffe, Marcel Duchamp, and Other Cross-Dressers*

## *Susan Fillin-Yeh*

Two photographs made in the same year, 1921, and in the same city, New York, offer the dandy's image to twentieth-century viewers. For studied singly and in their interrelationships, both Alfred Stieglitz's photograph of the painter Georgia O'Keeffe, dressed with uncompromising and elegant simplicity in an oversized man's hat, dark suit jacket, and white shirt open at the neck (fig. 4.1), and Man Ray's photograph of Dadaist Marcel Duchamp in drag (fig. 4.2) are alluring. As happens generally with portrait photographs, each photograph is a collaboration. In even the most ordinary of such photographs, the sitter poses her/himself for a photographer who in turn also has a visual agenda. But with these photographs, the situation was intensified, for photographer and sitter were partners in invention. These photographs are more than simply portraits; they are agents in the construction of new artistic, cultural, and sexual meanings, even of personal narrative. O'Keeffe once alluded to their passionate love affair when speaking of Stieglitz's photographs of her.[1] Her comment, one made in the 1970s, was unprecedented, a rare admission that her sexual life had a life in her art. As for the Duchamp/Ray collaboration, it insinuated the image of the Parisian femme fatale into the New York art world of the early twentieth century. That personage, an elegant, alluring, and mysterious woman, at ease in public space, had earlier been a central figure in nineteenth-century European literature and art (in the writing of Charles Baudelaire, and paintings by Gustav Moreau, Dante Gabriel Rossetti, and others). The femme fatale is central to what Christine

*Fig. 4.1.* Alfred Stieglitz, *Georgia O'Keeffe: A Portrait*, 1921, palladium photograph. National Gallery of Art, Washington, D.C. Alfred Stieglitz Collection. Reproduced by permission.

Buci-Glucksmann has felicitously termed "l'archaéologie de la modernité."[2] As Mary Ann Doane has pointed out, the femme fatale is a nexus for new, early-twentieth-century ideas about modernity and urbanization (she inhabits a new urban space of dance halls, streets, and restaurants), she figures in Freudian theory, and she is central to the new reproductive technologies of photography and film. A "sign of strength in an unwritten history" of the many feminisms, the femme fatale, as Doane has discussed her epistemology, carries with her the power of masquerade, a privileged, distanced, and disruptive anti-knowledge behind a cool facade.[3]

The Duchamp photograph charts the profound ambivalence about sexual difference characteristic of the late nineteenth century, for it is the image of a disguise, laced with witty subterfuge. Duchamp borrowed his fashionable hat with its wonderful patterned headband from

*Fig. 4.2.* Man Ray, *Marcel Duchamp Dressed as Rrose Sèlavy*, 1921, signed 1924, gelatin silver print, 8 1/2 × 16 3/16 in. Philadelphia Museum of Art. The Samuel S. White III and Vera White Collection. © 2000 Man Ray Trust/Artists Rights Society, New York/ADAGP, Paris. Reproduced by permission.

a friend, Germaine Everling, and it was Everling who posed for the hands. Duchamp finished his creation by retouching Ray's photograph, softening the lens' focus to exaggerate the shadowy, sultry image of a femme fatale's mysterious and elusive mobility.

But downtown Greenwich Village bohemia "in the know" recognized another kind of mobility: androgyny. They recognized Marcel Duchamp cut loose from conventional notions of gendered individuation to present himself as the woman he named Rrose Sélavy, a woman with veiled and shadowed eyes who has posed as if resting her elbows on a café table. Duchamp, so the image read to his audience, was double gendered, and—seemingly—changed his sexual aspect as easily as he changed clothing. And what of O'Keeffe? If the politics and mores of life in avant-garde circles influenced her dandyism, she also brought with her to New York by 1907 the disposition for cross-dressing not uncommon among middle-class young women born in the last decades of the nineteenth century.[4] These images of gender doubling and role reversal, the one of a man in the guise of a woman, the other one of a woman in Baudelaire's modern man's immaculate linen and stark black suiting (that "modern hero's" garb, Baudelaire wrote, which has "its own beauty"), once shaped an ambiance, and evoke it for us now: Greenwich Village in the 1910s, where aesthetic experimentation, feminism, and other kinds of political activism flourished in a new climate of personal liberation, liberated sexuality, and at least the beginnings of a new sexual freedom for women.[5] These photographs of artists all dressed up with, as one might say (and as their work attests), everywhere to go, are versions of a specialized expression of artifice, a modernist icon/pose/mode: the dandy. Defined conventionally as male—but also as female, as embodied in the dandyism of turn-of-the-century Gibson Girl shirtwaist fashions—the dandy was coolly elegant, detached but intensely aware of self and situation. As perhaps the best known among other artists they knew, O'Keeffe and Duchamp, as well as Florine Stettheimer (1871–1944), took up and deliberately altered that dandy's image inherited from the nineteenth century, refashioning it to their own needs and a new avant-garde art.[6]

It is hardly surprising that the model of Baudelaire's dandy translated so easily from French into English, from Paris of the boulevards to the newer and rawer avenues and cross-streets of New York of the 1910s. Clothed in his "eternal black suit," the dandy, a product of his fin de siècle history, transcended it.[7] Whether or not avant-garde artists in New York knew of the Baudelairean dandy's connections with utopian socialism, the Eight and Ash Can School painters, as well as artists of the Stieglitz and Arensberg circles, were predisposed to a vision of artistic identity as being of the moment, and of modernity as heroic. And lively models for dandyism existed: Stieglitz in his well-known black cloak and Duchamp (both as male and as female) with his consummate elegance (O'Keeffe once remarked on it).[8] The dandy's persona was seen as a vehicle for breaking with convention: New York artists shared Baudelaire's dandy's "burning need to make of oneself something original."[9]

Why was it that the dandy's image had such cogency for avant-garde art production in New York in the early twentieth century? It may be that the persona of the dandy is especially suited to urban modernism, beginning with Baudelaire's Paris, because, as we know it from his pronouncements, the type so clearly emerges as a composite: the dandy, stroller, observer, "the passionate spectator," and "the painter of modern life" who can be identified as "the perfect flâneur."[10] In the 1930s, Siegfried Kracauer commented on Baudelaire's thinking: "On the Boulevards, the dandies lived, so to speak, extraterritorially.[11] Kracauer's exile's empathies for dandyism surface in Walter Benjamin's flaneur/dandy, composedly present but "out of place," as Benjamin puts it, on city streets.[12]

Kracauer's and Benjamin's glosses on Baudelaire can suggest ways of looking at art produced earlier in the century in New York, for Duchamp, O'Keeffe, and Stettheimer each made work that draws attention to congruencies between the persona of the dandy and a climate of shifts and dislocations, that is, the paradox of the invigorating and empowering loss of belief in the certainties of past traditions, the intellectual and aesthetic loss of place within accepted conventions that is generally assumed in modernism's beginnings. Perhaps we need to remind ourselves that, as with postmodernism now, modernism too was once defined not only in relation to formal concerns but in cultural terms, and was oppositional.[13] New York art circles in Greenwich Village forged pragmatic definitions of modernism later submerged in the 1960s in discussions of self-contained and purified modes of modernism applied mostly to painting.[14]

Greenwich Villagers in the teens were proud of their distance from bourgeois life and conventional politics and celebrated their marginality. It was much more interesting where *they* were.[15] Thus it is no surprise that the attempts of New York modernists to relocate these new worlds within the shifting boundaries of their own art seem to inscribe the strolling dandy's fascination with boundary lines and moving across them, her/his familiarity with being marginal, "out of place," which also created a *new* place to stand.

Representations of dandies in nineteenth-century paintings make marginality explicit. They are rendered visible to us now in images of their up-to-the-minute fashion statements, for example, those déclassé artists and intellectuals self-defined by dress,[16] whose presence Baudelaire pointed out in the work of Constantin Guys, Eugène Lami, and Gavarni, and which we have learned to recognize in paintings by Tissot, Caillebotte, and Manet. Manet's barmaid of the *Bar at the Folies Bergère*, beautiful in her black Parisian dress, is their female equivalent. T. J. Clark has described this woman and other dandies, compelling personalities whose elegant appearance punctuated nineteenth-century images of urban capitalism. Elegance, masking, and self-construction loosened their class ties.[17] If the Folies Bergère barmaid is a person whose demeanor, as Anne Hanson has noted, is blunt and indifferent, at the same time, as Clark writes, her face has a "character [that] derives from its not being bourgeois—and having that fact almost hidden."[18] With their class status disguised by their fashionable appearance, both barmaid and flaneur had a new, if tenuous and chancy, social mobility; with their class not quite identifiable, some managed to transgress class lines. A linguistic concept that illuminates their new, late-nineteenth-century freedom of motion is that of the "shifter," a free-floating linguistic sign like "he/she," or "this/that," a word that takes on specific meaning only when used in context.[19]

The notion of a "shifter" is useful in explaining another aspect of the fit between dandyism and modernism, between dandyism as self-image and dandyism as self-defining artistic strategy, as absorbed into the ethos of New York's avant-garde. It is not only that the avant-garde encouraged shifting sexual freedom. There was also a significant distinction between New York's avant-garde and earlier ones: its many women artists. The notion of the "shifter" goes a long way in suggesting why the persona of the dandy was such a useful one tactically for women of the avant-garde in the early modern period, and why female dandies abounded in early modernism.[20] For if, like the men, avant-garde women relished their place apart from conventional art institutions, they differed from them in being *doubly* displaced, that is, intensely aware of the need to negotiate, to assert individuality within what was still *male* avant-garde culture.[21] O'Keeffe wrote in 1930, "I have had to go to the men as sources in my painting because the past has left us so small an inheritance of women's painting."[22] Stettheimer once commented ironically on a male photographer's arrogance, and his female subject's artistic revenge. Although the protagonists are unnamed, they are clearly Stieglitz and O'Keeffe.[23]

The presence of women put new pressure on androgyny. In a climate in which women's images and actions as independent artists were without precedent, they made themselves up as they went along, defining themselves in new—and shifting—contexts. Thus women's dandies' images took on meanings that empowered them. They posed a challenge to the dominant mode of male discourse by using its own symbols against it. The early twentieth century inherited such images as photographer Frances Benjamin Johnston's 1896 self-portrait smoking a cigarette, which mimics and flaunts male attributes and body language, and undermines the view that stereotypic male behavior was unnatural for a woman.[24] Although Johnston chose to show herself in women's clothing, her constructed pose was that of a cross-dresser, and her image operated then in the sense that Susan Gubar has discussed it: "Cross-dressing becomes a way of ad-dressing and re-dressing the inequities of culturally-defined categories of masculinity and femininity."[25] And, as Sandra Gilbert has written, "Feminist modernist costume imagery is radically revisionary in a political sense, for it implies that no one, male or female, can or should be confined to a uni-form, a single form or self."[26]

Female cross-dressers sometimes functioned as sex symbols for nineteenth-century men who attempted to eroticize and thus possess independent women or who repressed homosexual fantasies. But the New York avant-garde also had the examples of middle-class professional women.[27] Dr. Mary Walker wore men's clothing as a Civil War doctor, and described its importance to her: it gave her the power to do her job. "While bodies are caged in the petticoat badge of dependence," she wrote, "minds and souls . . . cannot command themselves."[28] Her choice of men's clothing for freedom of action was a tactic taken up by early feminists such as Madame Bernard Trouser, who lent her name to her sartorial invention, pants for women—"trousers."[29] Women in Greenwich Village may have had warm feelings for the stories of earlier women in the art world, for example, Rosa Bonheur, the French

painter of animal subjects, who obtained permission from the prefec-
ture of the city of Paris to wear men's clothing when she needed to visit
barnyards and stables.[30]

Late-nineteenth- and early-twentieth-century images of female
cross-dressing in America included photographs of fresh-faced, whole-
some-looking beauties like the popular actress Maude Adams, who
was famous at the turn of the century for playing men's roles on stage.
These images, and similar Gibson Girl advertising images of women in
men's hats and shirts, almost suggest a utopian vision of sexual equality, if only in consumerism. A photograph of O'Keeffe costumed in
men's formal clothing for a 1907 New York Art Students' League ball
can be placed within a tradition of snapshots depicting high-spirited
friendships among middle-class young women who wear men's clothing.[31] The photograph's high jinks portray O'Keeffe's youthful self, and
are predictive.

Markedly absent in O'Keeffe's photograph is the expression of pain
Gubar has discovered in many well-known late-nineteenth- and early-
twentieth-century images of women dressed like men, as for example,
in a self-portrait of 1923 by the expatriate painter Romaine Brooks.[32]
The image is startling in its similarities to Stieglitz's photograph of O'-
Keeffe, but it offers very different emotional messages. Brooks presented herself against a background of charred, bombed-out ruins, and
her painting reveals obvious signs of strain in her shaded eyes and face
and tense posture. The pose may suggest Brooks's sympathies with
Radclyffe Hall, who constructed an ambivalent and troubled fictional
characterization of Brooks in her book *The Well of Loneliness*. As
Gubar has noted, "Hall wrote about the frustration of a girl born to a
father who treats his daughter as the son he wanted. Since this is only a
slight exaggeration of the psychology of what growing up female can
be in patriarchy . . . Hall's analysis of her sense of freakishnes repeats
itself" in many women's biographies. [33]

But O'Keeffe's steady gaze, like Duchamp's masquerade, is confi-
dent. We recall that in Duchamp's image as Rrose Sélavy even the name
he made up for his alter ego was an exuberant joke, a pun: Rrose
Sélavy translates as "love—that's life," if the doubled *r* in Rrose is
rolled out French style and pronounced "eros," and Sélavy is anglicized
and interpreted as "c'est la vie." And as with O'Keeffe's, the image
gives us Duchamp's own wonderful good looks. His genuine allure as a
woman departs from the nineteenth-century tradition of men dressed

up as women who often look as gawky or deliberately awkward as New York Ash Can School painter John Sloan once did in 1894 when he dressed up as "Twillbee," the victim/heroine of a popular Victorian potboiler, in a theatrical spoof of George Du Maurier's *Trilby*.[34] Even Duchamp allowed himself to look awkward in one particular Ray/Duchamp photograph collaboration of 1921, a perfume bottle label for a Duchamp readymade, *Belle Haleine-Eau de Voilette (Beautiful Breath-Veil Water)*, in which the image makers leave no doubt that Duchamp really *is* a man.[35]

Images of the androgynous body multiplied in New York's avant-garde circles in a climate linking the artist's body and artistic radicalism. Both Stieglitz circle artists, many of whom explored organic imagery, and Dadaists, who took the mechanical world as a point of departure, constructed androgynous images as a format for unconventional, intimate portraits. Duchamp's *Large Glass/The Bride Stripped Bare by Her Bachelors, Even . . .* (1915–23) opened the possibilities for this new bridging, even for a new mode of sexuality, for *The Large Glass*, which offered contemporaries transparent images of the activities of amorous robots, featured "Bachelors" who were dandies of sorts. Even though Duchamp provided a different identity for each of them, all the bachelors wear abstracted versions of what is clearly the same generic "morning" coat.[36]

Their suiting is proper wedding attire and more. Duchamp characterized it as a "livery of uniforms," a phrase that vividly invokes Baudelaire's comments on the modern hero.[37] As with Baudelaire, Duchamp's list of professions even includes an undertaker (the others being a priest, department store delivery boy, *gendarme, cuirassier*, policeman, flunky, busboy).[38] And if, as with Baudelaire, who observed that "A uniform livery of affliction bears witness to equality," Duchamp's bachelor dandies in their "livery" are representatives of Baudelaire's "public soul," their representations are also Baudelairean because they are "the outer husk."[39]

Duchamp's construction in *The Large Glass* seemingly took Baudelaire literally, for in his eccentric system, the uniforms are empty clothing, clothing, that is, as a receptacle that waits for an identity to be supplied.[40] It is amusing to suppose that viewers of the glass, spectators who for Duchamp functioned as part of the tableau, offered their own diverse identities to the bachelors much in the way one poses for a photograph behind false painted billboard identities at a carnival. Even more than this borrowing, though, there is the fact that in Duchamp's eccentric system, the bachelors are "moulds" and they are "hollow." Their liveries have the possibility of filling with mysterious essences Duchamp invented ("illuminating gas," "provisional color"), which he called "eros' matrix."[41]

Duchamp's is far from the only double gendered image produced in New York avant-garde circles in the 1910s and 1920s. Paintings by Florine Stettheimer suggest how readily the implications of Duchamp's practices found acceptance. Stettheimer's 1923 *Portrait of Marcel Duchamp* even documents Duchamp in his dandy's doubled manifestations. Stettheimer painted Duchamp seated facing his alter ego, Rrose Sélavy, whom she chose to represent as a stylish female sylph who balances with impeccable poise on a stool at the top of a spring in a Rube Goldberg-like contraption that Duchamp manipulates.[42]

Stettheimer's paintings bring us New York in the 1920s and 1930s, taking in Greenwich Village and Forty-second Street, downtown bohemia, the upper crust, and popular culture; they offer a new mix of subject matter, for as Linda Nochlin has pointed out, Stettheimer populated her paintings of the city with personal friends, a shifting dandyesque world of public and private.[43] A lively participant in New York cultural life whose pictures contradict once conventionally held ideas that she was a recluse, Stettheimer gave parties that indexed the contemporary art scene.[44] Carl Springchorn's informal group portrait of art world guests at a party at the Stettheimer sisters' apartment includes Charles Demuth, Arnold Genthe, Carl Van Vechten, Isabel Lachaise, and Georgia O'Keeffe.[45]

Stettheimer herself was no stranger to the tactics of cross-dressing and dandyism. In androgynous self-portraits, among them *Portrait of Myself* (1923) and her cameo appearance in her 1933 *Family Portrait , II* (fig. 4.3), the one gendered aspect of Stettheimer's imaged self-construction enriches, plays against, and almost, but not quite, hides the other. Stettheimer's self-portraits offer new images of the androgynous body. *Portrait of Myself* gives us Florine in her female persona in flaming red, doubling as male in the black beret she wears, an accessory borrowed from among the attributes of the nineteenth-century romantic male artist. Her dress is nearly transparent and she has posed herself so that the garland of flowers she holds encircles her shadowy, hinted-at pubes.[46] Later, in *Family Portrait*, she is male in her black painting clothes—actually fashionable lounging pyjamas modeled on a man's

*Fig. 4.3.* Florine Stettheimer, *Family Portrait, II*, 1933, oil on canvas, 46 1/4 ×
64 5/8 in. The Museum of Modern Art, New York. Gift of Ettie Stettheimer.
Reproduced by permission.

suit. Except she also has on high-heeled red shoes. As with the earlier
portrait, it is the accessory that gives doubled gender to her image. Stettheimer was highly conscious of her sense of disguise. As one of her
poems describes it, "Occasionally / A human being / Saw my light /
Rushed in / Got singed / Got Scared / Rushed out / Called fire / Or it
happened / That he tried to subdue it . . . / Never did a friend / Enjoy
it . . . / So I learned to turn it low . . . a protection."[47] But even "turned
low," Stettheimer's cross-dressed self-images in paintings, self-con-
structions of a consummate dandy's personifications, offer evidence of
the very acceptability of role and rule changes in the New York art
world of the 1910s and 1920s, among a crowd that prized personal
and artistic leeway and room to maneuver. Duchamp's famous urinal,
R. Mutt's *Fountain* (1917) was, as William Camfield has argued very
convincingly, known in Stieglitz and Dadaist circles both as a male
Buddha and a female Madonna.[48] Influenced by Duchamp, Man Ray's
Dadaist "readymades" also embodied the new Dadaist aesthetic in

which sexual tensions and ambiguities resulted in a charged personal imagery. One of Ray's choices for a "readymade," or claimed object, was a kitchen utensil, an egg beater with quotidian but fundamental associations with food, even life (birth, the egg), and scrambled destruction. Ray photographed it and then called identical prints of the same photograph *Woman*—and *Man*.[49]

Another Ray and Duchamp collaborative photograph, *Rotary Glass Plates*, offers us Duchamp subsumed within the transparent body of a machine.[50] This machine and other Dadaist mechanomorphs were almost invariably defined as female in the iconography of New York Dada. "Man has made the machine in his own image," wrote Dadaist participant Paul Haviland in 1915, and went on to describe *her* lungs, *her* limbs, and so forth.[51] In a climate where both men and women sought to define themselves in terms of the other sex, Haviland's comment apparently seeks to annex some perceived notion of female power; it hints at sexual tension perhaps cranked up a notch because of the presence of an active, female avant-garde. "[W]hy," as Alice Jardine wondered in another not dissimilar context, "[did] all of these guys want to be wom*en*?"[52]

Along with anthropomorphic Dadaist representations possessing an ambiguous and doubled sexuality, Stieglitz circle artists also produced their own images of elusive and mysterious doublings that unfold into their opposites, or are bisexual or androgynous. O'Keeffe and Arthur G. Dove made paintings of plant and organic life whose recurrent themes reenact the dandy's personae:[53] shifting images—images sexually charged, but without a fixed gender—that are particularly modern. These are paintings of unmistakable but indefinable sexual content, whose sexual valences are impossible to pin down. Even if one were to apply the Freudian biologically based theories of gender often resorted to in avant-garde circles in the 1910s, the shapes in such paintings are simultaneously phallic and womblike.

Freudian definitions were not always taken seriously in the Greenwich Village art world, and were often misapplied. Perhaps they lost credence because they had become popular and overused so quickly. In 1915 Susan Glaspell and George Cram Cook of the Provincetown Players even wrote a play, *Suppressed Desires*, spoofing the use of Freudian definitions, which was billed as a Freudian Comedy. And Alfred Stieglitz repudiated Freudianism as passé in a well-publicized exhibition statement of 1921.[54] Even so, Freudian ideas were part of a common language in the New York art world throughout the 1910s and 1920s, and beginning in the 1910s, O'Keeffe's art was often defined in essentialist Freudian terms. These were definitions she was reluctant to accept. ("I would hear men saying, 'She is pretty good for a woman; she paints like a man.' That upset me.")[55]

Photographs documenting O'Keeffe's paintings raise other quite obvious questions about the climate for criticism in New York in the 1910s and 1920s, questions like "Whose Freudianism?" or "Who is doing the interpreting?" If phallic suggestions in O'Keeffe's sculpture and drawings in the 1910s seemed inescapable to her viewers then, still, it's useful to remember that it was Alfred Stieglitz who took the photographs that promote this reading, and that O'Keeffe and Stieglitz often disagreed on the work's meaning.[56] O'Keeffe's statements about her work deny a specific essentialist sexual content.[57]

Yet sexual images in O'Keeffe's art offer us a pervasive sexuality, one that floats loose from ties to fixed notions of gender; her imagery also shifts terms constantly to construct and reconstruct images. It is useful to recall that O'Keeffe's life-sized, breakthrough, abstract drawings of the 1910s were charged with unusual somatic resonances: O'Keeffe drew some of them while "crawling on the floor" over them.[58] These drawings were among O'Keeffe's first to take their cues from the generative forces in plant life. O'Keeffe, who designed Arts and Crafts movement Art Education programs when she taught in Texas public schools, adapted particularly the image of the budding, sprouting plant in her abstractions.[59] While reminding us that flowers are double sexed, the sexuality in O'Keeffe's flower imagery randomizes human impulses and anatomy, as for example in *Two Calla Lilies on Pink* (1928).[60] What is one to make of the petals in *Two Calla Lilies on Pink*? Are they female? And the yellow protrusions from the flower centers? Are they phallic?

Serial painting ensembles in black and white, which are typical of O'Keeffe's work beginning in the 1910s, pare away form to conflate a shifting and charged bisexuality with the studied presentation of the dandy's self-making. O'Keeffe, who had read Charlotte Perkins Gilman's articles on simplified clothing for liberated women in *The Forerunner,* in the 1910s began to dress exclusively in black or white, paring down and refining her fashion life at about the same time she reduced her palette.[61] In the *Shell and Old Shingle* series of 1926, successive paintings—significantly—lose their green pigment to leave us with the colors of a dandy's white linen and stark black suiting.[62] A suite of

*Fig. 4.4.* Georgia O'Keeffe, *Black and White*, 1930, oil on canvas, 36 ×
24 in. Whitney Museum of American Art, New York. Fiftieth Anniver-
sary Gift of Mr. and Mrs. R. Crosby Kemper. Photograph © 1999 Whitney Museum of American Art. © 2000 Georgia O'Keeffe Foundation/
Artists Rights Society, New York.

black and white paintings of around 1930, brought together for an exhibition at Stieglitz's gallery in 1932, is another celebration of the absence of color (fig. 4.4).[63] In these paintings, elegance alone remains. Stripped to the barest edge of legibility, they etch vibrating outlines with the rudiments of a flickering and pervasive human and vegetal sexuality.

It is instructive to compare the aesthetic dandyism of O'Keeffe and Stettheimer. If at first the two seem to have little in common, each carried over the dandy's artifice and shifting ambiguities from her person to her art. Unlike O'Keeffe, Stettheimer played with ultrafeminine tropes as if with masks, revamping the clichés of the feminine: jewels, flounces, lace. She claimed cellophane as an artistic material in sets she created in 1934 for the opera *Four Saints in Three Acts*, written by Gertrude Stein with music by Virgil Thomson.

Stettheimer's assumed naive imagery offers us an art that is dense, packed. She destroyed spatial illusion in order to leave room for things, describing her paintings in poems that are like lists: they are nonhierarchical with a lateral spread. Here is one in which Stettheimer describes herself in terms of objects, a set of desires:

> I like slippers gold
> I like oysters cold
> and my garden filled with flowers
> and the sky full of towers
> and traffic in the streets
> and Maillard's sweets
> and Bendel's clothes
> and Nat Lewis hose
> and Tappes window arrays
> and crystal fixtures
> and my pictures[64]

All this abundance would seem to be quite different from O'Keeffe's stripped-down sensibility. But in both, we have an art crafted out of excess—in Stettheimer's, an extreme materiality; in O'Keeffe's, an extreme reserve.

Perhaps the best way to suggest the importance of the dandy's persona as an artistic tactic in the art of O'Keeffe and Stettheimer is to compare paintings both made in the 1920s and 1930s in which startling objects float, dislocated, in the sky. In O'Keeffe paintings, these

*Fig. 4.5.* Georgia O'Keeffe, *Summer Days*, 1936, oil on canvas, 36 × 30 in. Whitney Museum of American Art, New York. Gift of Calvin Klein. Photograph © 1999 Whitney Museum of American Art. © 2000 Georgia O'Keeffe Foundation/Artists Rights Society, New York.

are mostly flowers, though she also chose bones and cow and deer skulls (fig. 4.5).[65] These paintings take on new meanings when compared with Stettheimer's *Family Portrait, II*, where numerous things, including a chandelier and its near look-alike in the form of a glowing and crystalline image of the Chrysler building, are suspended. Like O'-Keeffe, Stettheimer levitates silk flowers, crafted emblems of a stereotyped femininity.

These objects with their novel locations also have undergone disconcerting scale changes. Literally ungrounded, enormous, they are observed as spectacle, as panoply. And with this vision, artificed, ambiguous, and shifting, we are returned to the elegant and strolling flaneur/dandy, who takes on an artist's body. Stettheimer's self-image spells it out for us. If, in *Family Portrait, II* (as in other paintings), Stettheimer identifies herself as a painter, here where her mannish painting pyjamas separate her from her jeweled and begowned family, she also assumes the flaneur's aloof location at the side of her own painting—at its margin—the margin that offers her the most complete view of the panorama she has constructed for us.

Such dandyism in the work of both artists is a dandyism of locations, both psychic and physical, and a resultant dandyism of vision. In each case, objects have been drawn very close: the giant flowers and other floating things have been pushed to the foreground, nearly into our space. At the same time, the imagery, which looms against glowing skies, crowds the canvas. Stettheimer and O'Keeffe both suggest that certain things cannot be contained within boundaries, and so, psychologically, their images seem to push viewers back, displacing them. Thus, the viewers of Stettheimer's and O'Keeffe's paintings are brought to share the vision of the modernist artist, the flaneur/dandy "out of place," who privileges the view from the sidelines in images of distancing and dislocation while investing them with insight—and, perhaps, with the glamour of the unattainable.

And it is this dandy's consciousness of self and position that made that persona so useful an appropriation for all sorts of modernist dandies and cross-dressers, and especially for women artists, a persona that is inscribed in Stettheimer's dense narrations, in O'Keeffe's resonant severities, and the destabilizing spatial disjunctions seen in both. Each in her own way gives us images of modernism's mobile spaces in a vision of a world no longer grounded in certainty, no longer marked out in traditional perspective or rules of painting—or in clichéd sexual roles. If, as one might argue, modernism and the dandy constructed each other, women artists of New York's avant-garde shaped that construction to their own purposes as specially suited to their own paintings.[66] The visual imagery of dislocation that these early modernist dandies mapped out has come down to us now in a shifting, sometimes recalcitrant, subversive, and provocative masquerade.

NOTES

This essay is a revised version of the author's article that previously appeared in the *Oxford Art Journal* 18, no. 2 (1995): 33–44, and in *Women in Dada: Essays on Sex, Gender, and Identity*, ed. Naomi Sawelson-Gorse (Cambridge: MIT Press, 1999), and is reprinted with permission.

This paper has been brewing for a very long time; I benefited from the advice, enthusiasm, and insights of a great many people. I am grateful to my students at Yale and my students in Women, Art and Culture, at Hunter College. My thanks to the Whitney Humanities Center and the Women's Studies Program at Yale University for sponsoring the symposium, *New Art and the New Woman* (1987), where I presented the first version of this paper. I thank Laura Wexler, Christine Stansell, and Lois P. Rudnick for sharing ideas; and Laurie Lisle, Barbara Bloemink, and David Krapes for help with illustrations. Ellen Stauder, Nadine Fiedler, and Jen Yeh graciously read the manuscript, and Ellen Stauder and Charles Rhyne gave me opportunities in 1992–93 to present work in progress to their literature and art history classes at Reed College. This paper is dedicated to the memory of my parents and Milton W. Brown.

1. See Alfred Stieglitz, *Georgia O'Keeffe: A Portrait by Alfred Stieglitz, with an Introduction by Georgia O'Keeffe* (New York: Metropolitan Museum of Art, 1978).

2. Christine Buci-Glucksmann, *La Raison baroque: De Baudelaire à Benjamin* (Paris: Galilée, 1984), 34.

3. Mary Ann Doane, *Femmes Fatales: Feminism, Film Theory, Psychoanalysis* (New York: Routledge, 1991), 1, 3, 33–43. Although female masquerade has been conventionally discussed as reification and as a norm of femininity, I subscribe to the alternate reading Doane's analysis provides: that it is a destabilizing tactic and a way of breaking with clichés.

4. See Martha Banta, *Imaging American Women: Idea and Ideals in Cultural History* (New York: Columbia University Press, 1987); and Carroll Smith-Rosenberg, *Disorderly Conduct: Visions of Gender in Victorian America* (New York: Oxford University Press, 1985), 245–96. See also Doane's discussion in *Femmes Fatales* (24–25) of Freud's and Cixous's ideas about female transvestism, including "mastery over the image" and "the ease with which women can slip into male clothing." For an exemplary analysis of the cultural and political resonances of 1920s clothing in France that sheds light on the American version of the phenomenon, see Mary Louise Roberts, "Samson and Delilah Revisited: The Politics of Women's Fashion in 1920s France," *American Historical Review* 98, no. 3 (June 1993): 657–84. As Roberts points out, "Fashion was not 'politics' as we are used to conceiving of it, but the debates over its meaning . . . were profoundly political" (684). My thanks to Jacqueline

Dirks for giving me the Roberts article. For a photograph of O'Keeffe in men's formal clothing, see n. 31.

5. Charles Baudelaire, "Salon of 1846: On the Heroism of Modern Life," in *The Mirror of Art: Critical Studies*, trans. Jonathan Mayne (London: Phaidon, 1955), 127. O'Keeffe's art took shape in Greenwich Village circles that included Emma Goldman, Neith Boyce, and Charlotte Perkins Gilman. A letter of 25 August 1915 from O'Keeffe to Anita Politzer reads

> [T]hen 291 [the Stieglitz Gallery publication] came and I was so crazy about it that I sent for Number 2 and 3—and I think they are great—they just take my breath away—it is almost as good as going to 291 [Gallery]. I subscribed to it—it was too good to let it go by—and I had to have the *Masses* too. I got Jerome Eddy [*Cubists and Post Impressionism*, 1913] a long time ago and sent for Kandinsky. . . . I got Floyd Dell's *Women as World Builders* a few days ago and got quite excited over it.

Georgia O'Keeffe Papers, Yale Collection of American Literature, Beinecke Rare Book and Manuscript Library, Yale University (hereafter cited as Beinecke Library). See also Clive Giboire, ed., *Lovingly, Georgia: The Complete Correspondence of Georgia O'Keeffe and Anita Pollitzer* (New York: Touchstone, 1990), 15; and Jack Cowart and Juan Hamilton, *Georgia O'Keeffe: Art and Letters* (Washington, DC: National Gallery of Art, 1987), 143. For a study of Greenwich Village in the 1910s, see June Sochen, *The New Woman: Feminism in Greenwich Village, 1910–1920* (New York: Quadrangle, 1972); and for the decade in general, see also Adele Heller and Lois Rudnick, eds., *1915: The Cultural Moment: The New Politics, the New Woman, the New Psychology, the New Art, and the New Theatre in America* (New Brunswick, NJ: Rutgers University Press, 1991).

6. Among materials basic to study of the dandy's persona and cultural and political context are Baudelaire, "Salon of 1846: On the Heroism of Modern Life," 126–30; Charles Baudelaire, "The Painter of Modern Life" (1869), in *The Painter of Modern Life and Other Essays*, trans. and ed. Jonathan Mayne (London: Phaidon, 1970), 1–40; Walter Benjamin, "On Some Motifs in Baudelaire," in *Illuminations*, ed. Hannah Arendt, trans. Harry Zohn (New York: Schocken, 1976), 155–200; Ellen Moers, *The Dandy: Brummell to Beerbohm* (London: Secker and Warburg, 1960); Siegfried Kracauer, *Orpheus in Paris: Offenbach and the Paris of His Time* (New York: Knopf, 1938), 60–78; Valerie Steele, *Paris Fashion: A Cultural History* (New York: Oxford University Press, 1988), 79–96; Sandra M. Gilbert, "Costumes of the Mind: Transvestism as Metaphor in Modern Literature," *Critical Inquiry* 7, no. 2 (winter 1980): 391–417; and Susan Gubar, "Blessings in Disguise: Cross Dressing as Re-Dressing for Female Modernists," *Massachusetts Review* 22, no. 3 (autumn

1981): 477–508. See also Marjorie Garber, *Vested Interests: Cross Dressing and Cultural Anxiety* (New York: Routledge, 1992).

7. Steele, *Paris Fashion*, 92.

8. Stieglitz wears his cloak in Florine Stettheimer's 1928 portrait of him. For another example, see Marius de Zayas's caricature of Stieglitz, which has the double allusion of a cloak and a camera cover cloth, illustrated in Douglas Hyland, *Marius de Zayas: Conjurer of Souls* (Lawrence: Spencer Museum of Art, University of Kansas, 1981), cat. no. 23, 104–5. O'Keeffe described a studio tea party where Duchamp was present, perhaps in the summer of 1921. See Roxana Robinson, *Georgia O'Keeffe: A Life* (New York: Harper and Row, 1989), 246, 584 n. 26. See also Calvin Tomkins, "The Rose in the Eye Looked Pretty Fine," *New Yorker*, 4 March 1974, 44.

9. Baudelaire, "The Painter of Modern Life," 27–28.

10. Ibid., 9.

11. Kracauer, *Orpheus in Paris*, 68.

12. Benjamin, "On Some Motifs in Baudelaire," 172.

13. See Hal Foster, "Postmodernism: A Preface," commenting on Rosalind Krauss's 1979 essay "Sculpture in the Expanded Field," in *The Anti-Aesthetic: Essays on Postmodern Culture*, ed. Hal Foster (Seattle: Bay, 1983), xiii.

14. For a survey of critical attitudes, see Peninah R. Y. Petruck, *American Art Criticism, 1910–1939* (New York: Garland, 1981).

15. John Sloan's etching *Arch Conspirators* (1917), set on top of Washington Square Arch, commemorates a New Year's Eve party when Greenwich Villagers including Sloan and Duchamp decided as a joke to declare the Village an independent nation and secede from the United States.

16. Steele, *Paris Fashion*, 90–92.

17. T. J. Clark, *The Painting of Modern Life* (Princeton: Princeton University Press, 1984), 205–58.

18. Anne Hanson, *Manet and the Modern Tradition* (New Haven: Yale University Press, 1979), 204; Clark, *The Painting of Modern Life*, 253.

19. Roman Jakobson, "Shifters, Verbal Categories, and the Russian Verb," in *Selected Writings* (The Hague: Mouton, 1972), 2:130–36.

20. For a lively personal account, see Margaret Anderson, *My Thirty Years' War: An Autobiography* (New York: Covici, Friede, 1930).

21. For an informative article on "free love" and sexual inequity, see Ellen Kay Trimberger, "Feminism, Men, and Modern Love: Greenwich Village, 1900–1925," in *Powers of Desire: The Politics of Sexuality*, ed. Ann Snitow, Christine Stansell, and Sharon Thompson (New York: Monthly Review, 1983), 131–52. For the (most often male) critical reception of O'Keeffe, see Barbara Buhler Lynes, *O'Keeffe, Stieglitz, and the Critics, 1916–1929* (Chicago: University of Chicago Press, 1989).

22. Georgia O'Keeffe, quoted in an interview with Gladys Oaks, "Is Art

Life? Is Life Art? They Disagree: Radical Writer and Woman Artist Clash on Propaganda and Its Uses," *New York World*, 16 March 1930.

23. See Parker Tyler, *Florine Stettheimer: A Life in Art* (New York: Farrar, Straus, 1963), 90; Barbara Bloemink, *The Life and Art of Florine Stettheimer* (New Haven: Yale University Press, 1995), 136–37; and Donna Graves, "'In Spite of Alien Temperature and Alien Insistence': Emily Dickinson and Florine Stettheimer," *Women's Art Journal* 3, no. 2 (fall 1982–winter 1983): 26. *Crystal Flowers*, a volume of Stettheimer's poems, was published after her death by her sister, Ettie, and privately printed in 1949.

24. For an illustration, see Pete Daniel and Raymond Smock, *A Talent for Detail: The Photographs of Frances Benjamin Johnston, 1889–1910* (New York: Harmony, 1974), 31.

25. Gubar, "Blessings in Disguise," 479.

26. Gilbert, "Costumes of the Mind," 395.

27. My discussion focuses on middle-class experience. Working-class and farm women sometimes worked in men's clothing. See Steele's discussion of "Women in Trousers," in *Paris Fashion*, 162–76; and Julie Wheelwright, *Amazons and Military Maids: Women Who Dressed as Men in the Pursuit of Life, Liberty, and Happiness* (London: Pandora, 1989).

28. Mary Walker, quoted in Gubar, "Blessings in Disguise," 481. For an utterly compelling, funny, and useful account of George Sand's life, see Carolyn G. Heilbrun's discussion, quoting Ellen Moers, in *Writing a Woman's Life* (New York: Norton, 1988), 33–37.

29. For illustrations, see Banta, *Imaging American Women*, 35–36, figs. 32–33.

30. For a bibliography on Bonheur, see Whitney Chadwick, *Women, Art, and Society*, rev. ed. (New York: Thames and Hudson, 1996), 430–31.

31. For an illustration, see Susan Fillin-Yeh, "Dandies, Marginality, and Modernism," in *Women in Dada: Essays on Sex, Gender, and Identity*, ed. Naomi Sawelson-Gorse (Cambridge: MIT Press, 1999), 179, fig. 7.3.

32. See Adelyn D. Breeskin, *Romaine Brooks* (Washington, DC: National Collection of Fine Arts, 1986), 75.

33. Gubar, "Blessings in Disguise," 489–90.

34. See Banta, *Imaging American Women*, 268, 270, fig. 5.62. For a contemporary image, see "At Last a Male/Female," *New York Times*, 6 October 1987, sec. D, p. 36 (advertisement for a media consulting firm, Whittle Communications).

35. For an illustration, see Arturo Schwarz, *The Complete Works of Marcel Duchamp* (New York: Abrams, 1970), 310.

36. See Marcel Duchamp, *Notes and Projects for "The Large Glass,"* ed. Arturo Schwarz (New York: Abrams, 1969), 144–56.

37. Baudelaire, "Salon of 1846: On the Heroism of Modern Life," 127.

38. Duchamp, *Notes and Projects*, 144.

39. Baudelaire, "Salon of 1846: On the Heroism of Modern Life," 127.

40. I am indebted to Nina Felshin for the useful term "empty clothing."

41. Duchamp, *Notes and Projects*, 146–48.

42. For an illustration, see Henry McBride, *Florine Stettheimer* (New York: Museum of Modern Art, 1946), 27; this catalogue was produced for Stettheimer's memorial exhibition at the museum for which Duchamp was "Guest Director" (6). Duchamp appears in earlier Stettheimer paintings, *La Fête à Duchamp* (1917), *Sunday Afternoon in the Country* (1917), and *Picnic at Bedford Hills* (1918); see McBride, *Florine Stettheimer*, 12, 14, 15.

43. Linda Nochlin, "Florine Stettheimer: Rococco Subversive," in *Florine Stettheimer: Manhattan Fantastica*, by Elisabeth Sussman and Barbara Bloemink (New York: Whitney Museum of American Art, 1995), 97–116. Nochlin's essay first appeared in *Art in America* 68, no. 7 (September 1980): 68–83.

44. For a contemporary account, see Marsden Hartley, "The Paintings of Florine Stettheimer," *Creative Art* 9, no. 1 (July 1931): 18–23. For paintings of these parties, see McBride, *Florine Stettheimer*, 12, 14.

45. See Tyler, *Florine Stettheimer*, illustration following 146.

46. See Sussman and Bloemink, *Florine Stettheimer: Manhattan Fantastica*, for an illustration.

47. See Stettheimer, *Crystal Flowers*, 42.

48. William A. Camfield, *Marcel Duchamp: Fountain* (Houston: Menil Collection, 1989).

49. Among the publications that have reproduced this image is Arturo Schwarz, *New York Dada: Duchamp, Man Ray, Picabia* (Munich: Prestel, 1973), pl. 71.

50. Ibid., pl. 77.

51. Paul Haviland, "Statement," *291*, nos. 7–8 (September–October 1915).

52. Alice Jardine, "Opaque Texts and Transparent Contexts," in *The Poetics of Gender*, ed. Nancy K. Miller (New York: Columbia University Press, 1986), 103.

53. Among Dove's paintings that exemplify the category are *Based on Leaf Forms and Spaces* (1914), *Penetration* (1926), and *Dancing* (1934).

54. Alfred Stieglitz, "A Statement," published in the catalogue for his exhibition in 1921 at the Anderson Galleries, New York. For a facsimile reprint, see Beaumont Newhall, ed., *Photography: Essays and Images: Illustrated Readings in the History of Photography* (New York: Museum of Modern Art, 1980), 217.

55. O'Keeffe, quoted in "Is Art Life? Is Life Art? They Disagree."

56. For examples, see Stieglitz's photograph of O'Keeffe with a rare sculpture of 1917, and his photograph of the sculpture with her painting *Pink and*

*Blue Music,* both in the Wastebasket Collection, Georgia O'Keeffe Papers, Beinecke Library.

57. Sarah Greenough gives an excellent synopsis of O'Keeffe's ideas in her essay "From the Faraway," in Cowart and Hamilton, *Georgia O'Keeffe: Art and Letters,* 136–39.

58. O'Keeffe described making drawings by "crawling on the floor till I have cramps in my feet" in a letter to Pollitzer, 13 December 1915, Georgia O'Keeffe Papers, Beinecke Library. See also *Lovingly, Georgia,* 103.

59. Susan Fillin-Yeh, "Innovative Moderns: Arthur G. Dove and Georgia O'Keeffe," *Arts Magazine* 58, no. 10 (June 1982): 68–72, and also unpublished paper delivered at the Women's Caucus for Art Meetings, College Art Association annual conference, 1983.

60. For an illustration, see Georgia O'Keeffe, *Georgia O'Keeffe* (New York: Viking, 1978), pl. 28.

61. *Black Lines* (1916) and *Black Diagonal* (1917) are examples. See Charlotte Perkins Gilman, "The Dress of Women," *Forerunner* 6 (1915): 163, 192, 220, 250, 329. Gilman, "a smart old girl," as O'Keeffe once called her, sought to merge feminism and socialism. O'Keeffe, letter to Pollitzer, 27 November 1916, Georgia O'Keeffe Papers, Beinecke Library. See also Giboire, ed., *Lovingly, Georgia,* 216.

62. For illustrations, see O'Keeffe, *Georgia O'Keeffe,* 47–51.

63. For an installation photograph, see Waldo Frank et al., eds., *America and Alfred Stieglitz: A Collective Portrait* (Garden City, NY: Literary Guild, 1934), pl. XXVIII.B.

64. Stettheimer, *Crystal Flowers,* 23.

65. Examples are *Ram's Head—White Hollyhock—Little Hills, N.M.* (1935) and *From the Faraway Nearby* (1937).

66. There are very interesting parallels in this respect between O'Keeffe's art and the painting of her contemporary, the Canadian artist Emily Carr, active in Vancouver. For Carr, see Gerta Moray, *Unsettling Encounters: The "Indian" Pictures of Emily Carr* (Vancouver: University of British Columbia Press, in press).

### BIBLIOGRAPHY

Anderson, Margaret. *My Thirty Years' War: An Autobiography.* New York: Covici, Friede, 1930.

Banta, Martha. *Imaging American Women: Idea and Ideals in Cultural History.* New York: Columbia University Press, 1987.

Baudelaire, Charles. "The Painter of Modern Life." 1869. In *The Painter of*

*Modern Life and Other Essays,* trans. and ed. Jonathan Mayne. London: Phaidon, 1970.

Baudelaire, Charles. "Salon of 1846: On the Heroism of Modern Life." In *The Mirror of Art: Critical Studies,* trans. Jonathan Mayne. London: Phaidon, 1955.

Benjamin, Walter. "On Some Motifs in Baudelaire." In *Illuminations,* ed. Hannah Arendt, trans. Harry Zohn. New York: Schocken, 1976.

Bloemink, Barbara. *The Life and Art of Florine Stettheimer.* New Haven: Yale University Press, 1995.

Breeskin, Adelyn D. *Romaine Brooks.* Washington, DC: National Collection of Fine Arts, 1986.

Buci-Glucksmann, Christine. *La Raison baroque: De Baudelaire à Benjamin.* Paris: Galilée, 1984.

Camfield, William A. *Marcel Duchamp: Fountain.* Houston: Menil Collection, 1989.

Chadwick, Whitney. *Women, Art, and Society.* Rev. ed. New York: Thames and Hudson, 1996.

Clark, T. J. *The Painting of Modern Life.* Princeton: Princeton University Press, 1984.

Cowart, Jack, and Juan Hamilton. *Georgia O'Keeffe: Art and Letters.* Washington, DC: National Gallery of Art, 1987.

Daniel, Pete, and Raymond Smock. *A Talent for Detail: The Photographs of Frances Benjamin Johnston, 1889–1910.* New York: Harmony, 1974.

Doane, Mary Ann. *Femmes Fatales: Feminism, Film Theory, Psychoanalysis.* New York: Routledge, 1991.

Duchamp, Marcel. *Notes and Projects for "The Large Glass."* Ed. Arturo Schwarz. New York: Abrams, 1969.

Fillin-Yeh, Susan. "Dandies, Marginality, and Modernism." In *Women in Dada: Essays on Sex, Gender, and Identity,* ed. Naomi Sawelson-Gorse. Cambridge: MIT Press, 1999.

———. "Innovative Moderns: Arthur G. Dove and Georgia O'Keeffe." *Arts Magazine* 58, no. 10 (June 1982): 68–72.

Foster, Hal. "Postmodernism: A Preface." In *The Anti-Aesthetic: Essays on Postmodern Culture.* Ed. Hal Foster. Seattle: Bay, 1983.

Frank, Waldo, Lewis Mumford, Dorothy Norman, Paul Rosenfeld, and Harold Rugg, eds. *America and Alfred Stieglitz: A Collective Portrait.* Garden City, NY: Literary Guild, 1934.

Garber, Marjorie. *Vested Interests: Cross Dressing and Cultural Anxiety.* New York: Routledge, 1992.

Giboire, Clive, ed. *Lovingly, Georgia: The Complete Correspondence of Georgia O'Keeffe and Anita Pollitzer.* New York: Touchstone, 1990.

Gilbert, Sandra M. "Costumes of the Mind: Transvestism as a Metaphor in Modern Literature." *Critical Inquiry* 7, no. 2 (winter 1980): 391–417.

Gilman, Charlotte Perkins. "The Dress of Women." *Forerunner* 6 (1915): 163, 192, 220, 250, 329.

Graves, Donna. "'In Spite of Alien Temperature and Alien Insistence': Emily Dickinson and Florine Stettheimer." *Women's Art Journal* 3, no. 2 (fall 1982–winter 1983): 26.

Gubar, Susan. "Blessings in Disguise: Cross Dressing as Re-Dressing for Female Modernists." *Massachusetts Review* 22, no. 3 (autumn 1981): 477–508.

Hanson, Anne. *Manet and the Modern Tradition.* New Haven: Yale University Press, 1979.

Hartley, Marsden. "The Paintings of Florine Stettheimer." *Creative Art* 9, no. 1 (July 1931): 18–23.

Haviland, Paul. "Statement." *291*, nos. 7–8 (September–October 1915).

Heilbrun, Carolyn G. *Writing a Woman's Life.* New York: Norton, 1988.

Heller, Adele, and Lois Rudnick, eds. *1915: The Cultural Moment: The New Politics, the New Woman, the New Psychology, the New Art, and the New Theatre in America.* New Brunswick, NJ: Rutgers University Press, 1991.

Hyland, Douglas. *Marius de Zayas: Conjurer of Souls.* Lawrence: Spencer Museum of Art, University of Kansas, 1981.

Jakobson, Roman. "Shifters, Verbal Categories, and the Russian Verb." In *Selected Writings.* The Hague: Mouton, 1972.

Jardine, Alice. "Opaque Texts and Transparent Contexts." In *The Poetics of Gender,* ed. Nancy K. Miller. New York: Columbia University Press, 1986.

Kracauer, Siegfried. *Orpheus in Paris: Offenbach and the Paris of His Time.* New York: Knopf, 1938.

Lynes, Barbara Buhler. *O'Keeffe, Stieglitz, and the Critics, 1916–1929.* Chicago: University of Chicago Press, 1989.

McBride, Henry. *Florine Stettheimer.* New York: Museum of Modern Art, 1946.

Moers, Ellen. *The Dandy: Brummell to Beerbohm.* London: Secker and Warburg, 1960.

Moray, Gerta. *Unsettling Encounters: The "Indian" Pictures of Emily Carr.* Vancouver: University of British Columbia Press, in press.

Newhall, Beaumont, ed. *Photography: Essays and Images: Illustrated Readings in the History of Photography.* New York: Museum of Modern Art, 1980.

Nochlin, Linda. "Florine Stettheimer: Rococo Subversive." In *Florine Stettheimer: Manhattan Fantastica,* by Elisabeth Sussman and Barbara Bloemink. New York: Whitney Museum of American Art, 1995.

O'Keeffe, Georgia. *Georgia O'Keeffe.* New York: Viking, 1978.

———. *Georgia O'Keeffe Papers.* Yale Collection of American Literature, Beinecke Rare Book and Manuscript Library. Yale University.

O'Keeffe, Georgia. Quoted in an interview with Gladys Oaks, "Is Art Life? Is Life Art? They Disagree: Radical Writer and Woman Artist Clash on Propaganda and Its Uses." *New York World*, 16 March 1930.

Petruck, Peninah R. Y. *American Art Criticism, 1910–1939*. New York: Garland, 1981.

Roberts, Mary Louise. "Samson and Delilah Revisited: The Politics of Women's Fashion in 1920s France." *American Historical Review* 98, no. 3 (June 1993): 657–84.

Robinson, Roxana. *Georgia O'Keeffe: A Life*. New York: Harper and Row, 1989.

Schwarz, Arturo. *The Complete Works of Marcel Duchamp*. New York: Abrams, 1970.

———. *New York Dada: Duchamp, Man Ray, Picabia*. Munich: Prestel, 1973.

Smith-Rosenberg, Carroll. *Disorderly Conduct: Visions of Gender in Victorian America*. New York: Oxford University Press, 1985.

Sochen, June. *The New Woman: Feminism in Greenwich Village, 1910–1920*. New York: Quadrangle, 1972.

Steele, Valerie. *Paris Fashion: A Cultural History*. New York: Oxford University Press, 1988.

Stieglitz, Alfred. *Georgia O'Keeffe: A Portrait by Alfred Stieglitz, with an Introduction by Georgia O'Keeffe*. New York: Metropolitan Museum of Art, 1978.

Tomkins, Calvin. "The Rose in the Eye Looked Pretty Fine." *New Yorker*, 4 March 1974.

Trimberger, Ellen Kay. "Feminism, Men, and Modern Love: Greenwich Village, 1900–1925." In *Powers of Desire: The Politics of Sexuality*, ed. Ann Snitnow, Christine Stansell, and Sharon Thompson. New York: Monthly Review, 1983.

Tyler, Parker. *Florine Stettheimer: A Life in Art*. New York: Farrar, Straus, 1963.

Wheelwright, Julie. *Amazons and Military Maids: Women Who Dressed as Men in the Pursuit of Life, Liberty, and Happiness*. London: Pandora, 1989.

## Chapter 5

# "The Dandy in Me"
## *Romaine Brooks's 1923 Portraits*

## *Joe Lucchesi*

In a 1923 letter to her lover Natalie Barney, the American artist Romaine Brooks vividly described her social life in London, where she was painting several portraits. Although she was in London primarily for professional reasons, Brooks, at forty-seven, also kept an extremely busy social schedule. According to the correspondence, she frequented underground lesbian clubs and danced late into the night with a wide circle of acquaintances. After detailing a typical night of run-ins, dustups, and intrigues, Brooks commented, "Never have I had such a string of would-be admirers, and all for my black curly hair and white collars. They like the dandy in me and are in no way interested in my inner-self or value."[1] Her observation first suggests that Brooks understood and self-consciously exploited the symbolics of the dandy as a visible signifier of lesbian desire. She also implies that these sartorial displays were unconnected to what she perceived to be her "inner self." Even as a casually made remark, Brooks's statement is a significant revision of a very influential cultural notion of the time, one formulated by sexologists and psychologists and promoted in popular culture. They asserted that elegant, masculinely tailored clothing and tuxedos, when worn by women, were merely outward evidence of an inward pathology—homosexuality, or sexual inversion as it was more commonly known.[2] Brooks's comment is especially pertinent, however, because she translated her personal dandyism into a more permanent visual format. Her self-portrait of 1923 closely reproduces the dandified costume to which she refers, with its prominent white collar and short, dark hair partially hidden beneath her slightly oversized riding

*Fig. 5.1.* Romaine Brooks, *Self-Portrait*, 1923, oil on canvas, 46 1/4 × 26 7/8 in., National Museum of American Art, gift of the artist. Reproduced by permission.

hat (fig. 5.1). During that same trip to London, Brooks also produced two portraits: one of her friend Una, Lady Troubridge, and another of the British artist Gluck. Both adhere even more closely to the refined aesthetic accoutrements of the dandy, typically a dark, tailored costume, with exquisite formal details that frequently included cravats, high collars, and monocles, as well as short and often dashingly tousled hair (figs. 5.2, 5.3).

If the dandy in some sense functioned for Brooks as a performative marker of lesbian desire, the signifying range of her sitters' costume and her own was much more fluid and expansive. Most important, in another letter Natalie Barney comments that Gluck's portrait will make a good addition to Brooks's "series of modern women."[3] This chapter explores the possible interconnections between the dandy and the modern woman as markers of cultural identity and examines Brooks's specific use of them in her 1923 portraits. Through the visual rhetoric of the modern woman, Brooks transfigured the *male* cultural connotations of the dandy in early-twentieth-century Paris and London to suggest a potential *female* homoerotic sexuality as she explored the possibilities and limits of a visible lesbian identity within a culture based on normative heterosexuality. This was a particularly ambitious and risky project, given lesbianism's nearly complete cultural invisibility at that time and the consequent lack of well-established visual codes. As a result, Brooks and her sitters turned to the dandy as the most potent symbol available to them.[4]

Brooks's self-portrait, with its paradoxically confrontational and furtive sense of presence, has justifiably become her best-known and most reproduced image. It has traditionally been interpreted as a portrait of self-loathing, its androgyny read as a subject divided against itself through a kind of internalized homophobia.[5] Such readings, which are only beginning to be overturned, not only echo nineteenth-century sexologists' insistence on externally visible evidence of an internal deviance from cultural norms, but also assume an equivalence between artist and visual image. In other words, the portrait was considered a transparent window to Brooks's psyche. Her own words, however, associate the dandified costume with a playful homoeroticism and a public persona that may or may not have any relation to an "essential" self. Part of this portrait's potency indeed depends on the forceful bleakness of its setting and mood. I am interested, however, in rereading its psychology in less self-destructive terms. Whatever else this portrait may be, it is a manifesto of

*Fig. 5.2.* Romaine Brooks, *Una, Lady Troubridge,* 1924, oil on canvas, 50 1/8 × 30 1/4 in. National Museum of American Art. Reproduced by permission.

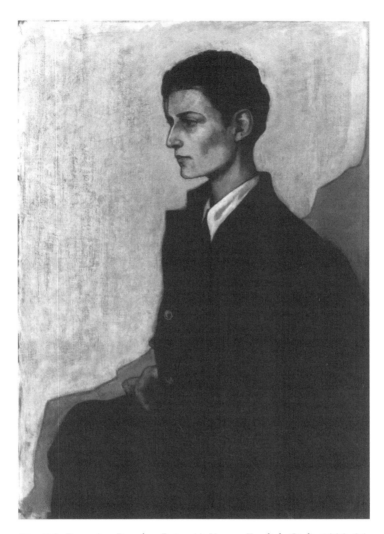

*Fig. 5.3.* Romaine Brooks, *Peter (A Young English Girl)*, 1923–24, oil on canvas, 36 × 24 1/2 in. National Museum of American Art. Reproduced by permission.

Brooks's artistic self-identity, that is, her identity *as an artist*, and was also a centerpiece to the 1925 exhibition of her work.

As an image of artistic self-identity, Brooks's portrait challenged the predominant conception of artistic creativity as a male enterprise, a conception once again flourishing in the avant-garde circles of postwar Paris, her usual home.[6] Her investigation of contemporary sexual and gender identity politics quite naturally manifests itself through specifically artistic issues and conventions. She perfected an aesthetic style and technique that led to critical assessments of her "masculine vitality," as John Usher of *International Studio* called it, in this and other works.[7] In describing the portrait, fashion authority *Vogue* (not surprisingly) focused on Brooks's appearance, first noting the costume's tight, masculinized tailoring, then that her hair is "hidden under a man's felt hat, from under which her gaze lurks with intelligence."[8] The writer suggested that secrecy and a vaguely predatory intelligence were at the center of the artist's self-representation. Brooks's penetrating gaze is arguably the conceptual heart of the work, an implacable look that issues a compelling visual challenge. The stiff centrality of the artist's cloaked figure and the starkly aggressive black and white color contrasts underscore the inflexible character of her gaze. Her unsmiling mouth, carefully modulated in dull rose tones, and her exaggeratedly pale skin darken the mood and deepen the shadows from which her look emanates. The bright flash of red from the medal on her lapel is the only visual relief from the intense monochromy of the work. The prominently placed red spot paradoxically intensifies the effect of the modulated grays. As the *Vogue* commentary makes clear, Brooks organizes her self-portrait around her partially veiled but arresting glance. Although the connection is only tenuously hinted in *Vogue*, other viewers made a more explicit connection between her appearance and her character, displacing the masculine attributes of her clothing to her activity as an artist and to her visual aesthetics, implicitly gendering both as masculine. Along with insightful and rational judgment, calm intelligence, and control, the artist is bestowed many epithets not normally associated at this time with a woman's stereotypic "feminine" sensibility. In its review of the show, the *Mercure de France* declared her talent "sober, a little severe . . . affirmed in portraits [that are] very clear, very cleanly cut, singularly intuitive."[9] Similarly, *Vogue* noted that Brooks painted her subjects with "wisdom, in which intelligence and talent overflow" in equal parts.[10] And Louis Vauxcelles defined her paintings as an "art of a totally cerebral sensuality," thus undermining any purely emotional eroticism and making that eroticism purely intellectual and rational.[11] Vauxcelles particularly attributed these qualities to her monochromatic palette, as well as her precise and authoritative design. Taken together, these comments create a strikingly consistent representation of Brooks as an artist with a masterful and masculine character, expressed through her uniquely controlled style and execution.

While her self-portrait individually plays along and against these gendered boundaries, Brooks further questions the masculine and implicitly heterosexual basis of artistic identity and creativity, for the artist engaged her visual self-image in a complicated dialogue with three prominent European artistic figures, who are themselves complexly tangled together: the Italian portraitist Giovanni Boldini, the French patron Count Robert de Montesquiou-Fezensac, and the American expatriate painter James Abbott McNeill Whistler. In her unpublished autobiography, Brooks identified Boldini as the artist whom she believed to be her main competition in the refined social circles they both inhabited before World War I.[12] In at least one case, they painted dueling portraits of the same sitter, the eccentric Marchesa Luisa Casati. But it was Whistler with whom Brooks's artistic career was most closely intertwined and in constant negotiation. Throughout her career, critical reviews of Brooks's work consistently referred to its "whistlerian" qualities.[13] Aimed primarily at her mature style, this usually referred to her sophisticated palette of carefully modulated blacks, whites, and grays. While she distanced herself from the connection in written statements, Brooks's visual style seems to court the comparison.

As an expression of her artistic identity, the 1923 self-portrait is the work in which she most overtly grapples with this particular artistic legacy. While the subtle palette echoes the "symphonies" of color associated with Whistler, the background landscape of the work most directly challenges her designation as Whistler's imitator. Scholars often interpret this landscape simply as a reinforcement of the gloomy atmosphere of the entire work, a blasted allegorical landscape read as an external projection of the artist's interior mental morbidity.[14] The sketchy execution and the muted tonalities of the scene, however, strongly evoke Whistler's nocturnes, for example, the 1864–68 *Grey and Silver: Chelsea Wharf*. Brooks's scene has a similar soft handling and atmospheric mood: the distant background is held in tension with the flat, banded areas of color, and she echoes Whistler's skeletal architectural forms. She also reproduces the thinly painted skeins of oil that were the primary carrier for his moody fog.

Significantly, Brooks's only assessment of Whistler and his work held that his painting contained "no surprise, no paradox, no complexity." "My own disturbed temperament," she wrote, "was to aspire to more indeterminate moods."[15] Her reference to her "disturbed temperament" acknowledges the neo-Romantic outlook that informed her artistic self; Brooks's self-portrait before this particular landscape suggests some of the visual implications of her critique of Whistler. The visual form of the setting invokes, yet thoroughly reworks, Whistler's tonal aesthetic with a more psychologically charged and emotional aesthetic.

In 1897 Brooks's rival Giovanni Boldini painted a portrait of his friend Whistler (fig. 5.4). That portrait and Brooks's later self-portrait share much conceptual ground in visualizing the dandy ideal so important to both Brooks and Whistler. Boldini presents Whistler as the consummate gentleman artist, a dandified image that Whistler himself carefully cultivated. Elegantly slouched in a chair, the sinuous curve of Whistler's body leads the viewer's eye to his face, whose animated expression emerges from the picture's darkness and dominates the composition. The delicate, attenuated fingers of his hand, the extravagantly curly hair, the barely suppressed smile, and the flushed cheeks all create a sense of a refined and creative personality, an artist momentarily pausing in the midst of some nervous or inspired activity. Brooks's portrait revisits this persona of the artist-dandy exemplified by Whistler. The two figures share the black jacket, standing white collar, and starched cuffs, and Brooks wears a slightly oversized black hat similar to the one Whistler holds in his lap. She replaces Boldini's portrayal of Whistler's rakish wit with a monumental stillness and seriousness of tone. Nevertheless, her gesture of hooking her finger into her jacket gives Brooks the same air of self-assurance conveyed by Whistler, with his hand to his forehead.

Another visual detail binds the portraits together more directly and connects the two artists they portray more explicitly. In Boldini's portrait, a bravura dash of red glints out of the darkness on the center right of the canvas. This single paint stroke refers to Whistler's chevalier's medal, which the French Legion of Honor awarded him, and which he nearly always wore on his lapel. In Brooks's portrait that slash of red reappears, also on her left lapel. The Legion of Honor also awarded Brooks the chevalier's medal, to acknowledge her exhibi-

*Fig. 5.4.* Giovanni Boldini, *James McNeill Whistler*, 1987, oil on canvas, 67 1/8 × 37 3/16 in. The Brooklyn Museum, New York, gift of A. Augustus Healy (09.849). Reproduced by permission.

tion-based fundraising efforts in France during World War I.[16] Boldini's tiny mark, already loaded with meaning, reemerges in Brooks's painting with increased insistence. It is the only spot of pure, unmodulated color in the work, and she places it at the exact measured center of the canvas.

In addition to Giovanni Boldini and Whistler, the third person with whom Brooks's artistic identity was in dialogue was their friend and professional associate the Count Robert de Montesquiou-Fezensac. Known as the "Prince of Aesthetes," during the opening decades of the twentieth century Montesquiou was the embodiment of the aristocratic dandy in Parisian society.[17] His decade-long support of Whistler has been well documented.[18] But it is less well known that Montesquiou also became Romaine Brooks's principal mentor and social impresario on her arrival in Paris around 1905. Her mother's death had left her both alone and immensely wealthy. Her inheritance gave her unlimited access to important social connections that culminated with her entry into Montesquiou's coterie of aristocrats, artists, and intellectuals.[19] Among other gestures of support, the count wrote a lengthy review of Brooks's first one-woman show in 1911, in which he coined the lasting nickname "Thief of Souls" to acknowledge her psychologically penetrating portrait style.[20]

In 1897 Giovanni Boldini produced a seated portrait of Montesquiou that is thematically similar to his portrait of Whistler. The half-length pose and spare geometry of the composition focus attention on the count's centralized figure, and Boldini carefully details Montesquiou's fine and expensive ensemble. As Brooks would later do, Boldini restricts his palette to a series of earth and brown tonalities, increasing the seriousness of the tone yet not fully muting his subject's flamboyance. Montesquiou's tailored coat, which narrows at the waist, his white kid gloves, starched cuffs, black top hat, and cane are all emblematic of his finely tuned sense of taste and decorum. The angular sharpness of his features, including his elaborate mustache, and the slow curve of his body underline the sense of aristocratic refinement and elegance. As in Brooks's self-portrait, Montesquiou's face is brightly lit, and his proud features enframed by the trademark dark, curly hair and white collar of the dandy. Brooks's adaptation of this particular format and conception is also relevant to her portrait of "Peter" (the British artist Gluck), who appears against a neutral background in profile view.

Although Boldini's portrait of Robert de Montesquiou also shares a general aesthetic impulse with Brooks's later self-portrait, her revisitation of the dandy relates even more directly to Whistler's famous *Arrangement in Black and Gold*, first shown in 1894 at the annual exhibition of the Société Nationale des Beaux-Arts in Paris. In this work, Montesquiou is shown full-length in formal black eveningwear, with impeccable white shirt and tie, gray kid gloves, and draped wrap emerging from the somber darkness. While the painting's exhibition caused a popular sensation, its critical reception was mixed.[21] Most critics, though, immediately seized on the sartorial aristocracy of both the model and the artist. Gustave Geffroy, for example, wrote that "the creator of such beautiful . . . portraits must have been tempted, given his own dandyism, by the dandyism of Monsiuer de Montesquiou."[22] Montesquiou prominently displayed the portrait in his homes, including the Pavillon des Muses, where Brooks could have seen it during her frequent visits to the Pavillon during her first days on the Paris scene.[23] It is clear that her own self-portrait owes an iconographic debt to her former mentor and to Whistler's portrait of him, a painting that visually encoded the image of the rarefied dandy, the Prince of Aesthetes, in the French cultural imagination.

Up to this point in the discussion, Brooks's reworkings of the dandy might be read simply as a female artist negotiating the gendered spaces of artistic authority. But the specifically homoerotic vector of her project becomes more clear with Whistler's portrait of Montesquiou. Displays of sartorial finesse personified by Whistler and Montesquiou and visually articulated in these portraits had traditionally been associated with a sort of gentlemanly aristocratic privilege; however, by 1923, when Brooks revisited the theme, the dandy had distinctly different connotations. After Oscar Wilde's 1895 sodomy conviction, the image of the elegantly attired gentleman became indelibly associated with decadent male homosexuality, to the extent that simply calling someone an "Oscar Wilde type" was sufficient to invoke the damaging link.[24] This link is one that Brooks understood fully, particularly since, during an earlier stay in London, her primary social companion was Alfred, Lord Douglas, one of the main figures implicated in Wilde's trial. According to her autobiography, she was attracted to Douglas's friendship precisely because she saw him as a *lapidé*, an outsider, because he was a "friend of Oscar Wilde."[25]

Robert de Montesquiou invoked these underlying associations between the dandy and "sexual inversion" throughout his life.[26] As Brooks would later do, Montesquiou asserted his class privilege to insulate himself from public censure and cultivated both his publicly aesthetic image and the open secret of his homosexuality. In fact, the count's "inversion" was so well known that he became the model for two notorious literary explorations of decadence as "deviant" sexuality—des Esseintes in J. K. Huysman's *À rebours* in 1884; and more pointedly, the Baron de Charlus, Marcel Proust's sympathetic yet scabrous portrait of effete male homosexuality. Proust's *Sodom and Gomorrah* was first published in 1923, nearly simultaneous to Brooks's first public exhibition of her dandy portraits.[27]

Whistler's portrait of Montesquiou, appearing mere months before Wilde's 1895 conviction, would have been caught up in this complex, shifting set of associations, and there are ample clues to suggest that its subtext was already recognizably established. An 1894 caricature from *Punch*, for example, exaggerates the sway of Montesquiou's pose, the droop of his shoulders, and the details of his exquisite outfit. The figure is decidedly lacking in the "masculine vitality" stereotypically assigned to heterosexual men. These homosexual implications would only strengthen over time. Many years later (around 1950), Graham Robertson, himself a member of this social circle, would retrospectively lament that the portrait's pose is "limp, weak, gone at the knees" and, paraphrasing Montesquiou himself, described him as a "squiggly little worm" in this picture. As an attempted corrective, Robertson noted that "Robert was beautiful," although immediately qualifying that as "a strange epithet to apply to a man."[28]

These, then, are the various cultural discourses that Brooks brings to bear in her self-portrait. Through her visual exploration of "the dandy in me," Brooks marked out her specific artistic identity in dialogue with and in opposition to Boldini, whom she considered her chief artistic rival, and Whistler, to whom she was endlessly compared. By self-consciously embracing the "feminized" masculinity of Robert de Montesquiou's dandy, Brooks underscored the homoerotics of her own image, undermined a privileged heterosexuality of artistic creativity, and simultaneously explored the possibilities of a visual lesbian self-identity.[29]

Like others who adopted it, Brooks was well aware of the class privilege that subtended the image of the dandy. Domna Stanton argues in her book *The Aristocrat as Art* that gaining class superiority has always involved a strategy of self-perfection in which the self is transformed into a sign system including the body as well as its gestures, manners, speech, and adornments. For Stanton, one example of this visual imposition of social superiority is the dandy. As she demonstrates, aristocracy contains an inherently aesthetic impulse.[30] By the beginning of the twentieth century, this sign system had solidified into an elaborate network of visual and artistic symbols of social superiority. This conflation of wealth, aristocratic privilege, and sartorial finesse received perhaps its most precise articulation in the Prince of Aesthetes, Robert de Montesquiou.

Using the same visual sign system, Brooks's self-portrait foregrounds her own elevated social standing. It compares closely to John Singer Sargent's earlier portrait of *Lord Ribblesdale* (1902) in its format, concept, and dress, a portrait that the art historian Albert Boime mentions as a "case study" in Sargent's efforts to create a visual paradigm for England's fashionable and influential elite in the opening decades of the century.[31] Within the quickly changing social alliances of Britain's high society, portraits like Ribblesdale's became a visual marker of class status, used to shore up traditional aristocratic associations through visual appearance. Like Brooks's self-portrait, Ribblesdale appears against an almost monochromatic background that emphasizes his solitary and monumental figure. He wears full riding regalia that contain many accoutrements echoed in her later image, particularly the black top hat, loose-fitting and slightly oversized riding coat, and gray kid gloves. Ribblesdale's costume not only makes reference to his skill as an equestrian, it also makes manifest his otherwise unseen wealth: the stable of horses and the lands on which he conducts the hunt.[32]

Brooks's portraits are deeply indebted to the tradition of portraiture epitomized by Sargent, and their class assertions would have been clear to viewers familiar with the visual system.[33] By the 1920s, her portraits would have appeared to be closely aligned with such a conservative pictorial tradition, particularly given the formal experimentations of Cubist portraiture and the emotionally interpretive portraits of the Fauves and Expressionists that were exhibited throughout Europe at this time.[34]

The issue of class status is intimately linked to any potential expression of Brooks's lesbian sexuality. As Montesquiou had done, Brooks asserted her social privilege in order to insulate herself from the potentially devastating social consequences of a public disclosure of her sexual identity.

Katrina Rolley has studied the visual codes of masculine clothing for upper-class lesbians and the question of cultural recognition in the 1920s. Her analysis is particularly relevant here because it is a case study of Brooks's friends (and sitter) Una Troubridge and Radclyffe Hall. Rolley concludes that while some viewers certainly understood the lesbian significance of their dandified attire, other viewers, particularly those of a different class, might "(mis)read [their costumes] as part of an aristocratic tradition of eccentricity," or merely as a kind of "high-brow modernism."[35] So while, as Domna Stanton noted, "only those with sufficient economic freedom and prestige can easily express their artistic impulses," that very visual assertion of privilege might actually obscure what the sartorial strategy might otherwise convey.[36]

But at the same time, in the wake of the late nineteenth-century cultures of "decadence," the notion of the refined aristocrat and particularly the dandy had been indelibly associated with so-called deviant sexualities. While this was particularly true for men, by the 1920s it had become more generally part of the cultural imagination for both sexes.[37] The generalization was commonplace enough that in his monumental analysis of "deviant" female sexuality, the sexologist Havelock Ellis drew an explicit link between elevated class position and lesbianism:

> the English girl, especially of the lower and middle classes, whether she has lost her virtue or not, is extremely fettered by conventional notions. It is, therefore, among the upper ranks, alike of society and prostitution, that Lesbianism is most definitely to be met with for here we have much greater liberty of action, and much greater freedom from prejudices.[38]

Ellis introduces class as a factor in determining both the frequency and the visibility of lesbian sexuality. He also credits this to upper-class women's freedom from strict bourgeois sexual mores as well as their insulation from social censure.

In her portrait of Una Troubridge, also from 1923, Brooks continues this subversive reworking of the dandy's sartorial signification (fig. 5.2). Una, the wife of Lord Troubridge, maintained an uneasy connection to her social backgrounds, as she had just left her husband to begin a lifelong relationship with Radclyffe Hall, the author of the lesbian novel *The Well of Loneliness*.[39] The generically aristocratic associations of her costume would have been entirely appropriate for her elevated class position. Troubridge's slightly parodic pose both excruciatingly and humorously re-creates the dandy's aristocratic pretensions, and Brooks's correspondence makes it clear that a humorous undertone to the work was deliberate. Throughout the portrait's progress, Brooks directed her efforts on capturing Troubridge's "unusual sartorial effect. A sign of the age which may amuse some future feminists."[40] Aside from her eerie prescience, Brooks's comment reveals her absolute clarity about this painting's purpose and its link to a wider cultural arena whose interest was the visual definition and interpretation of the female body.[41] Further, her appeal to future feminists underscores the oppositional underpinnings of her overall project in this portrait series. But the humor she hopes they find there keeps the question open as to the subversive potential embodied in Lady Troubridge.

Whether ironically funny or politically subversive (or both), a gendered play with appearances is everywhere evident in this portrait. Una Troubridge's dandified figure produces the "unusual sartorial effect" that Brooks exploits to maximum effect. As in her own self-portrait, the image most closely resembles a conventional male society portrait. The rigid centrality and minimal background underscore the importance of the figure, and the details of her costume re-emphasize the (supposed) seriousness of the presentation. The finely tailored lines of her jacket, the stiff whiteness of the linen shirt, and the binding cravat encircling her extraordinarily high collar parallel both the class consciousness of John Singer Sargent's Lord Ribblesdale and the aesthetic refinement of Robert de Montesquiou. Her outfit, as well as the tight execution of the painting itself, also suggests a kind of "masculine" control, a mood reinforced by the finger Troubridge slips under her dog's collar, pulling it to attentive devotion.[42] But several "feminized" accents unsettle the deadpan sincerity of this reading. Lady Troubridge's stylishly cropped and curled hair, her archly plucked eyebrows and rouged lips, and the very prominent pearl earrings seemingly contradict the masculinized attributes of social prominence and decorum. Given the thoroughly contradictory gender encodings in the portrait, Una Troubridge's flat look and slightly pinched mouth begin to take on a distinctly mocking air.

The general mood and tone of Brooks's portrait of the British artist Gluck, exhibited as Peter (*A Young English Girl*), differ considerably from Troubridge's portrait (fig. 5.3). Gluck, like Troubridge and others in Brooks's social circle, was from a wealthy background; her family had founded Britain's J. Lyons catering empire.[43] Brooks retains the simplicity of the composition, but the incidental details of wardrobe and appearance are greatly reduced in favor of a more austere conception, executed with less finish and polish. Also, the intense sense of privacy that permeates Peter's portrait, suggested by the half-turned face and introspective expression, replaces Troubridge's active engagement with the viewer. Finally, the solemn gravity of Peter's representation replaces the more sardonic tone and satiric wit suggested in Troubridge's faint smile and generalized exaggeration bordering on parody.

Gluck's suit, tie, hat, and closely cropped hair carry the full weight of a masculine signification. But Brooks's title pointedly disrupts this transparent reading, forcing viewers to reconsider their understanding. In the only specific reference to this painting from reviews of the 1925 exhibitions, an unnamed correspondent for the society *Daily Graphic* acknowledges the success of the artist's gambit. "Peter was shingled, dark, handsome, dressed like a boy, and looked like a boy, and yet I was assured that Peter was '*jeune fille anglaise*.'"[44] This viewer's skepticism before the portrait also explicitly underscores the terms of the ambiguity in the image. Peter's masculinity is apparently confirmed by the details of costume, and Brooks employs an even more reductively schematized black and white palette than in her self-portrait. Her "precise and authoritative design" is articulated through the careful black line that outlines Peter's face, shirt collar, and fingers, as well as through the stable geometry of the composition, a central pyramid offset by the diagonal that cuts from upper right to lower left behind the figure. But the picture's title undercuts the security of this purportedly "masculine" representation, and Peter's lack of an Adam's apple is the only tenuous evidence of her biological difference. So the viewer begins to reexamine the face carefully, perhaps deciding that the figure's features are somewhat "feminized." Under these visual and textual rhetorical pressures, the image fluctuates between Peter the young Englishman and Peter the young English girl. Both impressions are there, forcefully articulated by the stark black and white contrasts. Yet they do not appear simultaneously. The images seem superimposed, slipping in and out of focus like an optical illusion—the figure is neither one nor the other *and* both. Gendered polarities begin to break down and destabilize in the face of Peter's portrait, to be replaced by a profound androgyny. And the invocation of the dandy ensured that androgyny registered the presence of a visible homoerotics. With its shifting gender expectations, and in its play on representational structures and with gendered identity, Brooks's portrait of Peter undermines the visual status quo.

In all three of these portraits, Brooks uses the dandiacal visual codes to open up the possibility of a specifically lesbian female subjectivity within the very traditional format of the portrait and in the equally traditional viewing context of the art gallery. But other things about their clothing itself also mark these women as different: not only was the tradition of the dandy specifically reserved for men, the fashions that they wear were, by 1925, almost thirty years out of date. The fashionably dandified costume for men abruptly ended with Oscar Wilde's conviction, and with the notable exception of Robert de Montesquiou, gay men abandoned the exuberance of the outfit and its signifying possibilities. So when Brooks's portraits appeared in 1925, the outmoded quality of their sartorial iconography would have held an additional dissonant note for spectators.

This dissonance, however, extended far beyond the hothouse confines of reconfigured aristocratic portraiture. Brooks's portraits not only look backward to the 1890s visual rhetoric of the dandy, they also look forward to the emerging cultural discourse of the "modern woman." Just as Brooks and her sitters began dressing in masculinely tailored clothing, the gendered contours of contemporary fashion were experiencing a profound revision, manifested most visibly in the figure of the modern woman. By the artist's own admission, her portraits participate in formulating the iconography of this controversial figure, while simultaneously forcing the homoerotic subtexts already implicit in the modern woman's supposedly "masculinized" character.

Natalie Barney's use of the term "modern women" to describe Brooks's portrait project of the 1920s was hardly casual or coincidental. In fact, the concept of the modern woman was one of the most contentiously debated gender issues in post–World War I Europe. In the wake of the social upheavals, loss of life, and depopulation the war had caused, this cultural construct emerged as a destabilizing foil in the redefinition of bourgeois heterosexual masculinity after the war.[45] While supposedly defined by social roles and psychological disposition, the modern woman's identity crucially depended on what she looked like and her visible public behavior. The inordinate preoccupation with women's sartorial styles in the postwar European press, and more specifically the French press, occurred because these observers interpreted dress as a visual language for and visible sign of the larger societal shifts. Descriptive analyses of the visual style of the modern woman formed a starting point for a more profound attempt both to define and to fix the figure within European culture. That is, once she was identified by her clothing and her demeanor, the modern woman's sartorial style quickly became an indicator of deeper psychological and physiological traits that specifically positioned her within the dense context of contemporary gender politics.

Hosts of literary and popular accounts codified the modern woman's visual characteristics. To cite just one typical example, an anxious reader of *Progrès Civique* in 1925 presented this encapsulated litany of her qualities, calling modern women "these beings . . . who smoke, work, argue and box like the boys, who, at night in the Bois de Boulogne, their brains drowning with cocktails, search for juicy and acrobatic pleasures on the tobacco-colored cushions of a five horsepower Citroën: these are not young women!"[46] Naturally, contemporary fashion became a central focus in this debate: according to many troubled observers, women were cutting their hair, putting on men's clothes, and giving themselves the profile of sticks or *bâtons*.

There was an implicit, and thoroughly suppressed, subtext to these discussions about the modern woman's "difference": lesbian sexuality.[47] In fact, lesbianism appears to be the logical extension to the list of fears that the figure evoked. In a rare acknowledgment, the literary critic Pierre Lièvre explicitly recognized this connection with the modern woman when he claimed in 1927 that "the species felt itself endangered by a growing inversion [*uranisme*]. No more hips, no more breasts, no more hair."[48] Applying the standard list of physical characteristics others used to identify the *femme moderne*, Lièvre expressly links such visible signs of a troubling difference and female homosexuality.[49]

While Brooks and her sitters skillfully engage the visual rhetoric of the *femme moderne*, it is important to emphasize that her portraits are not entirely commensurate with other images of the modern woman. More broadly, while there was a near conflation in the European cultural imagination between the figure of the modern woman and the lesbian, they were not synonymous. As Mary Louise Roberts's book *Civilization without Sexes* amply demonstrates, the modern woman developed within the explicitly heterosexual framework of bourgeois sexual norms. As such, the figure's transgressive potential could also be reinscribed somewhat safely within those dominant social codes. In other words, the boundaries of bourgeois sexuality were flexible enough to accommodate and recontain the modern woman. The fashion historian Anne Hollander argued in her 1994 book on sexuality and men's fashion that the visual effect of masculinely tailored clothing on women often merely increases their perceived difference and solidifies gendered boundaries more rigidly. In tracing the history of upper-class sports clothes, specifically the woman's riding habit, Hollander concluded that "in the imitation of male style, eroticism and frivolity were only intensified by the look of severely tailored jackets artfully molded to feminine torsos," and such outfits remained "noticeably sexy" in mimicking men.[50] She further argues that although by 1916 "surface masculinity" was influencing daytime fashions, this was because fashion for the first time tried to reveal female sexuality "in direct bodily terms."[51] In other words, rather than sublimating female sexuality through frills and exaggerated volumes, fashion in the early twentieth century employed the form-fitting contours of *male* fashion to demonstrate female bodily realities.

So beneath the negative criticisms of the modern woman's appearance often lay a covert appreciation of its ultimately chic sensuality, or what one male viewer in 1926 bluntly termed "a certain spice" in appraising the effects of tuxedos on women.[52] Complaints about missing breasts and hips therefore may often have had less to do with the clothes themselves and their sometimes disturbing societal connotations than the fact that vocal male commentators found them unattractive. These and other comments imply that attractiveness *to men* was the real issue, and further that this enticing allure (of "surface masculinization") itself was enough to secure the true "womanliness" of the modern woman. Real anxiety occurred only when *all* womanly signifiers were erased. The writer Maurice Prax, for instance, frankly averred that "the weaker sex is completely destroying its charm, in order to be, from whatever angle one considers it, nothing more than a rigid, straight line."[53] While contemporary fashions might afford greater comfort, ease, and mobility to women, at least to some observers it seemed to rob them of their physical charms, metaphorically turning them into sticks and lines.

The French photographer Jacques-Henri Lartigue produced a myriad of photographs that charted the changes in women's clothing in the opening decades of the twentieth century. His pictures traced the evolution of women's fashion, and their popularity went a long way toward producing a definitive visual image of *la femme* in the public eye. He precisely charted the changing social signifiers of women's status and particularly focused on the emergence of the modern woman.[54] In 1925, for example, Lartigue undertook an extensive photo series titled *Les Dames aux cigarettes*, including over twenty portraits of young, attractive women smoking cigarettes.[55]

Lartigue's photograph of his wife, Bibi, and her friends from 1928 neatly captures the modern woman's ambiguous dynamic, somewhere between troubling social symbol and enticing sex object. Lartigue's wife is transformed into and showcased as an erotic and dandified modern woman. Bibi's central figure dominates the composition and becomes a visual catalogue of the type: her hair is short, she wears a bow tie and jacket and jauntily smokes a cigarette, sitting on the bumper of the car she no doubt drives. Her difference from the other women is emphasized through her every gesture and detail. The demure passivity of the figure on the left, for example, visually contrasts with the modern woman's dynamically tilted pose, and her enveloping cloak and floral corsage are a sharp contrast to Bibi's closely tailored suit and pocket handkerchief. The two women to the right gaze down at Lartigue's wife with what can only be called carefully staged desire, a sexual innuendo that in the end merely titillates the presumed male viewer (Lartigue himself?) rather than dangerously subverting sexual roles.

While Lartigue's photograph alludes to a homoerotic element situated in visual androgyny, like most other cultural texts of its kind, it contains a kind of compensatory mark of "femininity" that effectively undercuts the modern woman's subversive sexual potential. In this case, it is Bibi's prominently displayed legs, emerging from her skirt and forming the central visual axis of the picture. As this makes clear, any consideration of these figures as men or as threateningly male-identified women literally and metaphorically stops at the waist. In the myriad literary equivalents to Lartigue's picture, the fictional modern women almost always recanted and found ultimate happiness in marriage and bourgeois respectability. Lartigue makes this dynamic explicitly clear when he discusses the photograph in his diary. He invokes Victor Margueritte's notorious 1926 novel *La Garçonne* as a frame of reference for the women his picture contains. He notes that many women find dressing like boys "amusingly perverse," a kind of toothlessly threatening deviance. As if to underscore the reinscription of the modern woman within a heterosexual dynamic of desire, Lartigue refers to the group of women as his "harem."[56]

If, as Anne Hollander has suggested, masculinely tailored, form-fitting clothing on women registers an active sexual imagination, and further, if borrowing clothing from the other sex underscores sexual pleasure, then the modern woman's erotic charge would be equally visible to men *and* women.[57] And while dominant (heterosexual) culture rigorously suppressed a direct connection between the modern woman's character and the lesbian's, lesbians themselves definitely did not. They seized on and exploited the figure's sartorial erotic potential. Brooks's own observations about her "black curly hair and white collars" proceed immediately from a discussion of "being sensual like a man"—as she understood it, possessing an *active* sexual desire. Significantly, this discussion takes place in the larger context of Brooks's experiences in London's underground lesbian clubs, which she frequently attended while painting in 1923. Indeed, it was within these hidden social spaces, in both London and Paris, that the modern woman's look became codified as a sartorial symbol of lesbian sexual desire.

Not only did many lesbians adopt masculinized dress for wide-ranging self-identifying practices, they also strategically played the similarities with the modern woman to their advantage. If critics and observers decried the modern woman for her refusal of domestic propriety (read: marriage) and the obligations of motherhood, these same criteria could be easily transferred to lesbian women and the relationships they developed. Already nervous about this new female type and her "active" sexuality, the European cultural imagination tried vigorously to avoid the corollary notion that such an active sexual desire might decide to turn itself *away* from men. Although few commentators addressed this fear directly or articulated it overtly, the construction of the modern woman nevertheless circulated around the position of a proscribed lesbian sexuality. Thus lesbians adopted the signifying dress of the modern woman as a way of expressing their sexuality yet also linking it to a similar but less dangerous figure. Essentially, they "masqueraded" as modern women.[58] Masquerading as modern women helped them at least partially escape the disastrous consequences and absolute disapprobation of a public lesbian identity.

It is across the razor-thin edge between the images of Lartigue's modern woman and the lesbian that Brooks's 1923 self-portrait and her portraits of Peter and Una Troubridge operate. Her portraits resonate within both the heterosexual matrix of *la femme moderne* and the more marginalized network of lesbian sociality. Much of the visual tension of those portraits derives from the dilemma of women caught in this social and sexual rubric. Involving far more than fashion critiques, negative assessments of the modern woman illuminate the crucial importance of "womanly" markers in her sartorial style and the reassurances those markers provided men threatened by the social changes she represented.

That she considered her 1923 portraits part of a "series of modern women" confirms that Brooks's pictures are in direct dialogue with this complex and ongoing cultural concern. Unlike the prevailing version of the modern woman, however, her portraits provide none of those reassurances of ultimate femininity that attempted to dilute the figure's potential threat to prevailing gender norms. Significantly, all three women are seen only from the waist up. While we might know from other evidence that, unlike Gluck, Brooks and Troubridge always wore skirts, that question is suspended in the pictures themselves and ultimately left unresolved. The effect is most notable with Troubridge—seen nearly three-quarters length, the striped material below suggests both trousers and a skirt, but settles on neither.[59]

Each painting has a slightly different valence, but taken as a group they resolutely refuse to read the aesthetic of the modern woman as ultimately attractive to, and addressed to, heterosexual male desire. Romaine's confrontational and secretive "predatory" gaze peering from underneath her hat diametrically opposes the open and inviting frankness of the central figure's look in Lartigue's photograph. Her morbidly white flesh and lividly painted lips mock the desire for healthy and robust appearances, conducive (by extension) to the nation's health. Una Troubridge's sardonic presence and puckered reserve are far from the conventional idea of an inviting allure. The crisp contours of her figure exaggerate the tight tailoring of her costume and, consequently, her thinness, and do not accentuate her breasts, hips, and other details of a "feminine" silhouette routinely mentioned in popular descriptions. The feminized accents of her costume work only to reinforce the essential "masculinity" of the overall image rather than undercut its slightly imperious confidence. The portrait of Peter, meanwhile, carries even further a refusal to address the (male) spectator directly, its format ensuring its closed and self-involved presence. This resolute refusal underscores the title's very tenuous identification of this as a woman at all, an identification not strongly supported by the picture itself. When Brooks exhibited Gluck's portrait in 1925 as *Peter (A Young English*

*Girl*), even the title highlighted the oscillating and contradictory terms under which each portrait constructs its sitter's identity.

Taken together, these three portraits essentially reverse the terms under which secure identification as alluring, heterosexual, cross-dressing modern women is possible. They cannot be interpreted unequivocally as (straight) modern women, thus they register simultaneously as heterosexual women *and* as lesbians, and Brooks's deliberate undermining of the form makes the latter interpretation a compelling one. This is not to suggest that viewers of these paintings ever explicitly acknowledged that content. In fact there is no contemporary source that identifies Brooks's portraits in this manner. However, reviewers' excruciatingly studied imprecisions when discussing the works begin to seem almost panicked in their attempts to overlook exactly what their ephebic androgyny and disconcerting qualities might actually be.

Such was the difficult and often conflicted cultural terrain Brooks had to negotiate in 1923. Her response was to recombine two disparate strands of sartorial address, making each one newly strange and opening up new signifying possibilities. In her 1923 portraits, Brooks replaced those inevitable marks of "real" womanhood in the contemporary modern woman with the outward signs of the dandy, a visually anachronistic figure inextricably tied to notions of an active homosexual desire. Through this means Brooks amplified the feared homosexual implications of the modern woman and pushed to the foreground the overlapping conceptual discourses regarding the modern woman and the lesbian. In all of this, Brooks retained the connection Hollander has since described between "sex and suits." But she and her sitters literally invented a new definition of that "certain spice," a sexual allure that emerges from the clothes they wear, the self-confidence of their transgression, and their acknowledgment of lesbian identity and desire.

In her 1923 portraits, Romaine Brooks redeployed the (male) homoerotic associations of the dandy into female portraits. She also recombined the dandy's sartorial strategies with the modern woman's in an effort to fashion a different visual identity, one specifically and deliberately infused with homoerotic possibilities at a cultural moment when the visual signs of lesbian desire and identity were just beginning to emerge in dominant culture. Moreover, she suggested that all visual identities, whether straight or inverted, might not be related to any coherent, internal self at all. These possibilities created an unsettling and ambiguous resonance, one that, judging from critical responses, French and British viewers on some level understood. Louis Vauxcelles's commentary on the pictures is exemplary in this regard. He writes that "In her images there's a *je ne sais quoi* that disconcerts the French sensibility; certain young women look like ephebes, showing us what overturns our traditions."[60] What is this *je ne sais quoi* that Vauxcelles acknowledges but coyly refuses to name? What visual qualities in Brooks's portraits, her "modern women," disturbed French sensitivities and disrupted tradition? I would argue that it was precisely the dandy in her. Although resolutely marginalized, even in critical responses to these paintings, this nearly invisible specter of lesbian sexuality and subjectivity nevertheless maintained the power to haunt the limits of vision and cultural identity.

NOTES

1. Romaine Brooks to Natalie Barney, June 23, 1923, Bibliothèque Jacques Doucet, Paris, NCBC2.2445.57.

2. Theories of homosexuality proliferated in 1920s Europe, and by far the most influential was "sexual inversion." This term was commonly used in theories of homosexuality and was popularized as the title to the first volume of the sexologist Havelock Ellis's *Psychology of Sex*. Havelock Ellis and J. A. Symonds, *Sexual Inversion*, vol. 1 of *The Psychology of Sex* (London: Wilson and Macmillan, 1897). See Jeffrey Weeks, "Havelock Ellis and Sexual Inversion," in *Coming Out: Homosexual Politics in Britain from the Nineteenth Century to the Present* (London: Quartet Books, 1977), 57–67. See also Lucy Bland and Laura Doan, *Sexology Uncensored* (Chicago: University of Chicago Press, 1998) for recent critical examinations of sexology's cultural impact.

3. Natalie Barney to Romaine Brooks, Bibliothèque Jacques Doucet, Paris, NCBC2.2996. 38–39. Although the letter is undated, specific internal references date it securely to 1923.

4. See Weeks, *Coming Out*, in which Weeks has traced the emergence of lesbian identity into social discourse in late-nineteenth- and early-twentieth-century Europe. Like male homosexuality before it, lesbianism emerged in the context of its criminalization. As Weeks demonstrates, as late as 1921 lesbians were, for complex reasons, nearly invisible to dominant culture and still not subject to any criminal codes in Britain and France. Weeks establishes Radclyffe Hall's publication of the novel *The Well of Loneliness* in 1928 as a turning point in lesbian visibility. Brooks painted and exhibited her portraits several years before *The Well*'s publication, a time when ideas about "masculin-

ized" women and lesbianism were gaining rhetorical force that would crystallize with Hall's later novel.

Whitney Chadwick has linked the modern woman to the emergence of lesbianism in European culture, with particular reference to Brooks's 1923 portraits. See Whitney Chadwick, *Women, Art and Society* (New York: Thames and Hudson, 1990), 260–61. See also Bridget Elliott and Jo-Ann Wallace, *Women Artists and Writers: Modernist (Im)positionings* (London: Routledge, 1994), 31–56, 51, where the authors note that Brooks assumed the dandy costume to invoke "the cultural markers of a marginal, deviant, and illegal sexuality." See also Ellen Moers, *The Dandy* (Lincoln: University of Nebraska Press, 1962), 11–13, for her useful discussion of class and costume.

5. Susan Gubar, "Blessings in Disguise: Cross-Dressing as Re-Dressing for Female Modernists," *Massachusetts Review* 22, no. 3 (1981): 477–508. See also Shari Benstock, *Women of the Left Bank* (Austin: University of Texas Press, 1986), 304–7.

6. This is a central concern in Elliott and *Wallace, Women Artists and Writers*; they discuss this subject within a variety of media, including painting, poetry, and literature, during the 1910s and 1920s in France.

7. John Usher, "A True Painter of Personality," *International Studio*, February 1926, 46–50, 46.

8. "Romaine Brooks s'est peinte elle-même dans un strict tailleur masculin, les cheveux dissimulés sous un feutre d'homme, d'où le regard s'embusque avec intelligence." Jean Laporte, "Romaine Brooks interprête de la sensibilité internationale," *Vogue*, June 1, 1925, 34. The specific terminology here is important, since "*tailleur*" signifies specifically a woman's suit as opposed to a man's costume. So the term translates as "a strictly masculinized suit." Also, the verb "*s'embusquer*" means "to lie in ambush for." So the word "lurks," while not technically accurate, captures the spirit of the sentiment.

9. "Le talent sobre, un peu sévère, de Romaine Brooks s'affirme dans des portraits très nets, tres découpés, singulièrement intuitifs." *Mercure de France*, July 1, 1925.

10. "Elle la rend avec une sagacité où l'intelligence et le talent affleurement egalement." Laporte, "Romaine Brooks."

11. Louis Vauxcelles, *Paris-Soir*, May 25, 1925.

12. Romaine Brooks, "No Pleasant Memories" (Archives of American Art, Smithsonian Institution), 223. Brooks is typically dismissive of Boldini, writing only that "even his best paintings show that he could paint only [surface values.]"

13. The term "*whistlerien*" appears in a 1911 review of Brooks's solo exhibition at the Galeries Durand-Ruel in Paris (*Journal des Debats*, May 17, 1910). See also Pascal Forthuny, "Les petits salons," *Le Matin*, May 11, 1910; *New York Herald* (Paris edition), May 15, 1910. In 1925 London's *Daily Mirror* still called Brooks a "follower of Whistler" in its review of her 1925 exhibition (on June 14,

1925). The *Daily Mail* (June 5, 1925) and the *London Times* (June 16, 1925) echoed these sentiments.

14. See, in particular, Benstock, *Women of the Left Bank*.

15. Brooks, "No Pleasant Memories," 205.

16. Whistler became an officer of the Legion of Honor in 1892 after the Musée de Luxembourg purchased his *Portrait of the Painter's Mother*. See Véronique Weisinger, *Les Américains et la Légion d'Honneur* (exhibition catalogue) (Paris: Château de Blérancourt, 1993) for a complete survey of Americans who have been awarded the honor.

17. Philippe Jullian, *Prince of Aesthetes: Count Robert de Montesquiou* (New York: Viking, 1965) remains the definitive biography of Montesquiou.

18. See Edgar Munhall, *Whistler and Montesquiou: The Butterfly and the Bat* (Paris: Flammarion, 1995). See also Patrick Chaleyssin, *Robert de Montesquiou: Mécène et dandy* (Paris: Somogy, 1992) for a more complete study of Montesquiou's activities as a patron and as a leader of "dandified" aestheticism.

19. As Philippe Jullian colorfully described it, "Miss Brooks was madly in fashion," and Montesquiou set out to add her to his already fashionable circle. Jullian, *Prince of Aesthetes*, 230.

20. Robert de Montesquiou, "Cambrioleur d'Ames," *Figaro*, June 1910.

21. Munhall, *Whistler and Montesquiou*, 86–94.

22. Quoted in ibid., 93.

23. Among the extensive collection of Robert de Montesquiou's papers held at the Bibliothèque Nationale in Paris are several cards and letters from Brooks accepting invitations to parties, thanking the count for a variety of entertainments, and so on. See, for example, *Nouvelles Acquisitions* (NAF) 15084, p. 157; NAF 15144, pp. 168–82. Brooks later repudiated Montesquiou's elite social circles, referring to them in her autobiography as "the idle and stupid tribe called society." Brooks, "No Pleasant Memories," 240.

24. Weeks, *Coming Out*, 21, notes that Wilde himself realized that he had made his name a "synonym for folly." Weeks's text includes several examples invoking Wilde's name as a euphemism for homosexuality, including E. M. Forster's largely sympathetic main character in *Maurice*.

25. Brooks, "No Pleasant Memories," 205–6. Douglas was later engaged briefly to Natalie Barney in Paris.

26. Philippe Jullian documents the difficulties Montesquiou faced and the bold assertions he made during what Jullian calls "the Mauve Peril." See Jullian, *Prince of Aesthetes,* 101–15.

27. See Moers, *The Dandy*, 304. Jullian devotes an entire chapter to each of these literary characters in his biography of Montesquiou. See Jullian, *Prince of Aesthetes*, "Des Esseintes," 36–48, and "St. Charlus," 261–78. He carefully enumerates the similarities and differences of each man to Montesquiou's person as well as the count's reactions (often mixed) to the novels.

28. Quoted in Munhall, *Whistler and Montesquiou*, 90.

29. In dressing this way and painting these portraits, Brooks was certainly aware of the sort of homosexual "cross-dressing" in which she engaged. As Bridget Elliott and Jo-Ann Wallace have argued, the culturally dominant sexuality against which Romaine Brooks and her sitters defined themselves was male homosexuality, or at least male homosociality. See Elliott and Wallace, *Women Artists and Writers*, 53 ff.

30. Domna Stanton, *The Aristocrat as Art* (New York: Columbia University Press, 1980), esp. 1–12.

31. Albert Boime, "Sargent in Paris and London: A Portrait of the Artist as Dorian Gray," in *John Singer Sargent*, ed. Patricia Hills (New York: Abrams, 1987), 104.

32. Brooks uses a similar strategy in her portrait of the duchess of Clermont-Tonnère. In this portrait, unlike most others, the artist places the duchess before a recognizable landmark, the duchess's ancestral Parisian hôtel.

33. When she lived in London around 1905, Brooks rented the house just opposite Sargent's fashionable Tite Street studio. By all accounts, though, they never met. As she does with Whistler and Boldini, Romaine dismisses Sargent's work and its connections to her own, noting only that "his work did not interest me, and I never sought to know him." Brooks, "No Pleasant Memories," 201.

34. Elliott and Wallace have also discussed the "old-fashioned" quality of Romaine's portrait style. However, they are primarily interested in a rethinking of critical dichotomies that enforce the priority of "modernist" aesthetics. See Elliot and Wallace, *Women Artists and Writers*, 42–43.

35. Katrina Rolley, "Cutting a Dash: The Dress of Radclyffe Hall and Una Troubridge," *Feminist Review* 35 (summer 1990): 55–56.

36. Stanton, *The Aristocrat as Art*, 4. Stanton's comment occurs in relation to her reading of Thorstein Veblen's nineteenth-century text *The Theory of the Leisure Class*.

37. See Jeffrey Weeks, *Sex, Politics, and Society: The Regulation of Sexuality since 1800* (New York: Longman, 1981), 107–8.

38. Ellis and Symonds, *Sexual Inversion*, 84. Ellis's mention of prostitution can be read as an example of the often extreme moralizing that occurred when this supposedly scientific discourse dealt with "perversions" of female sexuality.

39. On Una Troubridge, see Richard Ormrod, *Una Troubridge: The Friend of Radclyffe Hall* (London: Jonathan Cape, 1984).

40. Bibliothèque Jacques Doucet, Paris, NCB2.2445.459. This letter is not written to Natalie Barney but to "Dorothy," probably Oscar Wilde's niece Dolly Wilde.

41. Twenty years later, Brooks echoed her sentiments about the historical implications of Troubridge's appearance when she described her as "a memento mori that is no longer gay." Bibliothèque Jacques Doucet, Paris, NCB2.2445.168.

42. The inclusion of Troubridge's dogs can be read as a witty play on two traditional motifs in painting. On the one hand, dogs have often appeared with women as an overtly erotic, often titillating substitute for female genitalia and sexual desire. Here, however, the coldness and formality of the image and Troubridge's grip on the dog completely alter the implied eroticism or exoticism in their interaction. On the other hand, dogs often accompany their (male) masters in aristocratic and royal portraiture, both as a sign of loyalty and to suggest the hunting activities in which such a man surely engaged. Purebred hunting dogs could be considered valuable property themselves, expensive to own and maintain. So the dogs signified not only a masculine sporting activity, but by extension, their owner's wealth as well as (indirectly) his estate and other possessions. Here, however, the proud hunting dogs are replaced with Troubridge's short and stubby dachshunds (Thor and Wotan) with decoratively studded collars and vacant expressions.

43. See Diana Souhami, *Gluck* (London: Pandora Press, 1988).

44. *Daily Graphic,* June 1, 1925.

45. In her study of gender politics in postwar France, Mary Louise Roberts identifies *la femme moderne* as one of the most pervasive images of female identity in the postwar arguments about women. According to Roberts, the idea of the modern woman was much more than one way of imagining the female self. The modern woman "provided a way of talking about the war's more general emotional trauma" as well as the trauma of rapid change, a way of "mak[ing] changes associated with the war comprehensible to the French." Mary Louise Roberts, *Civilization without Sexes: The Reconstruction of Gender in Postwar France, 1917–1927* (Chicago: University of Chicago Press, 1994), 9. These changes were hardly limited to France, and the sweeping cultural changes, and women's altered position within that culture, were just as evident in Great Britain. Bonnie Smith, *Changing Lives: Women in European History since 1700* (Lexington, MA: D. C. Heath, 1989) offers the best overview of these changes for British (as well as other European) women. See especially part 3, "A World Torn Asunder, 1875–1925," 272–409.

Laura Doan's recent study of women's fashions in 1920s Britain was published too recently to be considered fully in this essay. Doan usefully examines the British popular reaction to the modern woman phenomenon with particular reference to its potential lesbian significations. She focuses primarily on Radclyffe Hall, Una Troubridge, and Gluck. Doan also considers how older women like Hall and Troubridge used the modern woman's style, normally associated with a younger generation. See Laura Doan, "Passing Fashions: Reading Female Masculinities in the 1920s," *Feminist Studies* 24, no. 3 (fall 1998): 663–700.

46. "Ces êtres sans poitrines ni hanches, sans 'dessous,' qui fument, travaillent, discutent, et boxent comme les garçons et qui, dans la nuit de Bois de

Boulogne, le cerveau noyé sous quelques cocktails, recherchent sur les coussins havan de la 5 chevaux Citroën des sensations savoureuses et acrobatiques, ne sont pas des jeunes filles!" *Progrès Civique*, no. 304, June 13, 1925, 11. This assessment occurs as part of the journal's series of articles debating the value of new freedoms women enjoyed after the war.

47. In her discussion of Brooks and the modern woman, Whitney Chadwick notes that popular publications "altogether avoided mentioning" the emergence of lesbianism in postwar Europe. Chadwick, *Women, Art and Society*, 260.

48. Pierre Lièvre, "Reproches à une dame qui à coupé ses cheveux" (Paris: Le Divan, 1927). Quoted in Roberts, *Civilization without Sexes*, 70.

49. While surprising enough for its degree of biological determinism and trenchant homophobia, Lièvre's opinion is perhaps more startling because it occurs in a satiric tract ostensibly dedicated to contemporary women's hairstyles. In this context, his comment illustrates the often short conceptual distance between fashion and sexuality.

50. Anne Hollander, *Sex and Suits* (New York: Knopf, 1994), 124.

51. Ibid., 131.

52. "Le Smoking pour dames," February 24, 1926 (exact source unknown), Bibliothèque Marguerite Durand, Paris, Dossier Mode.

53. Maurice Prax, "Pour et contre," *Petit Parisien*, September 25, 1926. Quoted in Roberts, *Civilization without Sexes*, 68.

54. It was in fact in photography that images of the modern woman were primarily fixed and disseminated. Instances of the figure in painting are fairly uncommon, thus my use of Lartigue as a frame of reference for Brooks's painted portraits. The relative scarcity of painted versions of the modern woman would have made her work that much more unusual a subject in the gallery context.

55. Jacques-Henri Lartigue, *Les Dames aux cigarettes* (New York: Viking, 1980). See also *Jacques-Henri Lartigue et les femmes* (Paris: Editions des Chênes, 1973) for a pictorial overview of his photographs of women.

56. Jacques-Henri Lartigue, *Diary of a Century* (New York: Viking, 1970), n.p. On *La garçonne* and its controversies, see Roberts, *Civilization without Sexes*, 46–62.

57. This is part of Hollander's larger argument in *Sex and Suits*. See in particular the introduction and the chapter "Modernity."

58. In using the term "masquerade" here and "womanliness" earlier, I am deliberately invoking the psychoanalyst Joan Riviere's famous 1929 essay "Womanliness as Masquerade." Riviere posited that women professionals appeared hyperfeminine in order to mollify any perceived professional threat to their male colleagues. For Riviere, femininity involved masking women's masculinity beneath a decorative veneer. She suggested that femininity is therefore

not inherent but a social performance. I would like to retain Riviere's dynamic while reworking its particulars to examine a complex situation: lesbians hiding their perceived masculinity not beneath ultrafeminine appearances but rather through "masquerading" as the already problematic modern woman. The modern woman was already thought to be overly masculine, but her compensating "womanliness" offered lesbians a chance to openly perform their "masculinity" while at least partially dissembling its sexual implications. Riviere's essay is reprinted in Victor Burgin, James Donald, and Cora Kaplan, eds., *Formations of Fantasy* (New York: Routledge, 1986), 45–61.

59. Most extant photographs show that Una Troubridge wore stylishly tailored skirts and jackets. See, for example, the photographs in Rolley, "Cutting a Dash" and in Michael Baker, *Our Three Selves: The Life of Radclyffe Hall* (New York: William Morrow, 1985). Both authors also reproduce Gladys Hynes's 1937 painting *Private View*, which contains portraits of both Troubridge and Radclyffe Hall at a gallery opening. Troubridge wears a loose-fitting dress and fur stole, and Hall has on a tailored skirt and jacket. Rolley, like other writers, erroneously asserts that Una Troubridge wears "masculine dress" in her portrait by Brooks, in an effort to communicate her lesbian sexuality. On Brooks's part, her letters contain frequent and extensive descriptions of her latest dresses and skirts as well as instructions for Natalie Barney to buy her women's suits at particular shops and dressmakers. Diana Souhami lists the men's clothing stores at which Gluck ordered her outfits. In 1926 the artist had her photographic portrait done by Howard Coster, "Photographer of Men." Souhami, *Gluck*, 10–11. More generally, Anne Hollander has shown that until the end of the 1930s, skirts were "universal" in women's fashion and that trousers (including Gluck's) were a special, anomalous case. Hollander, *Sex and Suits*, 145.

60. "Il y a en ses images un je ne sais quoi qui déconcertent la sensibilité française; certaines jeunes femmes rassemblent à des éphèbes, mettons que cela bouscule nos habitudes." Vauxcelles, *Paris-Soir*, May 25, 1925.

## BIBLIOGRAPHY

Baker, Michael. *Our Three Selves: The Life of Radclyffe Hall*. New York: William Morrow, 1985.

Benstock, Shari. *Women of the Left Bank*. Austin: University of Texas Press, 1986.

Bland, Lucy, and Laura Doan. *Sexology Uncensored*. Chicago: University of Chicago Press, 1998.

Boime, Albert. "Sargent in Paris and London: A Portrait of the Artist as Dorian

Gray." In *John Singer Sargent*, edited by Patricia Hills. New York: Abrams, 1987.

Brooks, Romaine. "No Pleasant Memories." Archives of American Art, Washington, D.C.

Brooks, Romaine, and Natalie Barney. Correspondence. Bibliotheque Jacques Doucet. Paris.

Chadwick, Whitney. *Women, Art and Society*. New York: Thames and Hudson, 1990.

Chaleyssin, Patrick. *Robert de Montesquiou: Mécène et dandy*. Paris: Somogy, 1992.

Doan, Laura. "Passing Fashions: Reading Female Masculinities in the 1920s," *Feminist Studies* 24, no. 3 (fall 1998): 663–700.

Elliott, Bridget, and Jo-Ann Wallace, *Women Artists and Writers: Modernist (Im)positionings*. London: Routledge, 1994.

Feldman, Jessica. *Gender on the Divide: The Dandy in Modernist Literature*. Ithaca: Cornell University Press, 1993.

Garelick, Rhonda. *Rising Star: Dandyism, Gender and Performance in the Fin-de-Siècle*. Princeton: Princeton University Press, 1998.

Gubar, Susan. "Blessings in Disguise: Cross-Dressing as Re-Dressing for Female Modernists." *Massachusetts Review* 22, no. 3 (1981): 477–508.

Hollander, Anne. *Sex and Suits*. New York: Knopf, 1994.

Jullian, Philippe. *Prince of Aesthetes: Count Robert de Montesquiou*. New York: Viking, 1965.

Lartigue, Jacques-Henri. *Diary of a Century*. New York: Viking, 1970.

———. *Jacques-Henri Lartigue et les femmes*. Paris: Editions des chênes, 1973.

Lievre, Pierre. *Reproches à une dame qui à coupé ses cheveux*. Paris: Le Divan, 1927.

Moers, Ellen. *The Dandy: Brummell to Beerbohm*. Lincoln: University of Nebraska Press, 1962.

Munhall, Edgar. *Whistler and Montesquiou: The Butterfly and the Bat*. Paris: Flammarion, 1995.

Ormrod, Richard. *Una Troubridge: The Friend of Radclyffe Hall*. London: Jonathan Cape, 1984.

Riviere, Joan. "Womanliness as Masquerade." *International Journal of Psychoanalysis* 10 (1929). Reprinted in *Formations of Fantasy*, edited by Victor Burgin, James Donald, and Cora Kaplan, 45–61. New York: Routledge, 1986.

Roberts, Mary Louise. *Civilization without Sexes: The Reconstruction of Gender in Postwar France, 1917–1927*. Chicago: University of Chicago Press, 1994.

Rolley, Katrina. "Cutting a Dash: The Dress of Radclyffe Hall and Una Troubridge." *Feminist Review* 35 (summer 1990): 55–56.

Smith, Bonnie. *Changing Lives: Women in European History since 1700.* Lexington, MA: D. C. Heath, 1989.

Souhami, Diana. *Gluck.* London: Pandora Press, 1988.

Stanton, Domna. *The Aristocrat as Art.* New York: Columbia University Press, 1980.

Usher, John. "A True Painter of Personality." *International Studio,* February 1926, 46–50.

Weeks, Jeffrey. *Coming Out: Homosexual Politics in Britain from the Nineteenth Century to the Present.* London: Quartet Books, 1977.

——. *Sex, Politics, and Society: The Regulation of Sexuality since 1800.* New York: Longman, 1981.

Weisinger, Veronique. *Les Américains et la Légion d'Honneur.* Exhibition catalogue. Paris: Château de Blérancourt, 1993.

*Chapter 6*

# Claude Cahun, Dandy Provocateuse

*Jennifer Blessing*

Brouiller les cartes.
Masculin? féminin? [m]ais ça dépend des cas. Neutre
est le seul genre qui me convienne toujours. S'il existait
dans notre langue on n'observerait pas ce flottement
de ma pensée. Je serais pour de bon l'abeille ouvrière.
—Claude Cahun, *Aveux non avenus* (1930)

The excavation of the life and work of the French Surrealist writer-cum-artist Claude Cahun (1894–1954) has been fraught with confusion, a result of historians' neglect as well as the artist's own strategy of obfuscation. As a woman and a lesbian, Cahun was subject to erasure from the cultural history of 1930s Paris. Attempts to recuperate the artist in the 1980s at first generated little verifiable information and glaring errors.[1] References were made to Cahun using the masculine pronoun, a case of mistaken identity the artist might have enjoyed since she selected various masculine and ambiguous pseudonyms to replace her given name, Lucy.[2] In fact, most of Cahun's work promotes indeterminacy (or resistance to determination) as an aesthetic and political position; she uses paradoxical juxtapositions to suggest both/and rather than either/or. Her writing and her art indicate that she saw the personal as political, and that through the Surrealist espousal of unregulated expression—of dreams, of fantasies—as well as the generative possibilities of montage, she could expose social and political repression while she exposed and constructed herself.

Shortly after Cahun's work was introduced to American audiences in the 1985 exhibition *L'Amour fou*, the art historian and theorist Hal

Foster proclaimed her "a Cindy Sherman *avant la lettre* who deals in her self-portraits with masquerade."[3] Subsequent writers developed this suggestion, productively examining Cahun's work in terms of psychoanalytic theories of masquerade.[4] In this essay I will introduce the artist's photographic and literary production through the lens of masquerade and the presumption that gender is a kind of drag, exploring the specifically dandified aspect of much of Cahun's creative interrogation of identity, in general, and gender identity, in particular. There are significantly overlapping themes in the conceptual frameworks of masquerade and the dandy, such as an idealistic belief in self-creation and the notion that identity is constructed through artifice. Notwithstanding their current appeal (and thus perhaps anachronistic application to earlier production), both the psychoanalytic debate in which the theory of masquerade was developed and the literary articulation of the dandy formed a part of Cahun's intellectual milieu.

*Sous ce masque un autre masque.*    —*Claude Cahun*

In her self-portrait photographs Cahun creates a variety of hybrid personae, ranging from a bejewelled potentate with a Valentino stare to a pale Dracula with painted widow's peak to an Oscar Wilde dandy in velvet pants, all nominally "masculine" characters.[5] Her "feminine" protagonists are so exceedingly artificial and exaggerated that they appear to be drag queens: one frequently reproduced image depicts Claude as a Swiss Miss doll; another photograph of a feminine carnival-masked and bewigged Cahun is so elaborate that it raises the doubt that the artist is beneath the clothes at all.

The frequent comparison of Cahun to Sherman is prompted by images like these in which Cahun uses her own body as the basis of the construction. In these works, Cahun seems to be problematizing gender and subjectivity itself by taking on identities as she would a suit of clothes. This strategy is essentially one of performance, in which Cahun becomes the actor, a point that is emphasized by the artist's obsession with masks and her use of dolls as dramatis personae.[6] As the film theorist Annette Kuhn has noted, when an actor performs, s/he assumes the mask of an identity different from his or her own "'real self,'" constructing a distance between an assumed and "real" persona that emphasizes the "fluidity of subjectivity."[7] She has described cross-dressing as "a mode of performance in which—through play on the disjunction between clothes and body—the socially constructed nature of sexual difference is foregrounded and even subjected to comment: what appears natural, then, reveals itself as artifice."[8]

Cahun's elaborate characters reflect the overstated dramatic posing of silent screen actors and the kind of gender ambiguity that was popular in the late 1920s before the rise of fascism, the moralism of social realism, and the return to order of the postwar period. Just two examples of between-the-wars gender crossover are Virginia Woolf's *Orlando*, published in 1928, in which the protagonist's sex changes over the centuries, and Marlene Dietrich singing in drag in the 1930 film *Morocco*.[9]

This gender-bending should be viewed within the context of the "Great Debate" in the 1920s over the genesis of feminine identity, which divided the psychoanalytic community.[10] As one salvo in this battle, the analyst Joan Riviere published her article "Womanliness as Masquerade" in 1929.[11] Riviere based her argument on her analysis of a number of professional women, noting that they presented themselves in exaggeratedly ultrafeminine dress and demeanor in order to prevent the retribution they feared from the men whose prerogative they challenged simply through their presence in the public sphere. Their womanliness was a masquerade to prevent punishment from men for usurping their power. Riviere was vague about what might lie behind the mask, announcing at one point, "The reader may now ask how I define womanliness or where I draw the line between genuine womanliness and the 'masquerade.' My suggestion is not, however, that there is any such difference; whether radical or superficial, they are the same thing."[12]

In the mid-1970s, the film theorist Claire Johnston used Riviere's conception of masquerade to explain the dismal fate of the female protagonist in *Anne of the Indies*, who took on a male identity, represented visually in the film by her espousal of men's clothing, the sign of male authority.[13] Subsequently, Mary Ann Doane argued that Riviere's reasoning–in its portrayal of femininity as a form of disguise—allows for the possibility of a self-conscious masquerade with subversive potential.[14]

Cahun continued to play the signs of masculinity and femininity off one another in her photographic tableaux of enigmatic household and natural objects. Many of these images serve as illustrations for a 1937 book of children's poems written by Lise Deharme, entitled *Le Coeur de pic*.[15] In one assemblage a shoe and a glove lean on a wire-mesh dressmaker's form with a sword in it; another image includes a mound of down feathers, a pen projecting into space, and a tree branch bearing pen nibs in front of a satin backdrop. These components suggest a familiarity with the unconscious erotic connotations of ordinary forms and materials outlined in Sigmund Freud's *Interpretation of Dreams* (1900), which (like many of the analyst's texts) entered the Surrealist canon. Cahun's prominent use of flowers in the tableaux is ostensibly related to the botanical anthropomorphic imagery in Deharme's poems, but it could also be influenced by the radical philosopher Georges Bataille's short 1929 essay "The Language of Flowers," in which he argued that people and flowers share a similar displacement of signification.[16] Bataille noted that "[t]he sign of love" in a flower is displaced from the plant's reproductive organs (the pistil and stamens) to the corolla of petals around them, just as "the object of human love is never an organ but the person who has the organ."[17] He pointed out that the beauty of flowers and our attraction to them cannot be separated from their hideousness; "even the most beautiful flowers are spoiled in their centers by hairy sexual organs."[18] The implicit obscenity of plant components—the tuber root, for example—prompt the attribution of perversions to flowers as easily as the values of faith and constancy. Cahun's flowers, like her self-portraits, insist on these sublimated yet integral dimensions of signification. The flowers become actors in her elaborate scenarios, suggesting a miniature universe analogous to our own, and insisting that we confront the flip side of presumptions that a woman is as fresh and lovely as a rose, or a man is like a fine young sapling. There is no single monolithic reading of the meaning of a flower, nor a clear dichotomy between the sexes, nor a univocal way of describing identity. Cahun has created a *mise en abîme* of sexual signs that cancel each other out into infinity, so that any gender determination is indefinitely deferred. In a series of self-portrait photographs in which she appears as a kind of circus strong man, Cahun masks her body as well as her face: she wears white makeup and white clothing to simulate flesh; prosthetic nipples are sewn onto her shirt. In one particularly striking image, her made-up "masculine" face is countered by artificial "feminine" breasts. Masculine and feminine, seduction and repulsion, the beautiful and the grotesque are conflated and indistinguishable.

Cahun incorporated her self-portrait personae into photocollages, which she used to illustrate her 1930 book *Aveux non avenus*, a diaris-

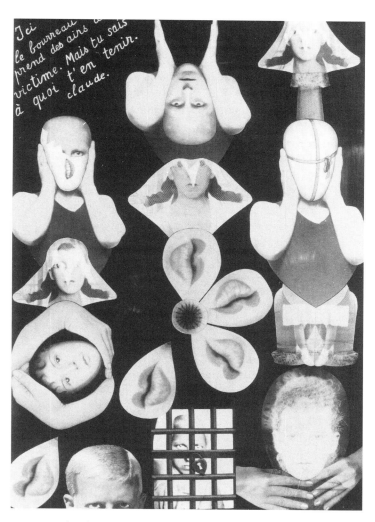

*Fig. 6.1.* Claude Cahun, *M. R. M. (Sex)*, 1930. Collection of Helen Kornblum. Photograph courtesy of the collector. Reproduced by permission.

tic compilation of extended poetic meditations, introspective missives, and quasi-philosophical dialogues. The photomontage constructions juxtapose found prints, photographs, and drawing into multivalent compositions foregrounding the excerpted self-portraits. In one work (fig. 6.1), the text in the upper left corner reads, "Ici le bourreau prend des airs de victime. Mais tu sais à quoi t'en tenir. claude."[19] All of the figures are Claude: Claude (as man?) in prison, at the bottom; Claude being strangled; Claude beheaded at the top, her reflection with shaved head, the traditional punishment of female adulterers. Is Claude the executioner taking on the poses of victim here? Her vamp-like lips suggest the seductress or femme fatale, a woman "executioner," but what of the young Claude protected in a woman's hands, at the left? This problematization of identity, positing a nonunitary or multiple conception of subjectivity, is the ostensible theme of Cahun's many self-images. The potential of such a strategy was underscored by the film theorist Mary Ann Doane in her influential 1982 evaluation of Riviere's masquerade article. Doane argued that the "misfit" of the mask, the schism between presumed identity and its representation, can allow women the possibility of playing with the masquerade. It can become a self-conscious ironic gesture, a question mark, a disruptive, transgressive act, and thus a source of power.[20]

During the 1930s Cahun strongly objected to Louis Aragon and other Surrealist poets who asserted that radical change warranted circumscribing their subject matter and stylistic options. Cahun argued that creative means cannot be disassociated from their end, and that revolutionary art may take many forms.[21] Her questioning and subversion of assumptions about gender have political implications, as is clear in a collage from the section "I.O.U. (self-pride)" in *Aveux non avenus* (fig. 6.2). On the left side of the image is a double column of eleven Claudes, surrounded by a handwritten text that reads, "Sous ce masque un autre masque. Je n'en finirai pas de soulever tous ces visages."[22] The uppermost heads look up with fear at a threatening triangle containing a nuclear family unit–and they are literally a unit, joined at the stomach. While the family was considered a repressive institution by avant-garde thinkers and writers in the nineteenth century, Cahun may also have been responding to the threat she could have perceived in the heavy pro-natalism campaign run by the French government after World War I. In her work, she represents procreation as a kind of assembly line of wooden dolls-within-dolls, led by the largest bearing a flag ironically inscribed "La sainte famille." In the text of the section this work illustrates, she wrote the diphthong OE in large type, and the statement "En vain j'essaye de remettre mon corps à sa place (mons corps avec ses dépendances), de me voir à la troisième personne. Le je est en moi comme l'e pris dans l'o."[23] This statement may be read

*Fig. 6.2.* Claude Cahun, *Aveux non avenus*, 1930, pl. 10. Reproduced by permission.

as an articulation of Cahun's desire to transcend the restrictions of an identity posited as monolithically unitary.

In 1991 the gender theorist Judith Butler outlined the problematic implications of any identity affiliation, contending that while it is important to "appear at political occasions under the sign of lesbian" in order to assert a subject position, she prefers "to have it permanently unclear what precisely that sign signifies."[24] Cahun's political stance seems to reflect, and to have encouraged, her revelry in just this lack of clarity.[25] Her work could illustrate what Butler later maintains, that "drag is not an imitation or a copy of some prior and true gender . . . drag enacts the very structure of impersonation by which *any gender* is assumed."[26] In her self-portraits, Cahun is both male and female impersonator. Neither position is more "real" or integrated, because, as Butler puts it, *"gender is a kind of imitation for which there is no original*; in fact, it is a kind of imitation that produces the very notion of the original as an *effect* and consequence of the imitation itself."[27]

> *La sirène succombe à sa propre voix.*   —Claude Cahun

Cahun's interest in identity and the manner in which she frames her explorations often manifest their indebtedness to the literary tradition in which the figure of the dandy was developed. As described by Charles Baudelaire in his essay "The Painter of Modern Life," the dandy is a product of modernity itself, an artistic spirit taxed by necessity–because of his temperament and his time–with fashioning his persona.[28] Asking what passion drives the dandy, Baudelaire answers, "It is first and foremost the burning need to create for oneself a personal originality, bounded only by the limits of the proprieties."[29] The means of this self-creation are found in demeanor and dress, in the artificial construction of identity through sartorial devices and postures. For Baudelaire, the dandy is haughty and diffident, a superior creature, one who is quite sure to present himself in the most elegant and *au courant* attire. A perfectly black suit was the epitome of his dandy's modern style.

The dandy was both a nineteenth-century social type and a figure of contemporaneous literature. Writers were thus inventing the character of the dandy as they reported it. According to the literary critic Jessica Feldman,

> the dandies of literature are often created by artists who are also dandies. The hall of mirrors is the dandy's ancestral home. In a dizzying reflexivity, the dandy created within the work of art—Pelham or Onegin or Don Juan—is actualized, rendered "real" in print by the living, breathing dandy-writer who chooses to make of himself and his daily life a fiction.[30]

The antinaturalism that structures Baudelaire's writing in general, and his conception of the dandy in particular, would also be central to Symbolism, the late-nineteenth-century French literary and artistic movement. As Cahun encountered the Surrealists, she was heir to this tradition; however, her personal and professional ties to the Symbolists predate her engagement with Surrealism and uniquely inform her work.

Cahun was born into a literary family: her father published a newspaper, and several of her relatives—including a grandfather, an uncle, and a great-uncle—were authors.[31] Educated in France and England, she began publishing her own work when she was nineteen. The breadth of her literary culture is clear in her writings. Her references include major Symbolist figures such as Arthur Rimbaud and Jules Laforgue, as well as twentieth-century authors like André Gide and Antonin Artaud. As a rule, Baudelaire's influence weighs heavily on the avant-garde movements of the late nineteenth and early twentieth centuries, and Cahun's debt to him is no exception. According to Feldman, Baudelaire's work characterizes "the three propelling forces of literary dandyism: metamorphosis, paradox, and analogy," all of which are devices Cahun frequently employs.[32] One quite literal example of her use of Baudelairean paradox is the line from the *Aveux non avenus* montage, "Ici le bourreau prend des airs de victime," which echoes Baudelaire's famous poetic pronouncement,

> Je suis la plaie et le couteau!
> Je suis le soufflet et la joue!
> Je suis les membres et la roue,
> Et la victime et le bourreau![33]

Like Baudelaire, Oscar Wilde is often associated with the dandy, both for his personal style and for his creation of dandies in fiction. Cahun's early interest in Wilde is obliquely manifested by the fact that her second published article was a report on an infamous British trial initiated by the lead actress in a private presentation of Wilde's *Salomé* during World War I.[34] The actress, along with the publicly banned performance's producer and many audience members, had been accused by a right-wing journalist of being morally depraved and hence practically a wartime collaborator. Cahun used this opportunity to deride the earlier persecution of Wilde and to argue for artistic freedom in the face of moralistic condemnations. She surely would have espoused Wilde's well-known art-for-art's-sake proclamation, "There is no such thing as a moral or an immoral book. Books are well written, or badly written. That is all."[35]

Wilde's own defenses of artistic freedom must have appealed to Cahun, as well as his interest in the artifice of dress and the construction of identity through flamboyant display. The dandy's cult of self, his creative narcissism, underlies Wilde's preoccupation with his *toilette* as it informs his art. Cahun's biographer, François Leperlier, argues for her affinities with Wilde:

> Sa propre ambivalence psychologique, alimentée par un narcissisme déclaré qui orientera l'oeuvre dans le sens d'une célébration du double (le miroir, le masque) d'une apologie de l'artifice, sa recherche de la singularité, son allergie aux moeurs établies, etc. . . . [V]oilà qui témoignent d'affinités profondes avec l'auteur du *Portrait de Dorian Gray*.[36]

In a number of early photographic self-portraits, Cahun presents herself as a dandy. One of the most striking images shows her, head shaved in the style of Baudelaire, sporting a dark jacket and velvet pants (fig. 6.3).[37] Her white cravat and jaunty pocket handkerchief call attention to her face, which features a commanding stare. Her attitude—eyes focused directly at the camera/viewer, one hand on her hip, the other in a fist at her side—suggests an aloof and perhaps combative person. In another self-portrait, this one a stark profile with close-cropped hair and dark corduroy jacket, Cahun's full lips and chin recall Wilde himself.[38]

During World War II Cahun anonymously distributed reproductions of Wilde with Alfred Douglas, which she incorporated into anti-Nazi photomontages intended as resistance propaganda. Her goal was certainly to irritate and probably implicitly to indict the Nazis through the proliferation of reminders of a persecuted "decadent" artist. By selecting the photo of Wilde with Douglas, however, she seems to be covertly allying herself with Wilde in a secret act of defiance. Douglas was Wilde's lover and, as the translator of *Salomé* into English, his collaborator. Cahun's lover and collaborator in art as well as resistance activities was Suzanne Malherbe, who also used the name Marcel Moore. Among their joint projects was a Cahun text containing illustrations by Moore that are greatly indebted to the style of Aubrey Beardsley's famous illustrations for Douglas's translation of *Salomé*.[39]

For Cahun, the figure of the dandy provided both an aesthetic and stylistic model for her writing, as well as her self-presentation. The tra-

*Fig. 6.3.* Claude Cahun, *Self-Portrait*, ca. 1921. Collection of Richard and Ronay Menschel. Photograph by Ellen Labenski. Reproduced by permission.

dition of the dandy was one in which she was thoroughly immersed; however, it required a particular kind of self-reflexivity and self-consciousness for Cahun as a female subject. The dandy's suggestion of an androgynous persona—typically a male character with "feminine" aesthetic sensibilities—was a legacy of the Symbolists that Cahun could look to as a gender-blending model. But the literary elaboration of the dandy, while it privileged traits stereotypically associated with female sensibility, was at the same time deeply misogynistic. Baudelaire's articulation is perhaps the best known but certainly not the only example.[40] His espousal of artifice against the evils of the natural includes his paean to feminine disguise in the section "In Praise of Cosmetics" in "The Painter of Modern Life," yet he continually describes woman herself as a debased creature, "a kind of idol, stupid perhaps," who is socially obligated to display her artificially elaborated charms.[41]

Baudelaire's description of the dandy as "an I with the insatiable appetite for the 'non-I'" could serve as an epigraph for the questions about identity that Cahun insistently addresses in both her literary and her artistic production.[42] For Cahun, as a woman-loving woman, the *je/autre* distinction is uniquely inflected. The dandy is a subject that represents an oscillation between gender positions, rather than a fixed status. This placement outside the dichotomous distinctions of unalloyed masculine versus feminine is the aspect of the androgyne, and the dandy as a category of androgynous subject, that draws Cahun.[43] Yet for her, both the subject and the object of desire can be a female figure; both herself and a (female) other. In a provocative involution, she is a woman (thus according to Baudelaire, she has greatest access to the artifice of physical self-transformation), yet the identity that she wears most comfortably—that appears to be most transparent, most "natural"—is that of a presumably male dandy.[44]

By referring to Cahun as female, or a lesbian, or as a woman who dresses like a man, I do not wish to reinstate fixed identity positions; in fact, the study of Cahun's work and life constantly renders such classifications meaningless. Rather, I hope to indicate something of Cahun's struggle within and against these labels. Similarly, the theoretical notions of masquerade, or the dandy, offer rhetorical devices with which to understand and position her work, while dragging along with them a certain amount of problematic baggage. The masquerade implies that there is some hidden essence of femininity behind the mask, or else nothing at all (femininity itself is a masquerade).[45] In its most thorough articulations, the dandy is conceived as a superior male subject who skims off the best feminine character traits while leaving the dregs of femininity behind for the abject female. Clearly we have yet to create a structure within which to adequately describe, much less understand, gender. Yet work like Cahun's, in its specifically queer take on the cult of the self, reimagines the legacy of the nineteenth century while it exemplifies the twentieth.

## NOTES

Portions of this essay have appeared in modified form in J. Blessing, "Resisting Determination: An Introduction to the Work of Claude Cahun, Surrealist Artist and Writer," *Found Object* 1 (fall 1992): 68–78. I am grateful to Mark Luttrell and Virginia Zabriskie at Zabriskie Gallery, New York, who graciously provided information on current owners of photographs, and Helen Kornblum, who promptly provided a photograph of a Cahun in her collection.

1. For example, the biographical notes stating that Cahun was killed in a Nazi death camp. See Edouard Jaguer, *Les Mystères de la chambre noire: Le Surréalisme et la photographie* (Paris: Flammarion, 1982), 108; and Rosalind Krauss and Jane Livingston, *L'Amour fou: Photography and Surrealism* (New York: Abbeville Press, 1985), 205.

2. Her full name was Lucy Schwob. Other pseudonyms included Claude Courlis and Daniel Douglas. For Cahun's biography, see François Leperlier, *Claude Cahun: L'Écart et la métamorphose* (Paris: Jean-Michel Place, 1992).

3. Hal Foster, "L'Amour faux," *Art in America* 74 (January 1986): 118. The exhibition appeared at the Corcoran Gallery of Art.

4. See Therese Lichtenstein, "A Mutable Mirror: Claude Cahun," *Artforum* 30 (April 1992): 64–67; Honor Lasalle and Abigail Solomon-Godeau, "Surrealist Confession: Claude Cahun's Photomontages," *Afterimage* 19 (March 1992): 10–13; Blessing, "Resisting Determination," 68–78; Laurie J. Monahan, "Claude Cahuns radikale Transformationen," *Texte zur Kunst* 3 (September 1993), reprinted as "Radical Transformations: Claude Cahun and the Masquerade of Womanliness," in *Inside the Visible*, ed. M. Catherine de Zegher (Cambridge: MIT Press, 1996), 125–33; David Bate, "The Mise en Scène of Desire," in *Mise en Scène: Claude Cahun, Tacita Dean, Virginia Nimarkoh* (London: Institute of Contemporary Arts, 1994), 5–15; Élisabeth Lebovici, "I Am in Training Don't Kiss Me," in *Claude Cahun photographe* (exhibition catalogue) (Paris: Jean-Michel Place, 1995), 17–23; and Katy Kline, "In or out of the Picture: Claude Cahun and Cindy Sherman," in *Mirror Images: Women, Surrealism, and Self-Representation*, ed. Whitney Chadwick (Cambridge: MIT Press, 1998), 66–81.

5. The most comprehensive source for reproductions of Cahun's photographic work is the "Werkzeichnis" section of the exhibition catalogue *Claude Cahun: Bilder*, eds. Heike Ander and Dirk Snauwaert (Munich: Schirmer/ Mosel 1997), 113–39.

6. Leperlier, *Claude Cahun*, 87–103, has documented Cahun's involvement

with two theatrical troupes in the 1920s, demonstrating that in a number of self-portraits the artist is posed in the costume of specific productions in which she played a part. This information establishes that the theatricality of Cahun's work is literal as well as structural and ideological. It does not diminish Cahun's role in the creation of her self-portraits since she was certainly instrumental in selecting the parts she played (both male and female), and her self-portrait photographs pre- and postdate her theatrical experiences. Furthermore, she incorporated her theatrical personae into her photomontages, thus indicating their centrality to her conception (as opposed to that of the playwright or director, for example). Her involvement with the theater seems more a logical extension of her interests than a point of initiation.

7. Annette Kuhn, *The Power of the Image: Essays on Representation and Sexuality* (London: Routledge and Kegan Paul, 1985), 52.

8. Ibid., 49.

9. This sexual modulation is charted in *Orlando* by documentary-style photographs, including a masquerading Vita Sackville-West, to whom the book is dedicated. Woolf outlines her conception of nonunitary identity when she writes (about Orlando), "For she had a great variety of selves to call upon, far more than we have been able to find room for, since a biography is considered complete if it merely accounts for six or seven selves, whereas a person may well have as many thousand." Virginia Woolf, *Orlando* (1928; New York: Harcourt Brace Jovanovich, 1973), 309.

10. For a review of this debate, see Juliet Mitchell, Introduction to *Feminine Sexuality: Jacques Lacan and the École Freudienne,* by Jacques Lacan, ed. Juliet Mitchell and Jacqueline Rose, trans. Jacqueline Rose (New York: Norton, 1982), 1–26.

11. Joan Riviere, "Womanliness as a Masquerade," *International Journal of Psychoanalysis* 10 (1929), reprinted in *Formations of Fantasy*, ed. Victor Burgin, James Donald, and Cora Kaplan (London: Routledge, 1986), 35–44; see also Stephen Heath, "Joan Riviere and the Masquerade," in the same volume, 45–61.

12. Riviere, "Womanliness as Masquerade," 38.

13. Claire Johnston, "Femininity and the Masquerade: Anne of the Indies," in *Jacques Tourneur*, ed. Claire Johnston and Paul Willemen (Edinburgh: Edinburgh Film Festival, 1975), 36–44. The first applications to film of Riviere's theory (via Lacan) appeared in Michèle Montrelay, "Recherches sur la féminité," *Critique* 26 (1970), revised version reprinted as "Inquiry into Femininity," in *French Feminist Thought: A Reader*, ed. Toril Moi (Oxford: Blackwell, 1987), 227–49; and *"Morocco* de Josef von Sternberg," *Cahiers du Cinéma*, no. 225 (November–December 1970), reprinted as *"Morocco,"* in *Sternberg*, ed. Peter Baxter (London: BFI, 1980), 81–94.

14. Mary Ann Doane, "Film and the Masquerade: Theorising the Female

Spectator," *Screen* 23 (September–October 1982), reprinted in *Femmes Fatales: Feminism, Film Theory, Psychoanalysis* (New York: Routledge, 1991).

15. Lise Deharme, *Le Coeur de pic* (Paris: José Corti, 1937).

16. Georges Bataille, "Le Langage des fleurs," *Documents* 3 (June 1929), reprinted in *Visions of Excess*, ed. Allan Stoekl (Minneapolis: University of Minnesota Press, 1985), 10–14. Freud outlined a dream he called "The Language of Flowers" in *The Interpretation of Dreams*, trans. and ed. James Strachey (New York: Avon, 1965), 350, 354, 360, 382–84, with which Bataille was undoubtedly familiar. Bataille notes, in "The Language of Flowers," "the value given to pointed or hollowed-out objects is fairly well-known" (11).

17. Bataille, "The Language of Flowers," 11.

18. Ibid., 12.

19. "Here the executioner takes on the airs of victim. But you know what to believe. claude." Unless otherwise indicated, all translations are mine, with the occasional kind assistance of Lysa Hochroth.

20. Doane, "Film and the Masquerade," 32. Doane writes, "The masquerade's resistance to patriarchal positioning would therefore lie in its denial of the production of femininity as closeness, as presence-to-itself, as, precisely, imagistic" (25).

21. See Claude Cahun, *Les Paris sont ouverts* (Paris: José Corti, 1934).

22. "Beneath this mask another mask. I will never be done lifting off all these faces."

23. "I try in vain to restore my body to its place (my body with its dependencies), to see myself in the third person. The 'I' is in me like the 'e' captured in the 'o.'" Claude Cahun, *Aveux non avenus* (Paris: Editions du Carrefour, 1930), 236.

24 Judith Butler, "Imitation and Gender Insubordination," in *Inside/Out: Lesbian Theories, Gay Theories*, ed. Diana Fuss (New York: Routledge, 1991), 14. Butler writes, "There is no question that gays and lesbians are threatened by the violence of public erasure, but the decision to counter that violence must be careful not to reinstall another in its place" (19).

25. See ibid., 14, where Butler notes the personal pleasure derived from this instability.

26. Ibid., 21.

27. Ibid.

28. Charles Baudelaire, "Le Peintre de la vie moderne," *Le Figaro* (November 26, 28, and December 3, 1863), reprinted as "The Painter of Modern Life," in *The Painter of Modern Life and Other Essays*, trans. and ed. Jonathan Mayne (London: Phaidon Press, 1964), 1–40.

29. Ibid., 27 (in the section entitled "The Dandy").

30. Jessica R. Feldman, *Gender on the Divide: The Dandy in Modernist Literature* (Ithaca: Cornell University Press, 1993), 3.

31. George Isaac Schwob, her paternal grandfather, went to school with Gustave Flaubert, knew Théophile Gautier, and published in a journal with Baudelaire, among others; her paternal grandmother's brother, Léon Cahun, was an essayist, novelist, and "ami des symbolistes"; her uncle Marcel Schwob was an influential Symbolist critic and translator of English literature. See Leperlier, *Claude Cahun*, 21–25.

32. Feldman, *Gender on the Divide*, 22.

33. Charles Baudelaire, "*L'Héautontimorouménos*," from *Les Fleurs du mal* (1861), in *The Flowers of Evil*, trans. James McGowan (Oxford: Oxford University Press, 1998), 156–57: "I am the wound, and rapier! / I am the cheek, I am the slap! / I am the limbs, I am the rack, / The prisoner, the torturer!"

34. Claude Cahun, "La 'Salomé' d'Oscar Wilde: Le Procès Billing et les 47 000 pervertis du livre noir," *Mercure de France*, no. 481 (July 1, 1918), as cited in Leperlier, *Claude Cahun*, 34–35, 293. Maud Allan, the star of *Salomé*, sued the journalist Noel Pemberton Billing, who had claimed she was included in a German prince's "Black Book of 47,000" supposed British perverts. See also Kline, "In or Out of the Picture," 81 n. 3.

35. Oscar Wilde, preface to *The Picture of Dorian Gray* (1891), in *The Portable Oscar Wilde*, rev. ed., ed. Richard Aldington and Stanley Weintraub (New York: Viking Penguin, 1981), 138. Note also that Marcel Schwob was Wilde's friend and translator and that, according to Leperlier, *Claude Cahun*, 25, Cahun intended to translate Wilde.

36. "Her own psychological ambivalence, fed by a declared narcissism that would orient the work in the sense of a celebration of the double (the mirror, the mask) of an apology of artifice, her quest for singularity, her allergy to established morals, etc. . . . All this is evidence of deep affinities with the author of *The Picture of Dorian Gray*." Leperlier, *Claude Cahun*, 35.

37. There are at least three variants of this image, which is dated circa 1921 by Leperlier. See *Claude Cahun photographe*, 138–39.

38. Leperlier, *Claude Cahun*, makes several brief references to the dandy aspects of Cahun's work. Perhaps the most suggestive comment is the following: "Il y a chez Claude Cahun une révolte jamais apaisée contre tout *donné*—la race, le sexe, l'anatomie, la famille, le nom—dont l'illégitimité ne cessera de crier tréfonds de son histoire. Tout en préfigurant certaines données de *l'art corporel*, elle semble précipiter la formule du dandysme (de Baudelaire à Oscar Wilde) en identifiant la poétique du corps à une sorte de 'théâtre intime de la cruauté'" (109).

39. Claude Cahun, *Vues et visions* (Paris: Georges Crès et Cie, 1919), as cited by Leperlier, *Claude Cahun*, 26–27, who includes two reproductions of Moore's designs. Note also that the story of Salome recurs in Cahun's writings (for example, in *Aveux non avenus* and among her essays on "Héroïnes"). For a provocative discussion of the place of the Salome story in French letters and

Wilde's work, see Charles Bernheimer, "Fetishism and Decadence: Salome's Severed Heads," in *Fetishism as Cultural Discourse*, ed. Emily Apter and William Pietz (Ithaca: Cornell University Press, 1993), 62–83. Bernheimer's discussion of the ambiguous sexuality depicted in Beardsley's illustrations serves to illuminate Cahun's and Moore's interest.

40. Feldman, *Gender on the Divide*, thoroughly explores this paradox, especially in her chapters devoted to the nineteenth-century French writers Jules-Amédée Barbey d'Aurevilly, Théophile Gautier, and Baudelaire (chaps. 2–4).

41. Baudelaire, "The Painter of Modern Life," 31–34, 30.

42. Ibid., 9. In this passage, Baudelaire is describing the ostensible subject of the essay, "Monsieur G." (the artist Constantin Guys), as a dandy and flaneur.

43. Interest in the androgyne overlaps with the Symbolist preoccupation with Narcissus. In fact, Cahun writes about Narcissus in the second chapter of *Aveux non avenus*, entitled "Moi-même (self-love)." The chapter begins, "Moi-même / (faute de mieux) / La sirène succombe à sa propre voix" (25). For discussions of Narcissus in Cahun's work, see Leperlier, *Claude Cahun*, 123 ff.; and Jennifer Shaw, "Cahun's *Narcissus*" (paper presented at the College Art Association conference, Los Angeles, February 11, 1999).

44. It should be noted that Cahun's forays into masculine masquerade also drew upon a legacy of female artists and writers who dressed as men (and often used male pseudonyms) in order to be taken more seriously professionally, and that lesbians in interwar Paris came out in elegant dandy attire.

45. For just one example of a rethinking of the theory of masquerade, see Mary Anne Doane, "Masquerade Reconsidered: Further Thoughts on the Female Spectator," *Discourse* 11, no. 1 (1988–89), reprinted in *Femmes Fatales*, 33–43.

BIBLIOGRAPHY

Bataille, Georges. "Le Langage des fleurs." *Documents* 3 (June 1929). Reprinted in *Visions of Excess*, edited by Allan Stoekl, 10–14. Minneapolis: University of Minnesota Press, 1985.

Bate, David. "The Mise en Scène of Desire." In *Mise en Scène: Claude Cahun, Tacita Dean, Virginia Nimarkoh*. London: Institute of Contemporary Arts, 1994.

Baudelaire, Charles. "L'Héautontimorouménos," from *Les Fleurs du mal* (1861). In *The Flowers of Evil*, translated by James McGowan, 156–57. Oxford: Oxford University Press, 1998.

———. "The Painter of Modern Life." In *The Painter of Modern Life and Other Essays*, edited and translated by Jonathan Mayne, 1–40. London: Phaidon Press, 1964.

Bernheimer, Charles. "Fetishism and Decadence: Salome's Severed Heads." In *Fetishism as Cultural Discourse*, edited by Emily Apter and William Pietz, 62–83. Ithaca: Cornell University Press, 1993.

Blessing, J. "Resisting Determination: An Introduction to the Work of Claude Cahun, Surrealist Artist and Writer." *Found Object* 1 (fall 1992): 68–78.

Butler, Judith. "Imitation and Gender Insubordination." In *Inside/Out: Lesbian Theories, Gay Theories*, edited by Diana Fuss. New York: Routledge, 1991.

Cahun, Claude. *Aveux non avenus*. Paris. Editions du Carrefour, 1930.

———. *Claude Cahun: Bilder*, edited by Heike Ander and Dirk Snauwaert. Munich: Schirmer/Mosel, 1997.

———. *Vues et visions*. Paris: Georges Crès et Cie, 1919.

Deharme, Lise. *Le Coeur de pic*. Paris: José Corti, 1937.

Doane, Mary Ann. "Film and the Masquerade: Theorising the Female Spectator." In *Femmes Fatales: Feminism, Film Theory, Psychoanalysis*. New York: Routledge, 1991.

Feldman, Jessica. *Gender on the Divide: The Dandy in Modernist Literature*. Ithaca: Cornell University Press, 1993.

Foster, Hal. "L'amour faux." *Art in America* 74 (January 1986): 118.

Freud, Sigmund. "The Language of Flowers." In *The Interpretation of Dreams*, edited and translated by James Strachey, 350, 354, 360, 382–84. New York: Avon, 1965.

Heath, Stephen. "Joan Riviere and the Masquerade." In *Formations of Fantasy*, edited by Victor Burgin, James Donald, and Cora Kaplan, 45–61. London: Routledge, 1986.

Jaguer, Edouard. Les Mystères de la chambre noire: Le Surréalisme et la photographie. Paris: Flammarion, 1982.

Johnston, Claire. "Femininity and the Masquerade: Anne of the Indies." In *Jacques Tourneur*, edited by Claire Johnston and Paul Willemen, 36–44. Edinburgh: Edinburgh Film Festival, 1975.

Kline, Katy. "In or out of the Picture: Claude Cahun and Cindy Sherman." In *Mirror Images: Women, Surrealism, and Self-Representation*, edited by Whitney Chadwick, 66–81. Cambridge: MIT Press, 1998.

Krauss, Rosalind, and Jane Livingston. L'Amour fou: Photography and Surrealism. New York: Abbeyville, 1985.

Kuhn, Annette. *The Power of the Image: Essays on Representation and Sexuality*. London: Routledge and Kegan Paul, 1985.

Lacan, Jacques. *Feminine Sexuality: Jacques Lacan and the École Freudienne*. Edited by Juliet Mitchell and Jacqueline Rose and translated by Jacqueline Rose. New York: Norton and Pantheon, 1985.

Lasalle, Honor, and Abigail Solomon-Godeau. "Surrealist Confession: Claude Cahun's Photomontages." *Afterimage* 19 (March 1992): 10–13.

Lebovici, Elizabeth. "I Am in Training Don't Kiss Me." In *Claude Cahun photographe*. Exhibition catalogue. Paris: Jean-Michel Place, 1995, 17–23.

Leperlier, Francois. *Claude Cahun: L'Ecart et la métamorphose*. Paris: Jean-Michel Place, 1992.

Lichtenstein, Therese. "A Mutable Mirror: Claude Cahun." *Artforum* 30 (April 1992): 64–67.

Mitchell, Juliet. Introduction to *Feminine Sexuality: Jacques Lacan and the Ecole Freudienne*, by Jacques Lacan, edited by Juliet Mitchell and Jacqueline Rose, translated by Jacqueline Rose, 1–26. New York: Norton, 1982.

Monahan, Laurie J. "Claude Cahuns radikale Transformationen." *Texte zur Kunst* 3 (September 1993): 101–9.

Montrelay, Michèle. "Inquiry into Femininity." In *French Feminist Thought: A Reader*, edited by Toril Moi, 227–49. Oxford: Blackwell, 1987.

"*Morocco* de Joseph von Sternberg." In *Cahiers du Cinéma*, no. 225 (November–December 1970). Reprinted as "*Morocco*" in *Sternberg*, edited by Peter Baxter, 81–94. London: BFI, 1980.

Riviere, Joan. "Womanliness as a Masquerade." *International Journal of Psychoanalysis* 10 (1929). Reprinted in *Formations of Fantasy*, edited by Victor Burgin, James Donald, and Cora Kaplan, 35–44. London: Routledge, 1986.

Shaw, Jennifer. "Cahun's *Narcissus*." Paper presented at the College Art Association conference, Los Angeles, February 11, 1999.

Wilde, Oscar. *The Picture of Dorian Gray*. 1891. Reprinted in *The Portable Oscar Wilde*. Rev. ed. Edited by Richard Aldington and Stanley Weintraub. New York: Viking Penguin, 1981.

Woolf, Virginia. *Orlando: A Biography*. 1928. Reprint, New York: Harcourt Brace Jovanovich, 1973.

## Chapter 7

# Cross-Dressing at the Crossroads
## *Mimic and Ambivalence in Yoruba Masked Performance*

### *Kimberly Miller*

In the West African countries of Nigeria and Benin, Gelede is one of the major masking traditions practiced among the Yoruba peoples. Like nearly all masquerades in West Africa, it is a tradition practiced exclusively by men.[1] Gelede, which takes place at the Yoruba marketplace, is a community performance considered to be a form of entertainment. Gelede is a visually stunning and powerful event, which combines the expertise of master carvers, skilled dancers, and powerful drummers, all of whom work together to create a multilayered and intellectually complex spectacle. Women, children, and nonmasked men are the audience. In front of an audience of family, friends, peers, and others, the Gelede maskers represent Yoruba women by focusing on and exaggerating female sexuality. In this community event, Yoruba men make themselves *into* and perform *as* women. Through mimicry and a display of gender ambivalence, the Gelede masquerade *appears* to be a powerful form of gender subversion. In theorizing the Gelede performer as a dandy figure, this essay offers an alternative interpretation of this complex performance. This essay will explore how the figure of the cross-dressed performer serves to reinforce, rather than subvert, divisions of gender and power in Yoruba society. As a display of cross-dressing and exaggerated sexuality, Gelede offers a new way to explore the complex meanings within the cross-dressed, dandy body.

Although women do not participate in Gelede masking, the female body plays a visually prominent role in the performance: Gelede costumes focus specifically on physical representations of women's bodies.

*Fig. 7.1.* Gelede mask called "Iju," symbolizing the woman Iju, whom the first settlers of Imasai, Nigeria, found when they reached there. Photograph by Henry John Drewal and Margaret Thompson Drewal, 1977. Slide no. A1992-028-00026. Henry John and Margaret Thompson Drewal Collection, Eliot Elisofon Photographic Archives, National Museum of African Art. Reproduced by permission.

The maskers wear wooden breastplates, partially covered with provocative transparent veils that are suggestively used to manipulate their movements during a dance.[2] Sometimes, the masker's breasts are left bare, with erect nipples prominently carved or drawn onto the tips (fig. 7.1). In addition, male maskers wear women's clothing (fig. 7.2). In their central text on the subject, *Gelede: Art and Female Power among the Yoruba*, Henry John Drewal and Margaret Thompson Drewal note that the Gelede costumes consist primarily of women's head ties, baby wrappers, and skirts, items of clothing borrowed from Yoruba women.[3] These articles are tied around the bodies of male maskers and layered in such a way that they suggest the female form. They are used to build up and exaggerate female hips and buttocks. Their variety of colors and textures contributes to the elegance and beauty of the entire spectacle. In each of these representations, parts of the female anatomy are visually accentuated and sexualized. The sexual anatomy of the

*Fig. 7.2.* Isale-Eko, Abo Gelede dancing, Isale-Eko, Lagos, Nigeria. Photograph by Margaret Thompson Drewal, 1978. Slide no. A1992-028-00769. Henry John and Margaret Thompson Drewal Collection, Eliot Elisofon Photographic Archives, National Museum of African Art. Reproduced by permission.

female body, breasts, buttocks, and by implication genitalia thus becomes the central means by which the masker defines and illustrates Yoruba women.[4] The multigendered audience understands through these means that the masker has fully *become* a woman. On a material level, the Gelede spectacle accentuates the sexualized anatomy of women.

This emphasis on body parts can be further seen in the word *Gelede* itself. As the Drewals translate it, the center portion of the word "*ele* refers to a woman's private parts."[5] Physical imagery also appears in Gelede song, where the vagina is repeatedly described as a source of power that engenders fear among Yoruba men. It is deemed a private part that "symbolize[s] the secrets that women will never reveal to men."[6] The following verse describes female genitalia as a source of male fear:

> Old bird did not warm herself by the fire.
> Sick bird did not warm herself in the sun.
> Something secret was buried in the mother's house.
> Mother whose vagina causes fear to all
> Mother whose pubic hair bundles up in knots.
> Mother who set a trap, set a trap.[7]

This verse indicates that, as a source of female power, the vagina is feared by men due in part to its hidden nature: the invisibility of female genitalia engenders a fear of the unknown, the unseen. These verses specifically refer to the "secrecy" of female genitalia as a "trap." Drewal quotes a Yoruba male informant who describes a powerful woman as "the one whose vagina we can never approach."[8] The informant understands her power not in political, economic, or intellectual terms, but solely in terms of her sexualized anatomy.

Yet it is not merely a woman's concealed genitalia that bears threatening overtones. Within the beauty and temptation of the female breast lies a potential for destruction too. Adefioye Oyesakin tells us that breasts are what help make "women so attractive and irresistible to men." Despite these attractions, women are a "sort of danger to men and for that reason, in dealing with them, men should be very careful, else, they will be ruined."[9] Physically, breasts contribute to a woman's outer beauty: "The breasts of a woman are her invaluable possessions and not only do these breasts attract men, but also tempt them."[10] Physical attraction is, Oyesakin suggests, something a man should approach with caution, and Oyesakin cites the Ifa Literary Corpus to illustrate these ambivalent attitudes toward female power and the body. The following are two separate examples:

> Handy solid breasts are the pride of a woman . . .
> The nipples of woman's pointed
> Breasts,
> Pinch our (men's) eyes.
>
> Ifa divination was performed for Eledumare.
> Who was about to send women,
> From heaven on to the earth.
> And the devil was planted on their
> chests.[11]

In the first example, the pleasure of looking at the female body is bound to physical pain. In the second, the Yoruba supreme creator warns Yoruba men of the immorality and deviance hidden beneath external female beauty. Both verses describe female sexuality as dangerous.

Yoruba men who perform the Gelede masquerade materialize the female anatomical parts that they deem threatening, presenting their understanding of Yoruba women through an elaborate construction and performance of anatomy. The breasts and buttocks are exaggerated and both in costume and dance, the Gelede spectacle accentuates female sexuality.

The Gelede dance supports the exaggerated sexuality suggested by the costume. While performing, the masker manipulates his costume in a manner that draws attention to this sexuality.[12] He may hold onto the ends of the cloth covering the breasts, manipulating its movement.[13] At times, the specific dance movements of the Gelede masker accentuate the breasts and buttocks, as described by Benedict Ibitokun:

> Her exaggeratedly protruding breasts draw hilarious laughter from youths. Her present positioning has the dramatic function of drawing admiration from the inquisitive crowd who crane their necks to see more of her. . . . Here is a big nippled-mask-dancer whose show of physical force in dancing goes beyond that of the second sex. With relentlessness she dances, piercing the air with quick, brisk thrusts. She dances with all her body . . . with her sensuous breasts standing erect, her buttocks; jutted back provocatively and her arms in full swing. . . . [A]t other times, two arms extend backwards, making the breasts stand out in sharper relief. . . . [T]he breasts shake with all imaginable sensuousness, blending their

own emotional tensions and appeals with those of the drums and of the other participants.[14]

Ibitokun's eyewitness account describes how one Yoruba man experiences Gelede as a member of the audience. The masker celebrates her pronounced breasts and buttocks during the performance, and Ibitokun's gaze, therefore, falls primarily on the sexualized anatomy of this fully "female" performer. For Ibitokun, the female body parts and the way they move effectively transform the masker into a woman. In his text, Ibitokun refers to the masker as "she"; the Yoruba masker transforms himself completely in order to define the essence of the Yoruba woman.

While the bodies and movements of these performers most certainly form a representation of women, there is an undeniable ambivalence present. Unlike most West African masking traditions in which the face of a masker is completely concealed and his identity temporarily suspended, in the Gelede performance we can at times literally see the face and body of the man who wears the costume (fig. 7.3). In most West African masked performances this is virtually unheard of and would be considered shocking, even dangerous, to witness. This phenomenon of the revealed face of the masker is unique to Gelede; a masker's identity is always concealed from his audience in other West African masking traditions.

In addition, masked performance mandates that a masker communicate with his audience through another individual, a mediator, or solely through body language. A masked performer never communicates directly with his spectators. Both of these qualities enforce the authority and spirituality of the masker, yet both are undone in Gelede. In fact, Babatunde Lawal states that the identity of the Gelede masker is not a secret, that the masker can even unmask in public and speak in a natural voice: "Behind any mask is a man."[15] This creates an undeniable ambivalence; while the masker appears at first to be making the female gender through clothing, body parts, and behavior, this construction is destabilized by the appearance of the masker's male face. Not only is the audience aware that there is a male body beneath the mask, they also witness his body in combination with that of the female he so effectively represents. His disguise is intentionally incomplete. This creates a degree of uncertainty: what is happening here? Are these maskers changing sex, or simply changing clothes?[16]

*Fig. 7.3.* Gelede masker, Gelede Egbado Yoruba peoples, Illaro, Nigeria. Photo-graph by Margaret Thompson Drewal, 1977. Slide no. A1992-028-01130. Henry John and Margaret Thompson Drewal Collection, Eliot Elisofon Photographic Archives, National Museum of African Art. Reproduced by permission.

If we read the Gelede figure as a cross-dressed, dandy figure, the multilayered junctions of sex and gender may be retheorized as they are performed. The dandy is a figure of ambivalence. On the surface, he is a figure of subversion. The dandy, like the transvestite that Marjorie Garber describes in her 1992 book, *Vested Interests: Cross-Dressing and Cultural Anxiety*, is one who defines the space of crisis negotiation, and hence of cultural redefinition or transformation.[17] He exists in a space between or beyond that of "male" or "female," for he is at once both and neither. The transvestite/dandy "confounds our sense of identity while at the same time constructing who we are."[18] Explaining him is difficult; defining him is impossible. In Gelede performances, the masker creates a tension between the sex of the performer and the gender of the performance.

He is, therefore, a trickster figure, the Gelede dandy. He confounds our perceptions of what makes a male or a female, our perceptions of sex and gender. He is a "shifter," as described by Susan Fillin-Yeh in her 1995 essay on dandies.[19] The notion is particularly useful in this case, as Gelede performers intentionally create a confusion between sexuality, gender identity, and power. The complexities of these categories are revealed within his figure, for in our confusion over what it is, we are permitted to think beyond the regulatory discourses and images that lead us to accept fixed notions of sex and gender.

The main marketplace, where Gelede occurs, is in itself a place of ambivalence and uncertainty. Often situated at a crossroads, the Yoruba marketplace is the realm of Esu, the Yoruba trickster figure. It is therefore a liminal space, a site of tricks and uncertainty where anything might happen, as Esu governs its activities. In the marketplace deals are made, money is exchanged, crowds of people congregate to socialize and do business. Tempers rise and fall. It is also a space where spirits intermingle with humans.[20] The space where Gelede is performed both underscores and supports the ambivalence of the performance.

In the marketplace, lines between male and female gender roles blur, for in Yorubaland, the marketplace is also the domain of women. It is where women's economic and intellectual powers are realized. It is a public, female space and has historically been so for hundreds of years. Yoruba women's control over trade and economy in the marketplace not only withstood the impact of colonialism, but increased because of it.[21] Moreover, the more recent expansion of a market economy has resulted in increased female economic activity and power.[22] The market is a site of female independence and movement where women's "collective social power is most consciously felt."[23] It is clearly a site of female empowerment.

Within this space, the role of the marketwoman is a crucial part of a Yoruba woman's identity. The Drewals note that outside the marketplace, the Yoruba are a polygamous and patriarchal society where men's and women's roles are more clearly defined: "Although women have economic independence, they have less overt power in their domestic roles."[24] As members of large, polygamous compounds, women have been described as being, at times, strangers in their own homes. Outside the market, many Yoruba women exert less control over their daily lives. The marketplace affords them a certain freedom and mobility. Yoruba women are, therefore, testing the boundaries of their culturally ascribed gender roles while they are at work. Here they exert control over their own bodies and actions. Yoruba men recognize this role: in Gelede and other Yoruba masked performances, one image that illustrates female power is that of the marketwoman at work. It is a recurring image of female power.

Perhaps this is what Gelede's male transvestite maskers are responding to—it is their own way of questioning gender norms and categories. Yoruba women maintain the market, while Yoruba men cross-dress within its borders. I like to call it cross-dressing at the crossroads. Within this space, women take on "masculine" attributes of power, decision making, and control whereas men take on "feminine" bodies.

In contrast to other West African masking traditions, however, the Gelede performer does not try to be completely convincing. Ultimately, the Gelede masker fails to successfully mimic a Yoruba woman. This "failure" on the part of the male masker is intentional. The Gelede performance affords the Yoruba men beneath the masks an acceptable space in which to experiment with their own sexuality. For a time, they publicly get to "be" women. Yet the fear of actually becoming women vanishes as the male faces and bodies appear from beneath the masks. In front of their audience, this display of ambiguity allows the maskers to retain their identities as men. Gelede thus serves as more than a vehicle expressing female power, for it concurrently mimics and stereotypes women, questions the idea of female power, and offers support for phallocentric control.

The Gelede spectacle and the marketplace are therefore both spaces of possibility. They are privileged sites of transgression: of play, change, and uncertainty. Yet while Gelede performances and transvestism seem to express a fluidity of gender perceptions, or even a lack of gender boundaries, the imaging of women by men continues to have ramifications in Yoruba society outside this protective space. In their sexually charged representations, maskers confirm certain sexual expectations or gendered norms beyond the performance. They work to maintain so-called traditional attitudes outside Gelede. The maskers intrude into a powerful female space and make themselves into female "objects" within this realm of female agency. Contesting this agency, this power, the maskers reassert their ultimate power over women and their representations.

Using cross-dressing to invoke gender ambivalence, the Gelede masquerade appears to be a powerful form of subversion. My contention is that Gelede is not subversive but is, ultimately, a complicated means of confirming the male/female binaries that maintain oppressive structures of gendered power. Through the ambivalent representation of gender mimicry and ambivalence, indeed, through the figure of the dandy, the female body is performed and presented in ways that complicate and possibly even support the powers of patriarchy. The Gelede masker is not always the humorous, subversive stereotype that he appears to be. Although Yoruba women are central to the Gelede performance, the men harness the transformative powers of the mask, and the women become spectators of their own womanhood. Beyond the performance, though, the agency of masquerade resides with men, and male maskers ultimately insure their own power as they create, present, and perform ideas about Yoruba womanhood.

### NOTES

Research for this essay was supported by a graduate fellowship at the National Museum of African Art, Smithsonian Institution. I would like to thank my fellowship advisors, Christraud Geary and the late Phillip Ravenhill, for their guidance and support. I also extend great thanks to Henry John Drewal and Margaret Thompson Drewal for allowing me to use their collection of fieldwork photographs, which are held in the Smithsonian's Eliot Elisofon Photographic Archives. These photographs were the inspiration for and now form the visual basis of this essay.

1. There is only one known performance in all of Africa where women perform wearing wooden masks: the Sande masquerade among the Mende peoples in Liberia and Sierra Leone.

2. Henry John Drewal and Margaret Thompson Drewal, *Gelede: Art and Female Power among the Yoruba* (Bloomington: Indiana University Press, 1990), 125.

3. The most extensive work on Gelede has been done by Henry John Drewal and Margaret Thompson Drewal. In their work, the Drewals argue persuasively for the spiritual and social powers of women within the Gelede masked performance. They are among the first scholars of African arts to make gender a focus in their study of masquerade.

4. See Sander Gilman, *Difference and Pathology: Stereotypes of Sexuality, Race, and Madness* (Ithaca: Cornell University Press, 1985). Gilman makes clear the visual connections and ideological implications between representations of female buttocks and genitalia.

5. Drewal and Drewal, *Gelede*, xv.

6. Ibid., 42.

7. Henry John Drewal and Margaret Thompson Drewal, "Gelede Dance of the Western Yoruba," *African Arts* 8, no. 2 (1974): 44.

8. Henry John Drewal, "Gelede Masquerade: Imagery and Motif," *African Arts* 7, no. 4 (1974): 8.

9. Adefioye Oyesakin, "The Image of Women in the Ifa Literary Corpus," *Nigeria Magazine* 141 (1982): 16.

10. Ibid., 17.

11. Ibid..

12. The Gelede dance is best understood in person or on videotape. See Henry John Drewal, *Efe/Gelede Ceremonies among the Westhern Yoruba*, videocassette (Madison: Ashe Works, 1970).

13. Drewal and Drewal, *Gelede*, 125.

14. Benedict Ibitokun, *Dance as Ritual Drama and Entertainment in the Gelede of the Ketu-Yorua Subgroup in West Africa: A Study in Traditional African Feminism* (Ile-Ife: Obafemi Awolowo University Press, 1993), 97.

15. Babatunde Lawal, "New Light on Gelede," *African Arts* 11, no. 2 (1978): 69.

16. Gender ambivalence also exists in the texts that describe Gelede performances. Some texts, like Ibitokun's account cited in note 14, refer to the maskers who represent female characters as "she," For these authors, the maskers actually become women. Other accounts refer to the maskers as "he"; the maskers remain men.

17. Marjorie Garber, *Vested Interests: Cross-Dressing and Cultural Anxiety* (New York: Routledge, 1992), 10.

18. Ibid.

19. Susan Fillin-Yeh, "Dandies, Marginality and Modernism: Georgia O'-Keeffe, Marcel Duchamp and Other Cross-Dressers," *Oxford Art Journal* 18, no. 2 (1995): 36.

20. Drewal and Drewal, *Gelede*, 10.

21. For an extensive study of Yoruba women in the marketplace, a fascinating picture of the economic and social adaptations that Yoruba marketwomen have made in changing Yoruba society, see Niara Sudarkasa, *Where Women Work: A Study of Yoruba Women in the Marketplace and in the Home* (Ann Arbor: University of Michigan Press, 1973).

22. Ibid., 37.

23. Drewal and Drewal, *Gelede*, 10.

24. Ibid., 53.

### BIBLIOGRAPHY

Beier, Ulli. "Gelede Masks." *Odu: A Journal of Yoruba and Related Studies* 6 (June 1958): 5–23.

Cole, Herbert M., ed. Introduction to *I Am Not Myself: The Art of African Masquerade*. Los Angeles: University of California, Museum of Cultural History, 1985.

Drewal, Henry John. "African Art Studies Today." In *African Art Studies: The State of the Discipline*, 29–62. Washington, DC: National Museum of African Art, 1987.

———. *Efe/Gelede Ceremonies among the Western Yoruba*. Videocassette. Produced and directed by Henry John Drewal. 27 min. Ashe Works, Madison, WI, 1970.

———. "Gelede Masquerade: Imagery and Motif." *African Arts* 7, no. 4 (1974): 8–18, 62–63, 95–96.

Drewal, Henry John, and Margaret Thompson Drewal. *Gelede: Art and Female Power among the Yoruba*. Bloomington: Indiana University Press, 1990.

———. "Gelede Dance of the Western Yoruba." *African Arts* 8, no. 2 (1974): 36–45.

Drewal, Margaret Thompson. *Yoruba Ritual: Performers, Play, Agency*. Bloomington: Indiana University Press, 1991.

Fillin-Yeh, Susan. "Dandies, Marginality and Modernism: Georgia O'Keeffe, Marcel Duchamp and Other Cross-Dressers." *Oxford Art Journal* 18, no. 2 (1995): 33–44.

Garber, Marjorie. *Vested Interests: Cross Dressing and Cultural Anxiety*. New York: Routledge, 1992.

Gilman, Sander. *Difference and Pathology: Stereotypes of Sexuality, Race and Madness*. Ithaca: Cornell University Press, 1985.

Ibitokun, Benedict. *Dance as Ritual Drama and Entertainment in the Gelede of the Ketu-Yoruba Subgroup in West Africa: A Study in Traditional African Feminism*. Ile-Ife: Obafemi Awolowo University Press, 1993.

Kasfir, Sidney L. "Introduction: Masquerading as a Cultural System." In *West African Masks and Cultural Systems*, edited by Sidney L. Kasfir. Tervuren: Musée Royal de l'Afrique Centrale, 1988.

Lawal, Babatunde. *The Gelede Spectacle: Art, Gender, and Social Harmony in an African Culture*. Seattle: University of Washington Press, 1996.

———. "New Light on Gelede." *African Arts* 11, no. 2 (1978): 65–70.

Murray, Sarah E. "Dragon Ladies, Draggin' Men: Some Reflections on Gender, Drag and Homosexual Communities." *Public Culture* 6 (1994): 343–63.

Oyesakin, Adefioye. "The Image of Women in the Ifa Literary Corpus." *Nigeria Magazine* 141 (1982): 16–24.

Renne, Elisha. "Wives, Chiefs and Weavers: Gender Relations in Bunu Yoruba Society." Ph.D. diss., New York University, 1990.

Sudarkasa, Niara. *Where Women Work: A Study of Yoruba Women in the Marketplace and in the Home*. Ann Arbor: University of Michigan Press, 1973.

Tester, Keith, ed. *The Flaneur*. New York: Routledge, 1994.

## Chapter 8

# Sartor Africanus

## Richard J. Powell

"Why does the sight of a Negro dressed in European fashion provoke the laugh of the white man" is the question which Bergson asked himself in his study on Laughter. "Because the white man thinks the Negro is disguised," is his answer.
—*La Revue du Monde Noir*, 1932

Ideology and style are the same thing.
—Imamu Amiri Baraka, *In Our Terribleness*, 1970

While conducting archival research, I came across a grainy photograph from a June 1927 issue of the *Chicago Defender* (fig. 8.1). The photograph was of a black man, identified in the caption as "Boisey Johnson of Georgia," in a double-breasted suit, standing in front of a crowd of onlookers on the avenue des Champs-Élysées in Paris, France. He wore a body-hugging jacket, bell-bottom pants, and a short cape around his shoulders (not to mention a head-hugging derby, dangling pocket handkerchief, white gloves, and an ornament-studded walking cane), and I couldn't help but marvel at his bold fashion statement—radical even for the *artistes* of Jazz Age Paris—and nervy sense of self-display and confidence.[1]

After discovering this picture I also found myself reflecting on the above epigraph from *La Revue du Monde Noir*, a Paris-based black literary journal of the early 1930s.[2] The intent of the editors, of course, was to sarcastically present the philosopher Henri Bergson's observation that because blacks were perceived as so fundamentally oppositional to

*Fig. 8.1.* Anonymous, *"Struttin' His Onions,"* photograph from *Chicago Defender*, June 4, 1927. Perkins Library, Duke University, Durham, North Carolina. Reproduced by permission.

whites, the very idea of them wearing European fashions was unfathomable, absurd, and therefore hilarious.[3]

Bergson followed his published statement about "the Negro in disguise" with another observation, all the more salient and relevant to the subject at hand: "It might be said that ceremonies are to the social body what clothing is to the individual body: they owe their seriousness to the fact that they are identified, in our minds, with the serious object with which custom associates them, and when we isolate them in imagination, they forthwith lose their seriousness." Thus Bergson qualifies his previous statement by seeing the "Negro in disguise" not just in imaginative isolation, which he would argue prompts laughter, but in a historical and cultural context, which introduces serious contemplation of the scene.[4]

With Bergson's proviso in mind, what does one make of "Boisey Johnson of Georgia"? Why is he in Paris and so far away from home? What are the differences in this instance between dressing in "European fashion" and "struttin' his onions" (the *Chicago Defender*'s caption for this photograph)? Had the editors at *La Revue du Monde Noir* seen Johnson in person, or this photograph of him? Would they have acknowledged that a late spring sighting of Johnson in full regalia on a busy Parisian avenue at high noon might justifiably cause heads to turn, mouths to cluck, and cameras to flash? Is Mr. Johnson's manner of dress simply about ostentatious self-promotion, or is it about something else?[5]

Admittedly, I can only surmise answers to these questions, but their emergence in a discussion of black male sartorial expressivity underscores the sentiments of the second epigraph, by the renowned poet and playwright Amiri Baraka: an analysis of a particular political, economic, and social class of people includes an analysis of their outwardly expressive, aesthetic selves. In another part of Baraka's text, he further describes this equivalency between ideology and style, but in a slightly different way:

> Our terribleness is our survival as beautiful beings, any where.
> Who can dig that? Any where, even flying through space like we
> all doing, even faced with the iceman, the abominable snowman,
> the beast for whom there is no answer, but change in fire light
> and heat for the world
>
> To be bad is one level
> But to be terrible, is to be
> badder dan nat[6]

Baraka would no doubt concur with the assessment that when the subject matter is male and black, one must marshal a distinct body of historical experiences, political realities, and cultural phenomena in order to explicate that individual's status, condition, and image. As hinted at in the *Chicago Defender* photograph, Boisey Johnson's particular status, condition, and image are informed by a larger racial and social dimension that, in spite of the more conventional definitions of the dandy, provides us with an even greater part of his story.

The racial and social baggage that Boisey Johnson bore as a black dandy includes his exposure to white spectatorship, his personal embodiment of cultural difference, and (to quote Baraka) his aesthetic "terribleness." Johnson's lineage can be traced back a hundred years, to a moment in history when black people (and specifically black men) were being transformed in the popular American imagination. Much has been written about this new racial typecasting, focusing on blackface minstrelsy and its unconscious desire to perform white male working-class anxieties via racist, stereotypic versions of blackness. Less commonly discussed than blackface minstrelsy, however, are the black dandy and real flesh-and-blood, fashionable nineteenth-century black men.[7]

These black men who were called "dandies"—the occasionally dressed-up and highly visible common laborers, domestics, and unskilled workers in the free, urban underclass—became the butt of many a joke in New York, Philadelphia, and other northern cities during the antebellum period in the United States. Although they were constantly referenced and ridiculed by European and American diarists, very little that is meaningful has been said about these men, other than the descriptive sightings and critiques that emphasized their foppish demeanor, a vanity that verged on the narcissistic, and (as Bergson observed many years later) their comic incongruity. These commentaries fueled the imaginations of many a white musician, playwright, illustrator, and satirist, who in turn added this new black character type—variously referred to as "Dandy Jim," "Zip Coon," and "Long Tail Blue"—to an already existing roster of broad, stereotypic characterizations in the American popular theater.[8]

The New York–based lithographer George Endicott employed his creative talents toward visualizing this iconic black male figure in an 1843 sheet music depiction of "Dandy Jim from Carolina," the spectatorial subject of this "popular Negro melody" (fig 8.2). Dressed to the hilt in a tight, body-hugging cutaway coat, tartan morning vest with matching trousers, and ascot with a jewel stickpin, gold chain, and pocket watch, Dandy Jim sticks out his chest, juts out his large derriere, and stands like a proud peacock. Gazing and gesturing at his own

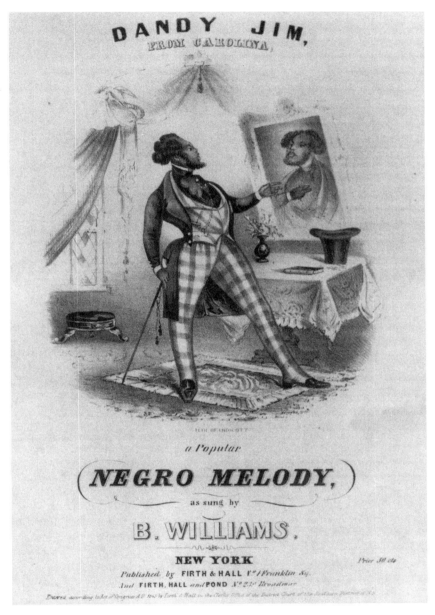

Fig. 8.2. George Endicott, *Dandy Jim from Carolina*, 1843, lithograph. Rare Book, Manuscript, and Special Collections, Perkins Library, Duke University, Durham, North Carolina. Reproduced by permission.

handsome image in an elaborately framed mirror that hangs in an elegantly decorated room, the bearded and wooly-haired Jim strikes a pose that, curiously, is both performative (in terms of its dramatic display) and introspective (in terms of his touching self-absorption).[9]

It was perhaps this encoded duality in Dandy Jim's body (in which elegance is fused with outrageousness, and drama paired with contemplation) that, in tandem with the double entendres in the song's ribald lyrics, created an image of the black dandy that was carnal and irrational, yet also ambitious and corrupt.[10] In a society that sought comfort in clearly defined social roles and a spatially predictable landscape (despite idealistic claims of a broad-based democracy and upward social mobility), the black dandy's striking, audacious appearance on America's street corners disrupted the white majority's false notions of social order, racial homogeneity, and cultural superiority. Dandy Jim's two greatest sins—visibility and indiscretion—can be understood as transgressions only in the context of a society where black people (and specifically black men) had clearly demarcated positions and identities and posed a challenge to the American body politic when they failed to conform to white expectations.

Coinciding with the flurry of visual, musical, and literary depictions of the black dandy during the antebellum period were black men who not only dressed the part, but also spoke out vehemently against slavery, racial violence, and all forms of black disenfranchisement. Based in U.S. cities like Boston, Albany, New York, and Philadelphia (and in foreign cities like London and Edinburgh), many of these black dandies traveled far and wide to preach about America's ills, and thus made their spectatorial flagrance and impropriety a broadly based offense against the white American cultural mainstream. Through their words and their presence, black activist dandies like the novelist William Wells Brown, the artist Robert Douglass Jr., the elocutionist William Craft, and of course the legendary orator Frederick Douglass made an indelible mark on the abolitionist lecture circuit. Standing before audiences at public antislavery events, filled with the emotional fire and fervor of advocates representing a people maligned and unfairly treated, these black men dressed in what would have been considered "white men's clothing"—a formal suit, vest, dress shirt, and cravat—and thus challenged their audiences even before uttering a word.[11]

Of the black activist dandies of the antebellum period, Frederick Douglass was probably the best known and most widely portrayed by

*Fig. 8.3.* Samuel J. Miller, *Frederick Douglass*, 1847–52, cased half-plate daguerreotype, 14 × 10.6 cm. The Art Institute of Chicago, Major Acquisitions Centennial Endowment, 1996.433. Photograph © 1999 by the Art Institute of Chicago. All rights reserved. Reproduced by permission.

painters, graphic artists, and photographers. Looking at a daguerreotype of Douglass by the Akron, Ohio, photographer Samuel J. Miller (circa 1847–52), one can perhaps understand just how striking a figure he was for audiences (fig. 8.3). A man of imposing height (over six feet), strong, masculine features, and wavy, mane-like black hair, Douglass often wore (as seen in this daguerreotype) the most elegant suits, vests, and neckties. His impressive attire, combined with his handsome features, deep, rousing voice, and dramatic delivery, converted the susceptible and startled the unassuming. The famous nineteenth-century spiritualist Margaret Fox wrote to a friend after an encounter with Douglass that "Frederick is as fine looking as Ever . . . I think he is the finest looking gentleman I have seen since I have been in Cincinnati." Fox's added observation that beholding Douglass "would set the people *Crazy*" illustrates the almost hypnotic power that he and other black dandies had over observers: a perceptual potency that combined race, gender, and culture in its dominion over social expectations and stratification.[12]

Just at the time that "Dandy Jim from Carolina" and Frederick Douglass were being critiqued in American cultural circles, several European artists and intellectuals also made note of this distinct social type, frequently writing about these dapper, postrevolutionary figures and their fashionable accoutrements, manners, and airs. The objects of both literary fascination and social scorn in the nineteenth century, dandies nonetheless functioned as pivotal figures in modern Europe, serving as exemplars of a cultural alternative to mainstream bourgeois society and its fawning adherence to republican values, old and new. Unlike a predictable, categorical citizen of the emerging European nation-state, the dandy was ideologically anachronistic as well as socially anarchistic, dressing and acting the part of a latter-day aristocrat, a willful outcast from the conventional lives and appearances of most European men, and a human work of art.[13]

Is it surprising, then, that alongside detailed descriptions of such legendary European dandies as Beau Brummell, Eugene Delacroix, and Paul Garvarni, one is hard pressed to find *any* references at all to black dandies? Bergson observed that the mere suggestion of "a Negro dressed in European fashion" was so antithetical to Eurocentric logic that the only place for such a concept was in the realm of the hilarious and absurd. In contrast, European authors like Jules Lemaître magnified and deified European men who personified this particular cultural icon:

> From an ensemble of insignificant and useless practices he fashions a craft which bears his personal stamp, and which appeals and seduces in the manner of a work of art. He confers on minute signs of costume, bearing and language, a meaning and a power they do not naturally possess. *In short, he makes us believe in what does not exist.*[14]

While one was more likely to read such metaphorical descriptions about dandies in the writings of Lemaître, Honoré de Balzac, and Charles Baudelaire, references to black dandies were more likely to be found in either a satirical or diaristic American context, and they were almost always couched in negative terms.

For example, Thomas Worth, an illustrator of the highly popular and unabashedly racist *Darktown* cartoon series for the important New York City–based lithographers Currier and Ives, inadvertently mentions a black dandy in one of his reminiscences:

> One day I had been in and sold him [Mr. Ives] a couple of sketches. On leaving . . . we met a big crowd about the front window, looking and laughing at the "Darktown" picture. There was one well dressed darky who took exception to the Darktown part of the show and he was expressing himself very forcibly. He said "he would just like to once get hold of the fellow who drawed dem 'scanlous' pictures of de poor colored man." The quick-witted Ives took in the situation. He said to the coon he would give him an introduction to the artist "who drawed dem pictures." . . . The man who boxed the goods was a tremendous big Dutchman, a perfect Hercules. Ives explained the situation to him, and presented him to the complaining coon who took one look at him, sneaked off and vanished . . . in a hurry, without getting hold of the man who "drawed dem pictures."[15]

Recounted to further ridicule African Americans and to justify his visual assaults on them in his *Darktown* series, Thomas Worth's narrative situates his "well dressed darky" in the public (read: white/urban) sphere, making him a spectacle *both* in front of Currier and Ives's picture gallery *and* via his "reenactments" of Worth's drawings, in Currier and Ives's display window. Even more revealing, Worth's narrative places the "well dressed darky" in an adversarial position vis-à-vis the white status quo and, similarly, in opposition to the bigger, more classically proportioned white "Dutchman." The fact that this "complaining coon" is well dressed is, in all likelihood, Worth's encoded way of categorizing him as a dandy, which, in this instance, affirms his disruptive, audacious presence in a white world, in addition to the less threatening attribute of being ludicrous.

What these and the other early references to the black dandy suggest is that, unlike the artistic reflections and poetic musings directed toward his European counterpart, there is little in the pre–civil rights era

American imagination that celebrates black male sartorial expressivity. Rather, what guides the critiques in the United States is not only an imaginative, isolation-engendering call to laughter, but a racially motivated fear of black male agency and, by inference, black enfranchisement. While in the late nineteenth and early twentieth centuries the European dandy was largely tolerated (and in some instances even lionized) for his sartorial and behavioral excesses, during this same period in many parts of the United States African American men who had the audacity to "dress up" and "strut their onions" were publicly ridiculed, sometimes attacked on the streets, and frequently lynched. For black men *and* women well into the middle of the twentieth century, the accusation of "not knowing your place" referred not only to transgressed spatial demarcations based on race, but violations of the perceptual restrictions on a black person's appearance in the presence of whites. In the context of American racism the black dandy has the potential to be metaphorically dressed in an even bolder array of social and cultural signifiers: a wardrobe that speaks of modernity, freedom, oppositionality, and power.[16]

These overtures to a personal strength and self-determination, manifested through a highly expressive, collective, and undeniable cultural presence in the world, were only possible for black dandies like Boisey Johnson in cities like Paris, New York, and Chicago: metropolises that, by the third decade of the twentieth century, were magnets for black men and women who envisioned themselves far differently and more provocatively than the white status quo perceived them. In Richard Wright's posthumously published first novel of the 1930s, *Lawd Today* (1963), he vividly describes the sartorial workings of one Depression-era dandy, Jake Jackson, as he readies himself for the streets on Chicago's southside:

> And because he was wearing the green suit, he decided on low-cut, brown suede shoes with high Cuban heels and toes that tapered to a point. He tied the shoestrings in a neat, tight bow. Spotlessly white spats capped the bargain. Next, he put on a soft-collared lavender shirt which contrasted pleasingly with his broad, red, elastic suspenders. Then he tried a black tie, a green tie, a brown tie, and a red tie. In the end he selected a wide yellow one studded with tiny blue halfmoons. He added a delicate finishing touch by inserting a huge imitation ruby that burned like a smear of fresh blood. Squaring his shoulders, he buttoned coat and vest and adjusted with sensitive fingers the purple embroidered orange

handkerchief that peeped out of his breast pocket. He sprayed each of his coat lapels with violet-scented perfume, then pivoted on his heels in the middle of the rug and brought himself to a sudden halt in front of the dresser mirror.

"Like a Maltese kitten," he said.[17]

Jake Jackson, like "Dandy Jim of Carolina," ponders and measures his artistic creation in the mirror and, after surveying the beautiful apparition, comments on it as if he were entirely detached from his own marvelous creation. This unabashed narcissism, borne out of necessity due to centuries of degradation and lives spent powerless, lifted many black men from the depths of invisibility to the exhilarating heights of personhood.[18]

Where there had once been self-hatred (and a closet full of muddy brogans, denim overalls, and hand-me-downs), the migration to cities where wider opportunities existed brought many African American men a greater self-confidence and, for the first time in their lives, the ability to reimagine themselves. Elegance and unruffability, paired with originality and autogeny, were the trademarks of countless black men who, because of their new cosmopolitan settings and, sometimes, their involvement in show business, could readily act on their desires to dandify. Boisey Johnson's fashion metamorphosis in Paris, simply unimaginable in his native Georgia, would be repeated time and time again by other migrants-turned-performing-artists. With broader vistas, fresher attitudes, and more fully realized talents, "hayseeds" like John Birks Gillespie, Richard Penniman, and James Marshall Hendrix would transform themselves into Dizzy Gillespie, Little Richard, and Jimi Hendrix, three of the most famed black dandies and performing artists of the twentieth century. Their aesthetic stance (like that of Wright's Jake Jackson) emphasized not only a sartorial inventiveness that pushed into the realm of the extreme, but graceful, choreographed physical bearings and, simultaneously, a steadfast control on one's emotions. Whether it was the sight of a beret- and goatee-sporting bopper on New York's Fifty-second Street, a zoot suit- and pompadour-clad rock 'n' roller in a Cleveland stage show, or an Afro-coifed and tie-dye-wearing electric guitarist at the Monterey Pop Festival, the final visual effects captured the imaginations of countless people in the Western world at midcentury and, consequently, put the heretofore neglected black dandy on the public's "radar screen," so to speak.[19]

It was this new visibility for black men during and just after the 1960s that catapulted them into an even broader spectatorial arena than previously experienced. Although black men in this period of expanded visibility and advances in civil rights essentially dressed in the same apparel that was available to white men, they often wore those clothes with a difference. That difference (in the long-standing tradition of the dandy) often had to do with being a master of "l'art de plaire en déplaisant," which in English roughly translates into "the art of seduction through transgression." The African American television news anchor and cultural critic Bryant Gumbel (himself a contemporary fashion plate for more conservative men's styles) more or less arrived at this same conclusion: "part of the reason why I think our clothes historically tend to be ahead of the curve is because there was always this desire, this need, to be recognized. We were so invisible to [the] majority [of] Americans for so long that, once we earned the option to choose, we adorned ourselves in a way that would force others to take notice."[20]

Black male cultural icons of the 1960s and 1970s (like the radical spokesperson Eldridge Cleaver, the entertainer James Brown, and the boxing great Muhammad Ali) often bedazzled people with their fascinating mix of political rhetoric, performative genius, and seductive physicality, buttressed with stylish fashion statements. Starting in the late 1960s, these and other black artists, athletes, and activists were joined by the ordinary man on the street in what seemed like a freewheeling and impromptu black urban fashion show. Late 1960s and early 1970s men's clothing—uncharacteristically fanciful, frequently countercultural, and *prêt-à-porter*—transformed these former "invisible men" into flesh and blood *and* leather-, dashiki-, and polyesterwearing embodiments of that era's resounding racial mantra: *black is beautiful*. During this same era of the sexual revolution and an altered life *after* the major civil rights crusades of yesteryear, many black men sartorially conveyed modern yet idiosyncratic interpretations of the classic dandy.[21]

In his book *Men of Color: Fashion, History, Fundamentals* (1998), Lloyd Boston describes this shift in the fashion sensibilities of African American men in the 1970s, linking it (in a breathless, offhanded, yet vivid manner) to examples in the entertainment industry, radical politics, and that era's changing definitions of traditional gendered identities:

The "slap-me-five-on-the-black-hand-side," gangster-leanin', jive-talkin', fist-picked seventies brought Black male attitude to international attention through soul music hits, political luminaries, and Blaxploitation films. Brothers bounced to William DeVaughn's seventies anthem "Be Thankful for What You've Got." Face-forward politicians such as Stokely Carmichael and Huey P. Newton spoke to the people. *Black Caesar* (1973) and *Black Belt Jones* (1974) brought Black male icons to the silver screen. The ideas, stances, and styles of such groups as the Black Panthers trickled down to the 'hood, turning those who were once our neighbors into our "brothers and sisters." Whether decked out in high-shined two-toned, Stacey Adams lace-up oxfords, stacked patch-work-leather platform boots, or maxi-length fur coats, supporters of the "player chic" aesthetic populated the streets.[22]

As suggested by Boston, cultural changes in black communities inaugurated changes in self-imaging for men: transformations that, curiously, brought into critical consciousness a 1970s version of the classic dandy. For Lemaître, Baudelaire, and others in late-nineteenth-century France, the dandy's aesthetic embraced striking, modish appearances that contributed to the social art of captivation. For the fashion historian Boston, the African American dandy's aesthetic also centered on an attitudinal flamboyance and brilliance that, as with Second Empire France or Victorian England, also had seduction and transgression as twin goals. Of course, what distinguished this latter moment of dandification was that by the 1970s, black nationalism, economic collapse, shifting sexual politics, and a growing dependency on illegal drugs hurled many black men into an identity tailspin, resulting in the adoption of "baaddd" styles or a "cool" demeanor that in turn provided these men with a debonair, resistant "cover" that (to paraphrase Amiri Baraka) served as an instrument for "their survival."[23]

Although not generally perceived as a late-twentieth-century talisman, the outrageous and often derided "player chic" aesthetic of the 1970s frequently functioned as much more than mere fashion foppery and excess. These clothes—voluminous, colorful, theatrical, and often complementary to their dark-skinned African American wearers—formed an aesthetic mantle and psychological shield around these men, protecting them from the cultural mainstream's imposed visual standards, while also providing them with an avenue of self-expression and creativity traditionally reserved for others, specifically women and

artists *proper.* While the term "player chic" privileges the flamboyant
fashion statements of pimps, street hustlers, and other disreputable
members of an African American demimonde, this same style of
dress—turtleneck sweaters, platform shoes, body-hugging jumpsuits,
wide-lapeled jackets in bold patterns and/or solid colors, leather pants
and maxicoats, and fur trimmings (real and artificial)—was worn by a
broad spectrum of black men in the 1970s, most of whom were not
connected at all with any illegal activities. However, the sense of illicit-
ness (and misogyny) in the term "player chic," and in the clothing that
it describes, perhaps accentuates the vicarious feelings of provocation
and transgression that many black men may have indeed felt who
donned these clothes and, in turn, assumed this outlaw persona.[24]

Playing on (and with) all of these narratives and metanarratives of
race, fashion, sexuality, and gender identity is the painter Barkley L.
Hendricks, a product of the Pennsylvania Academy of the Fine Arts
and Yale University School of Art. Making his mainstream museum
debut in the controversial Whitney Museum of American Art exhibition *Contemporary Black Artists in America* (1971), Hendricks has
long been fascinated by the idea of the black dandy and the notion of a
documentable and distinct black diasporic attitude, regardless of one's
specific cultural context, manner of dress, or sexual identity. A conflu-
ence of all of these theoretical interests was in evidence from that first
Whitney exhibition, when Hendricks's painting *Brown Sugar Vine*
(1970) was shown. This backgroundless, frontally posed portrait of a
tawny-complexioned black man—completely naked except for dark
sunglasses and a pompon-topped knitted ski-cap—fit with neither the
abstract works in the show nor the other figurative works, which were
either politically charged or tradition-bound but certainly not as pro-
fane as *Brown Sugar Vine.* Hendricks's preoccupation with an alluring
yet outrageous black male subject puts him at the core of any discussion about the black dandy and, by association, discussions about
shifting identities for African American men in the modern and contemporary periods.[25]

In another more recent but also controversial exhibition at the Whitney Museum of American Art, Hendricks's paintings of black men
again provided the exhibition's focal point and critical apex. Writing
about *Black Male: Representations of Masculinity in Contemporary
American Art* (1994) for the *New Yorker,* the reviewer and art critic
Adam Gopnik astutely noted that in Hendricks's three "very fine realist

portraits" *(George Jules Taylor, North Philly Niggah,* and *Tuff Tony)*, he placed the figures "against a white background, so that the soulful individual seems to be measuring himself against a conventional image." Gopnik's careful choice of words and argumentation, which juxtapose Hendricks's representations of an interior black male self with more accessible, orthodox constructions, illustrate a perceptive understanding of how Hendricks's painted subjects come alive for audiences and engage us with questions of identities, public and private. In these and other paintings by Hendricks (almost all with human figures placed against non-illusionistic, perspectiveless backgrounds), his black men seem introspective, looking within themselves and yet also pondering the voyeuristic assessments of their bodies, talents, and minds from the society-at-large and beyond, including us, as viewers.[26]

In Hendricks's oil and acrylic painting *Sir Charles, Alias Willie Harris* (1972), he continues to pursue these "interior/exterior" portrayals of black men, as well as representing with documentary precision the "player chic" aesthetic in African American men's fashions of the 1970s (fig. 8.4). The black male subject in this painting appears against Hendricks's typical stark white background but, atypically, multiplied and in three different positions: in full profile facing left; with his back turned toward viewers and facing left; and in quarter profile facing right. In each of these three aspects, the goateed, "Afro" hairstyle–wearing subject is dressed in a calf-length, bright red overcoat, a white turtleneck sweater (which disappears into the background), a black suit (with slightly flared trouser legs), and two-toned (white and tan), wing-tipped oxford shoes. The clothes, the poses, and the facial expressions all convey a masculine elegance and self-possession that recall the cool attitudes of 1970s-era professional male fashion models (and their nonprofessional counterparts).

The subtle repetitions of the subject's head, arms, legs, shoes, and coattail energize the composition. Indeed, the uninterrupted red coloring and fabric-like undulations that start at the shoulders of each figure and continue down to the hems of their coats stress the conceptual singularity of this tripartite image and (when viewed as a dark, contrasting silhouette against the white background) emphasize its ornamental, ogee-like formations.

While most art historians immediately would draw a conceptual link between Hendricks's *Sir Charles, Alias Willie Harris* and the Baroque master Anthony Van Dyck's well-known painting *Charles I in Three*

*Fig. 8.4.* Barkley L. Hendricks, *Sir Charles, Alias Willie Harris,* 1972, oil and acrylic on linen canvas, 84 1/8 × 72 in. National Gallery of Art, gift of the William C. Whitney Foundation. © 1999 by the Board of Trustees, National Gallery of Art, Washington, D.C. Reproduced by permission.

*Positions* (1635–36), Hendricks himself recounts a different, more complex lineage than just his encounters with portraits of royalty in European museums. Admitting that the roots for this painting's *other* important subject—the red coat—are in response to middle-class African American prohibitions against wearing the color red (which, historically, is regarded as conspicuous, uncouth, and thus a mark of belonging to the lower classes), Hendricks nonetheless states that his human subject was derived from a more pedestrian source. According to Hendricks, "Sir Charles" was a small-time New Haven, Connecticut, drug trafficker, who would frequently disappear with the hard-earned money of naive Yale University students, in a manner similar to the infamous yet physically absent character Willy Harris in Lorraine Hansberry's award-winning play *A Raisin in the Sun* (1959). Hence, the dual identities that are referenced in the title *Sir Charles, Alias Willie Harris* are, in sequential order, the nickname and the *nom de guerre* of the subject under discussion.[27]

Agreeing to pose for Hendricks on several of those rare occasions when he actually was present and accounted for, "Sir Charles" was, indeed, a black dandy and urban aristocrat who ruled over a minuscule corner of the pre–oil embargo U.S. market economy. Sir Charles's red coat not only signified his regal status in New Haven's "university of the streets"—the mostly black, inner-city community that borders Yale University near Dixwell Avenue—but signaled his refusal to aesthetically acquiesce to a black conservative *and* Ivy League standard of dress. Part hustler and wholly self-invented, Sir Charles morphs into a multiplicity of selves under Hendricks's eye, each one not quite sufficient unto itself to explicate the enigma of this handsome, chic, and elusive black man but, when seen as whole, evoking a simultaneity and choreographed action that evoke early-twentieth-century futurism. But Hendricks's ode is to a subversive future that is decidedly postmodern and black, with the omnipresent and yet evasive Sir Charles flickering in front of one's minimalist white vision like John Shaft, Sweet Sweetback, Superfly, and other assorted fictional black dandies from 1970s Blaxploitation films.[28]

Despite the centrality of the red coat (and fashion in general) in *Sir Charles, Alias Willie Harris,* clothes *alone* do not "make the man," nor do they create the painting's moods of masculine potentiality and self-possession. Rather, it is Sir Charles's attitude, as communicated in his facial expressions, bodily gestures, and physical carriage, that carry him and our fascination with him to a more exalted stage. In a manner similar to his brother "Dandy Jim from Carolina," Sir Charles exudes (thanks to Hendricks's multiple views) an inward-looking, contemplative side, a totally self-absorbed persona, as well as an aspect that acknowledges and indeed confronts us ever so slightly. With one hand tucked partially (and pretentiously) in his suit pocket and the other snugly set in the pocket of his red overcoat, Hendricks presents a rather ambiguous picture of Sir Charles: part effeminate fop, part macho idler. But the central figure's discernibly broad back, shoulders, and wide, open-legged stance seem to soft-pedal his more feminine side and, instead, push forward a tougher, more masculine personality, one that aligns itself with that period's preoccupation with what the cultural critic bell hooks calls a "phallocentric black masculinity." Yet one might also argue that, in spite of these willful overtures toward a kind of "masculine masquerade," it is Hendricks's greater reliance on an *ambiguous* black male identity in much of his work (as seen in *Sir Charles, Alias Willie Harris,* as well as in his nudes and other paintings that incorporate a complex, many-sided attitude for his subjects) that opposes a singular, social construction of black masculinity and thus makes these figures truly interesting.[29]

Of course, the appeal for many African American viewers in images like *Sir Charles, Alias Willie Harris* resided in its "realness" and in Hendricks's mastery of a painterly illusionism. When in 1972 it was still a novelty to see black people artistically depicted with any measure of truth—perceptual or conceptual—Hendricks's paintings filled a wide, cavernous void in artistic representations of blacks. Unarticulated in this African American–centered attraction to these paintings, however, was Hendricks's successful rendering of things *felt* when in the presence of a Sir Charles, but things *unspoken* and even, at times, *unspeakable.* For many viewers there was pure, unabashed pride in Sir Charles's confidence, his ability to put himself out there with such a bold, visual outburst. For others there was envy for his unrestrained self-imaging and social daring in the eye of an overly critical, hostile public. Still, for many others there was desire for Sir Charles, and knowing all too well that such an attraction was déclassé, forbidden, or just plain crazy. A major part of this appeal for a Sir Charles or, for that matter, for a Dandy Jim from Carolina, a Frederick Douglass, a Jake Jackson, and for the black dandy in general was their defiant, unapologetic existence outside social conventions, and their fervent (and perhaps mad) belief in a religion of stylish self-expression and, yes, the *self-as-art.* These were no doubt the unspoken feelings that compelled the Harlem Renaissance–era editors at the *Chicago Defender* to publish Boisey Johnson's photograph, and the same feelings that have intermittently drawn museum curators and art critics since the late 1960s to Barkley Hendricks's expansive portrait gallery of black dandies.

"Why not?" was Hendricks's response to someone who once questioned his fascination with these subjects and the significance of their respective styles of dress. "Rembrandt did it and so did Rubens and Van Dyke. I like it when the wrapper is interesting."[30]

Hendricks's comments can perhaps be elaborated on to suggest that not *only* does the wrapper make what is inside "interesting," but that which is inside the wrapper makes the whole affair compelling as well. Boisey Johnson does more than merely "strut his onions" on Paris's avenue des Champs-Élysées, he transforms himself and the world around him into a different place, where black people—and black men in particular—can no longer be reduced to fixed, immovable images of poverty, danger, and negativity. Whether just in the mind and imagination of the French philosopher Henri Bergson, or represented on the walls of the Whitney Museum of American Art, the black dandy inserts an aesthetic virus into the industrial age machines and technological age computers of European American standards of beauty and art, with his sartorial permutations, idiosyncratic attitudes, and, most important, his absolute humanity. As evidenced in countless representations of these "terrible . . . beautiful beings," the clothes do more than signify the aristocratic status of their wearers: they underscore the essentialness of art in life, as well as form a protective wall against white racism and its uncanny ability to render people of color invisible. The black dandy transforms and problematizes an unalloyed, one-dimensional definition of black masculinity via his sartorial splendor, his fastidious attention to ornament and detail, and his expansion of the parameters of desire across and within the traditional boundaries of gender and sexuality.

Finally, as both Amiri Baraka and Barkley L. Hendricks might agree, the black dandy is a cultural project that, in the face of the economic divide between an affluent minority and a poverty-stricken majority in the United States, begs for contemporary social analyses. The black dandy's cultural *absence* in the 1990s speaks to a kind of co-option of black male sartorial expressivity, as evidenced in the growth of such corporate fashion merchandising giants as Tommy Hilfiger, Karl Kani, and FUBU, who reappropriate innovative street styles and then target their marketing strategies of this apparel to young consumers, many of whom are black, Latino, and living below the poverty line. These changing economic tides, along with the proliferation in the media of sartorially imaginative, black male venture capitalists—from athletes like Dennis Rodman to entertainment moguls like Sean "Puffy" Combs—ultimately answer Baraka's rhetorical question in 1970: "Is it about Economics? Yesssssssssss definitely, my man." All of this suggests that, unlike the visual and conceptual assaults that a Boisey Johnson or a Sir Charles performed years ago, being a provocatively dressed black man *now* may not be as subversive as it once was.[31] Still, the interrogation of this phenomenon suggests that the black dandy's historical presence and aesthetic impact can still illuminate his contemporary absence, today's social scene, and what some may argue is his surviving legacy in this African American culture–saturated era: to understand and deconstruct the manifold examples of a modern and postmodern black style. As the *Chicago Defender* warned its readers in the caption for Boisey Johnson, "Get busy, you sheiks, he's a jump ahead of you."

NOTES

1. "Struttin' His Onions," *Chicago Defender,* 4 June 1927.

2. "Nos enquêtes/Question Corner," *La Revue du Monde Noir* 2 (1932): 60. The next issue of this journal published a series of fascinating replies to a question that followed Bergson's published statement, "How should Negroes living in Europe, dress?" Louis-Th. Achille, "Nos Enquêtes," *La Revue du Monde Noir* 3 (1932): 50–54.

3. Henri Bergson, *Laughter: An Essay on the Meaning of the Comic,* trans. Cloudesley Brereton and Fred Rothwell (1911; reprint, New York: Macmillan, 1928), 40–45.

4. Ibid. I am very grateful to my Duke University colleague Mark Antliff for sharing his insights on Bergson and nineteenth-century European aesthetics with me.

5. Boisey Johnson's spectacular appearance on one of Paris's busiest avenues brings to mind other Jazz Age–era discourses concerning black men and fashion, especially as presented in the writings of various Harlem Renaissance authors. For a somewhat parallel discussion of the pros and cons of European haberdashery, but from the vantage point of an African American connoisseur, see Claude McKay, *Home to Harlem* (1928; reprint, Boston: Northeastern University Press, 1987), 288–89.

6. Imamu Amiri Baraka, *In Our Terribleness (Some Elements and Meaning in Black Style)* (Indianapolis: Bobbs-Merrill, 1970), n.p.

7. An exception to this dearth of critical writing on the black dandy is Eric Lott, "'The Seeming Counterfeit': Early Blackface Acts, the Body, and Social

Consciousness,'" in *Love and Theft: Blackface Minstrelsy and the American Working Class* (New York: Oxford University Press, 1993), 111–35.

8. For published examples of these diaristic critiques of an emerging free black population, see Gary B. Nash, *Forging Freedom: The Formation of Philadelphia's Black Community, 1720–1840* (Cambridge: Harvard University Press, 1988). For a discussion of how whites often viewed free blacks in antebellum America, see Richard J. Powell, "Cinqué: Antislavery Portraiture and Patronage in Jacksonian America," *American Art* 11 (fall 1997): 48–73.

9. "Dandy Jim from Carolina: A Popular Negro Melody, as Sung by B. Williams" (New York: Firth and Hall, 1843). Courtesy of the Rare Book, Manuscript, and Special Collections Library, Duke University, Durham, NC.

10. The following two stanzas from "Dandy Jim from Carolina" illustrate the salacious characterization of this minstrel figure:

> The Niggers knew that she loved pork,
> That is the reason that she did snort;
> She went to hog with a perfect swine,
> For Dandy Jim of Caroline,
>
> Then every little nigger she has had,
> Is the very image of their dad;
> Their heels stick out three feet behind,
> Like Dandy Jim of Caroline.

For a fascinating discussion of the sexual symbolism that operates behind the image of the black dandy in blackface minstrelsy, see Barbara Lewis, "Daddy Blue: The Evolution of the Dark Dandy," in *Inside the Minstrel Mask: Readings in Nineteenth-Century Blackface Minstrelsy*, ed. Annemarie Bean, James V. Hatch, and Brooks McNamara (Hanover: Wesleyan University Press, 1996), 257–72.

11. For a general history of the role of black abolitionists in the American and British antislavery movements, see Benjamin Quarles, *Black Abolitionists* (1969; reprint, New York: Da Capo, 1991).

12. Colin L. Westerbeck, "Frederick Douglass Chooses His Moment," *Museum Studies* 24, *African Americans in Art: Selections from the Art Institute of Chicago* (1999): 144–61. Margaret Fox to Amy Post, undated letter (circa 1851), as quoted in William S. McFeely, *Frederick Douglass* (New York: Norton, 1991), 163.

13. For a critical study of the dandy in Europe during the eighteenth and nineteenth centuries, see Domna C. Stanton, *The Aristocrat as Art* (New York: Columbia University Press, 1980).

14. Jules Lemaître, *Les contemporains: Études et portraits littéraires* (Paris: H. Lecène and H. Oudin, 1895), 4:57.

15. Thomas Worth, as quoted in Harry T. Peters, *Currier and Ives, Print-makers to the American People* (1929; reprint, New York: Arno Press, 1976), 1:80, 82. I am grateful to the art historian Paul A. Roger, who brought this quote to my attention.

16. Blood-curdling accounts of white mobs who ruthlessly lynched black men, women, and children inundate the American public record during the first half of the twentieth century. News stories with captions like "Negro Veteran Lynched for Refusing to Doff Uniform" *(Chicago Defender,* 5 April 1919) prove that being a "black dandy" could be perceived by whites as transgressive and even provoke murder. For a compilation of these atrocities, see Ralph Ginzburg, *100 Years of Lynchings* (1962; reprint, Baltimore: Black Classic Press, 1988), 118.

17. Richard Wright, *Lawd Today* (1963; reprint, Boston: Northeastern University Press, 1986), 27, 28.

18. I explored the concept of a therapeutic and psychologically necessary narcissism in the life and imagery of Frederick Douglass in "Brown Narcissus" (lecture presented at the Art Institute of Chicago, 3 October 1997).

19. Countless books have attempted to link particular African American styles of dress, corporeal attitudes, and vernacular speech with selected moments and genres of African American musical culture. Of the many books that address these concerns, I have found the following to be the most useful and indispensable for me in formulating theories of music-engendered, twentieth-century black styles: Greil Marcus, *Mystery Train: Images of America in Rock 'n' Roll Music* (1975; reprint, New York: Dutton, 1976); Albert Murray, *Stomping the Blues* (New York: McGraw-Hill, 1976); Roy Carr, Brian Cross, and Fred Dellar, *The Hip: Hipsters, Jazz, and the Beat Generation* (London: Faber and Faber, 1986); Martha Bayles, *Hole in Our Soul: The Loss of Beauty and Meaning in American Popular Music* (New York: Free Press, 1994); and Bob Merlis and Davin Seay, *Heart and Soul: A Celebration of Black Music Style in America, 1930–1975* (New York: Stewart, Tabori and Chang, 1997).

20. Bryant Gumbel, as quoted in Lloyd Boston, *Men of Color: Fashion, History, Fundamentals* (New York: Artisan, 1998), 79.

21. For the spirit of the late 1960s and early 1970s (in terms of changing aesthetic standards for African American men), see Nikki Giovanni's poem "Beautiful Black Men (with Compliments and Apologies to All Not Mentioned by Name)" (1968), in *The Norton Anthology of African American Literature*, ed. Henry Louis Gates Jr. and Nellie Y. McKay (New York: Norton, 1997), 1984.

22. Boston, *Men of Color: Fashion, History, Fundamentals,* 90.

23. For a discussion of the various psychological states and protective sociocultural mechanisms that black males embrace in the modern and contem-

porary era, see Richard Majors and Janet Mancini Billson, *Cool Pose: The Dilemmas of Black Manhood in America* (New York: Lexington Books, 1992).

24. The most obvious example in the early 1970s of a broad-based celebration of the "player chic" aesthetic was the commercial success of *Superfly* (1972), a feature-length film directed by Gordon Parks Jr. about a black pimp and drug dealer, and its award-winning musical soundtrack, *Superfly* (Curtom 8014), by the noted rhythm 'n' blues composer Curtis Mayfield.

25. Robert Doty, *Contemporary Black Artists in America* (New York: Whitney Museum of American Art, 1971).

26. Adam Gopnik, "Black Studies," *New Yorker*, 5 December 1994, 135–40. Also see Thelma Golden, *Black Male: Representations of Masculinity in Contemporary American Art* (exhibition catalogue) (New York: Whitney Museum of American Art, 1994).

27. Barkley L. Hendricks, telephone interview with the author, 27 August 1999. For the original reference to the allusive "Willy Harris," see Lorraine Hansberry, *A Raisin in the Sun*, act 2, scene 3, in Gates and McKay, *Norton Anthology of African American Literature*, 1768–78.

28. For an excellent overview of the Blaxploitation era in America cinema (and its reverberations in fashion, music, and other forms of cultural statement during that period and later), see Darius James, *That's Blaxploitation: Roots of the Baadasssss 'Tude (Rated X by an All-Whyte Jury)* (New York: St. Martin's Griffin, 1995).

29. bell hooks, "Reconstructing Black Masculinity," in *The Masculine Masquerade: Masculinity and Representation*, ed. Andrew Perchuk and Helaine Posner (Cambridge: MIT Press, 1995), 69–88. Also see Jennifer Craik, "Fashioning Masculinity: Dressed for Comfort or Style," in *The Face of Fashion: Cultural Studies in Fashion* (London: Routledge, 1995), 176–203.

30. The focus on Hendricks's fascination with pictorial representations of *the real* span his career of over thirty years, as seen in the following two exhibition publications: Mary Schmidt Campbell, *Barkley L. Hendricks* (New York: Studio Museum in Harlem, 1980), and Thelma Golden, "My Brother," in *Black Male: Representations of Masculinity in Contemporary American Art*, 42. For comments by the artist, see Betty Tyler, "Barkley Hendricks: Contrast and Controversy," *Darien News-Review*, 11 February 1993.

31. For a recounting of the commercial successes that numerous contemporary fashion designers have achieved based on "street styles," see Suzanne Ryan, "Street Clothes: FUBU Fashions Get Their Energy from the Queens Homeboy Who Made the Firm into a $4,000,000 Business," *Boston Globe*, 29 January 1998; Sherryl Connelly, "His Highness of Hip-Hop: How White, Middle-Aged Tommy Hilfiger Became the Style Swami to Urban Youth," *Daily News* (New York), 28 June 1998; and "Urban Looks Upscale for Fall," *Women's Wear Daily*, 25 March 1999.

BIBLIOGRAPHY

Achille, Louis-Th. "Nos Enquêtes." *La Revue du Monde Noir* 3 (1932): 50–54.

Baraka, Imamu Amiri. *In Our Terribleness (Some Elements and Meaning in Black Style).* Indianapolis: Bobbs-Merrill, 1970.

Bayles, Martha. *Hole in Our Soul: The Loss of Beauty and Meaning in American Popular Music.* New York: Free Press, 1994.

Bergson, Henri. *Laughter: An Essay on the Meaning of the Comic.* Translated by Cloudesley Brereton and Fred Rothwell. 1911. Reprint. New York: Macmillan, 1928.

Boston, Lloyd. *Men of Color: Fashion, History, Fundamentals.* New York: Artisan, 1998.

Campbell, Mary Schmidt. *Barkley L. Hendricks.* Exhibition catalogue. New York: Studio Museum in Harlem, 1980.

Carr, Robert, Brian Cross, and Fred Dellar. *The Hip: Hipsters, Jazz, and the Beat Generation.* London: Faber and Faber, 1986.

Connelly, Sherryl. "His Highness of Hip-Hop: How White, Middle-Aged Tommy Hilfiger Became the Style Swami to Urban Youth." *New York Daily News,* 28 June 1998.

Craik, Jennifer. "Fashioning Masculinity: Dressed for Comfort or Style." In *The Face of Fashion: Cultural Studies in Fashion,* 176–203. London: Routledge, 1995.

"Dandy Jim from Carolina: A Popular Negro Melody as Sung by B. Williams." New York: Firth and Hall, 1843. Courtesy of the Rare Book, Manuscript and Special Collections Library, Duke University, Durham, NC.

Doty, Robert. *Contemporary Black Artists in America.* New York: Whitney Museum of American Art, 1971.

Ginzburg, Ralph. *100 Years of Lynchings.* 1962. Reprint, Baltimore: Black Classic Press, 1988.

Giovanni, Nikki. "Beautiful Black Men (with Compliments and Apologies to All Not Mentioned by Name)." 1968. In *The Norton Anthology of African American Literature,* edited by Henry Louis Gates Jr. and Nellie Y. McKay, 1984. New York: Norton, 1997.

Golden, Thelma. "My Brother." In *Black Male: Representations of Masculinity in Contemporary American Art.* Exhibition catalogue. New York: Whitney Museum of American Art, 1994.

Gopnik, Adam. "Black Studies." *New Yorker,* 5 December 1994, 135–40.

Hansberry, Lorraine. *A Raisin in the Sun.* In *The Norton Anthology of African American Literature,* edited by Henry Louis Gates Jr. and Nellie Y. McKay, 1768–78. New York: Norton, 1997.

hooks, bell. "Reconstructing Black Masculinity." In *The Masculine Masquer-*

*ade: Masculinity and Representation*, edited by Andrew Perchuk and Helaine Posner, 69–88. Cambridge: MIT Press, 1995.

James, Darius. *That's Blaxploitation: Roots of the Baadasssss 'Tude (Rated X by an All-Whyte Jury)*. New York: St. Martin's Griffin, 1995.

Lemaître, Jules. *Les contemporains: Études et portraits littéraires*. Vol. 4. Paris: H. Lecène and H. Oudin, 1895.

Lewis, Barbara. "Daddy Blue: The Evolution of the Dark Dandy." In *Inside the Minstrel Mask*, edited by Annemarie Bean, James V. Hatch, and Brooks Mc-Namara. Hanover: Wesleyan University Press, 1996.

Lott, Eric. "'The Seeming Counterfeit': Early Blackface Acts, the Body, and Social Consciousness." In *Love and Theft: Blackface Minstrelsy and the American Working Class*. New York: Oxford University Press, 1993.

Majors, Richard, and Janet Mancini Billson. *Cool Pose: The Dilemmas of Black Manhood in America*. New York: Lexington Books, 1992.

Marcus, Greil. *Mystery Train: Images of America in Rock 'n' Roll Music*. 1975. Reprint, New York: Dutton, 1976.

McFeely, William S. *Frederick Douglass*. New York: Norton, 1991.

McKay, Claude. *Home to Harlem*. 1928. Reprint, Boston: Northeastern University Press, 1987.

Merlis, Bob, and Davin Seay. *Heart and Soul: A Celebration of Black Music Style in America, 1930–1975*. New York: Stewart, Tabori and Chang, 1997.

Murray, Albert. *Stomping the Blues*. New York: McGraw-Hill, 1976.

Nash, Gary. *Forging Freedom: The Formation of Philadelphia's Black Community, 1720–1840*. Cambridge: Harvard University Press, 1988.

"Nos enquêtes/Question Corner." *La Revue du Monde Noir* 2 (1932): 60.

Peters, Harry. *Currier and Ives, Printmakers to the American People*. Vol. 1. 1929. Reprint, New York: Arno Press, 1976.

Powell, Richard J. "Brown Narcissus." Lecture presented at the Art Institute of Chicago, 3 October 1997.

———. "Cinqué: Antislavery Portraiture and Patronage in Jacksonian America." *American Art* 11 (fall 1997): 48–73.

Quarles, Benjamin. *Black Abolitionists*. 1969. Reprint, New York: Da Capo, 1991.

Ryan, Suzanne. "Street Clothes: FUBU Fashions Get Their Energy from the Queens Homeboy Who Made the Firm into a $4,000,000 Business." *Boston Globe*, 29 January 1998.

Stanton, Domna. *The Aristocrat as Art*. New York: Columbia University Press, 1980.

"Struttin' His Onions." *Chicago Defender*, 4 June 1927.

Tyler, Betty. "Barkley Hendricks: Contrast and Controversy." *Darien News-Review*, 11 February 1993.

"Urban Looks Upscale for Fall." *Women's Wear Daily*, 25 March 1999.

Westerbeck, Colin. "Frederick Douglass Chooses His Moment." *Museum Studies* 24, *African Americans in Art: Selections from the Art Institute of Chicago* (1999): 144–61.

Wright, Richard. *Lawd Today*. 1963. Reprint, Boston: Northeastern University Press, 1986.

## Chapter 9

# Twiggy and Trotsky
## *Or, What the Soviet Dandy Will Be Wearing This Next Five-Year Plan*

### *Mark Allen Svede*

SCENE ONE: A fashion catwalk festooned with red banners in a cavernous Kremlin-like chamber. A Cossack saws away on a violin as a heavyset woman, wearing a blue-gray burlap shift, *babushka,* and scowl, lumbers down the spotlit runway beneath a huge portrait of Vladimir Lenin.
*Announcer* [a female-impersonator in military drab, reads from clipboard]:
Nyext . . . *Day*-vear. *Veh*-ry nice!
[Applause from stony Politburo and sullen peasantry]

SCENE TWO: Same model in same housedress lumbers down same catwalk, but carries a massive flashlight.
*Announcer: Eve*-ningvear.
[Applause]

SCENE THREE: Same model, same housedress, same catwalk, but she carries a beachball covered with red stars.
*Announcer: Svim*-vear.

Before it was pulled from television broadcast amid charges of poor sportsmanship on the eve of the 1980 Moscow Olympic Games, the voice-over to the infamous "Russian Fashion Show" commercial for the fast-food chain Wendy's noted, "Having no choice is no fun." If dandyism stands for anything, it is choice—not so much in terms of wardrobe options, but more the ability to entertain antithetical propositions simultaneously. In his 1986 manifesto, "Le Dandy," Philippe Sollers declared,

About any topic the dandy can, and must, show that he could hold *all* of the possible discourses. He is simultaneously of the right and the left, nationalistic and antinationalistic, human and inhuman, for the maximum of Good as well as for the maximum of Evil. . . . A dandy of today, for example, can only have been Maoist. He is evidently the papist of our time. He is very traditional and very modern, but he abominates fashion and modernism.[1]

Despite the dandy's political and moral dichotomies, the challenge of describing in our familiar capitalist context what Jessica Feldman calls "dandyism's paradoxical, centerless, mobile truth" is further complicated in the communist realm by common Cold War–era assumptions regarding Soviet culture.[2] For example, the misperception that a dandy is purely the product of clothing is amplified in the supposition that one could have achieved the status of dandy in Soviet society by merely finding an alternative to the shapeless sack that cross-functioned as *dayvear/eveningvear/svimvear*. Yet, when we contemplate Soviet dandyism, perhaps the primary issue remains: How could sartorial self-construction transpire in a modern totalitarian environment where a state-planned economy determined the color, cut, and catechism of virtually every available garment? Of course, such contemplation still requires caveats about making clothes overly determinative of one's dandyism, or about failing to distinguish between Soviet material culture as it existed in the center of the empire and its deviations in peripheral regions, or, indeed, about qualifying a Soviet dandy as Soviet in any sense whatsoever. Such admonitions hardly rescue us from the slippery slope relished by dandies of all periods, places, and persuasions.

On the surface—if dandyism stands for anything, it is surface—dandyism in totalitarian culture would seem logistically impossible. Whether enforced by ideological limitations or industrial exigencies, the policing of sartorial nuance (never mind flamboyance) was routine during the early to middle Soviet era, and it was sometimes absurd. After Lenin's New Economic Program (NEP) of 1921 spawned the "flapper and foxtrotter" craze in Moscow and Petrograd, Bolshevik authorities swiftly condemned these "dandies . . . with bows, with fashionable boots, wearing the latest outfits over dirty underwear . . . dancing 'American' dances and having only one wish—to find 'a good fiancée.'"[3] In a characterization as scathing as any by Thomas Carlyle or other anti-dandiacals of the 1830s, the newspaper *Komsomol'skaia pravda* made an example of a certain (no doubt fictional) Boris Kliuev, worker and Komsomol member by day, dandy by night:

> In the evening after work this *komsomolets* can no longer be considered your colleague. You can't call him Boris, but imitating a nasal French accent you must call him "Bob." If you meet him somewhere in the park "with a well-known lady" . . . and start to talk to him about something related to the factory, he will cautiously glance back at the "madam" and without fail change the conversation.[4]

But with the rescission of the NEP, the dandy—however imperfectly and colloquially this term was applied in the first place—faced extinction.[5] Although visual and consumer culture during Josef Stalin's reign was governed by the sort of vulgar petit bourgeois taste against which dandies have always rebelled, opportunities for rebellion were limited, less by material scarcity than by the general climate of paranoia. Even a cultural monument as unassailably doctrinaire as Vera Mukhina's sculptural ensemble *Worker and Collective Farm Woman* atop the Soviet pavilion at the 1937 World Exposition in Paris, an argument for sober dress and sensible shoes if one ever existed, found itself the target of hostile rumors that the modeling of its drapery concealed the profile of the demonized Leon Trotsky.[6] More subversive, however, and presumably never remarked on by contemporaries, is the fact that the male laborer and the female farmer have identical faces, making their clothing the only mark of their gender.

On the other hand, an atmosphere of hostility and vigilance would not by itself prevent the existence of dandyism, for the phenomenon has always thrived on—indeed, perfected—such dispositions. Its commentators have often remarked on the sadomasochistic bent of the dandy's autonomous, differentiating dress and behavior, and in fact, the eighteenth-century dandies' term for excluding inferior company, *cutting*, names this violence, particularly its sadistic aspect, while the premium they placed on their own youthful beauty, novelty, and insouciance doomed themselves inevitably, masochistically, to obsolesence—that is, if internecine intrigue didn't cut them first. A Soviet dandy's potential to literalize Jean-Paul Sartre's image of the narcissistic dandy as a binary "executioner-victim" was, in the shadow of the gulag, unsurpassable.[7] Certain members of the Stalinist elite endeavored to dress and live exquisitely, but as shown in Ivan Dykhnovichnyi's film *Prorva*

(1992, released in the West as *Moscou Parade*), characters such as the dandiacal NKVD (state security) agents and their associates who believed themselves exempt from the leveling forces of collectivized society often paid a grim price for acquiring, indulging, and even flaunting foreign tastes.

After the demise of Stalinism with its civic ostentation and personal privation, visible means of identity construction continued to face circumscription during the Khrushchev period when the Party sanctioned a renewed functionalism, both as moral aesthetics and industrial pragmatics.[8] Nevertheless, aspects of later Soviet culture might be considered particularly conducive to dandyism, not so surprising since one finds dalliances between dandies and leftism well before Nikita Khrushchev and far afield. Granted, some evidence of this could be deemed circumstantial, but then, if dandyism stands for anything, it is the transcending of circumstances. For example, Sir Oswald Mosley, a British MP of the 1920s known as the "Dandy of the Revolution," reportedly modeled himself on Ferdinand Lassalle, the dandy who rivaled Karl Marx as leader of the German socialist movement.[9] During Mosley's tenure, a number of dandified British writers actively, if fleetingly, engaged with Bolshevism, an episode chronicled by Martin Green in his book *Children of the Sun*. Among Green's anecdotes is the 1937 publication of Cyril Connolly's satire, "Where Engels Fear to Tread," a spoof of Christian de Clavering's autobiography *From Oscar to Stalin*; in Connolly's version, de Clavering abandons his Wildean circle and

> picks up the idea that all writers must now be socialist and proletarian, and . . . changes his name to Cris Clay and starts threatening his literary rivals and potential reviewers . . . with political punishment. "A line is being drawn. . . . Those lines mean something. Tatatat! Yes, my dears, bullets—real bullets, the kind of bullets they keep for reviewers who step across the party line." In the last scene he is depicted going on a protest march through London, rather dismayed at seeing Peter [Quennell] and Robert [Byron] and Evelyn [Waugh] now standing at the window of White's Club with the peers he used to dominate and patronize. But then he finds some foreign nobility in the march with him, so happily begins instructing them in correct proletarian dress and manners.[10]

At roughly this same time in Madrid, the popular Basque writer Pío Baroja published his novella *Un dandy comunista*, whose title character, Adolfo Ruiz Santovenia, is a study of dramatic internal contradictions: meticulous in comportment but afflicted with St. Vitus' dance, self-aggrandizing in anecdote but a self-confessed liar, he is a white-shoed aristocrat who authors an article titled "Be Bolshevik." Prefiguring Sollers's strategic criterion for dandyism—that is, the individual must entertain polarities of morals, taste, and politics—Ruiz Santovenia survives in volatile pre–Civil War Spain precisely because of his dichotomous character, a mutability that later Soviet dandies would also find essential for their survival. "'It is true; sometimes I lie,' he admitted, 'imagination excites me; but there's truth in what I say.'" [11] When Ruiz Santovenia describes himself as an authoritarian anarchist, he is wholly undisturbed by the oxymoron.

Elsewhere in the literary world, and seemingly undisturbed about the grotesque nonchalance of his own observation, the dandiacal Wallace Stevens wrote in a letter dated 1945,

> What is terribly lacking from life today is the well developed individual . . . or the man who by his mere appearance convinces you that a mastery of life is possible. . . . The unfortunate part about [Stalin's contempt for the people] is that in the long run these people will hold him back, and, for my own part, I think they should.[12]

Stevens's prognosis is odd, given that most dandies neither suffer the people nor suffer from the reciprocal contempt. But then, he may have stopped short of considering Stalin a true dandy. Far less debatable is the notion that Stalin possessed what Martin Green once described, apropos of someone else, "all the requirements of a dandy's father—he was tyrannical, obsessive, philistine, crazy, and clever enough to be a good enemy."[13] The identification of Stalin as father figure returns us to that period in Soviet history when a number of dandyism's customary preconditions developed anew.[14]

In his essay "Le Dandy," Baudelaire located dandyism's occasion in an authoritarian culture experiencing decline:

> Dandyism appears especially in the transitory periods when democracy is not yet all-powerful, and when aristocracy is only partially unsettled and depreciated. In the confusion of such periods, some few men who are out of their sphere, disgusted and unoccupied, but are rich in natural force, may conceive the project of founding a new kind of aristocracy. . . . Dandyism is the last splendor of heroism in decadence.[15]

Usually taken to mean the Regency of George IV and the French Restoration, this account could pertain equally to the USSR during the period of destalinization and nominal democratization in the late 1950s and 1960s known as the Thaw.[16] The fact that groups of dandiacal young men suddenly emerged in certain Soviet cities following the repudiation and disappearance of Stalin in official Soviet culture after his death conforms to this pattern, just as it supports Françoise Dolto's theory that a dandy is the product of an absent father, a theory she first articulated at the very moment Soviet citizens were reckoning with their missing patriarch.[17] Dolto's image of the dandy as "solitary adolescent" recalls a connection drawn by Martin Green between dandyism and "the cult of the naïf at the core of thirties Marxism—the image of the sun-bronzed man with his shirt open, bringing the radiant candor of his gaze to bear on the mess the fathers have made of the world"—this, ironically, during the time Stalin, revered in Soviet popular imagination as "Wise Father," "Friend," and "Dear Grandpa," was making the worst mess imaginable of communist ideals.[18] Dolto goes on to describe the dandy as being "reduced to the artificial status of Adam," and indeed, the new breed of dandies in the USSR found themselves wandering a post-Edenic wilderness during the 1950s and 1960s, when it became safe to question the Stalinist slogan of the previous generation, "Life has become better, life has become jollier." Their ability to survive expulsion from utopia—and to do so in the name of fashion—is all the more poignant when one recalls a painting from 1924 by the Hungarian communist activist Sandor Bortnyik titled *The New Adam*.[19] A dandified bourgeois holding a boater and cane, and sporting checkered pants, white bow tie, white gloves, pointy shoes, spats, and a lacy handkerchief that peers from the pocket of a cinched black jacket is rendered by Bortnyik as little more than a mannequin atop a hand-cranked pedestal. The dandy's retardataire artifice stands in stark contrast to his constructivist surroundings: architecture comprised of floating trapezoidal planes and a schematic drawing of an industrial mechanism. The implication here is that the dandy's overpreened subjectivity will be obsolete in a utilitarian future. Yet thirty years hence and a couple of fraternal communist republics to the east, dandyism endured, as fully realized as in Bortnyik's vision of modernity, or perhaps even more so.

Depicted thus, it's understandable that dandies would abhor modernism (striving all the same to set sartorial standards for fellow moderns). On the other hand, because no dandy worth his snuff would settle for playing a sun-bronzed, open-shirted naïf in a socialist realist composition, the Soviet dandy came to inhabit a space opened by discrepancies between conventional representations of *homo sovieticus* and Soviet social reality. Dolto's more recent discussions of dandyism have been equally relevant to this scenario, if unwittingly so. In a 1986 interview she described the dialectics of the icon as conducive to the dandy's relation to the modern world, a world in which giant omnipresent photographic representations effect subject-formation much like mirrors do in Jacques Lacan's theory of the mirror stage of infant development: "this society in which [one is] before pictures of enormous fathers, a manner of infantilizing humans."[20] Dolto's point is unwitting in that she detects this dialectical relationship in any hypermediated society with its colossal faces emblazoned on billboards and movie screens, not specifically in Soviet visual culture where an indigenous Orthodox religious icon tradition segued into a program of monumental propaganda with its Red Square–sized hagiographic representations of Lenin and Stalin. There, lessons in dandiacal self-presentation could not have been made any clearer for aspirants. In marked contrast to winsome propagandistic images of smudge-faced coal miners and sunburnt tractor drivers, Stalin appears impeccably groomed (above and beyond the photo-retouchers' miracle of dermabrasion), immaculately dressed in a luminous yet restrained all-white uniform or car coat, and poised not only decorously but well in advance of any lowly physical exertion and often on a plane above the hoi polloi.

But apart from Leninist-Stalinist hagiography, what role did clothing play in common, lived experience in the USSR? It's little wonder that, surviving in the midst of Soviet material culture, a dandy—in accordance with Sollers's manifesto, but contrary to stereotype—would find fashion an abomination. If, as Baudelaire tells us, dandies react against the homogenizing tendency of democratization and its attendant mediocrity, the USSR would seem to offer unparalleled opportunity for revolt, for it was a land of bureaucratized fashion, which at its most imaginative moments favored gimmicky cut over quality construction and substituted gratuitous mixtures of materials for fabrics of any integrity. In practice, the Soviet analogue of the fashion industry problematized the dandy's relationship to clothing in interesting ways. Elsewhere, this relation had long ceased being problematic (or, some would argue, even definitional). In his 1962 essay "Dandyism and

Fashion," Roland Barthes proposed that fashion, in its late capitalist guises, killed dandyism, a notion worth quoting here at length:

> [F]ashion has exterminated all imagined singularity of garment, in taking charge tyrannically of institutional singularity. It is not the garment itself that is bureaucratized (like, for example, in societies without fashion), but more subtly its project of singularity. Inoculating all contemporary clothing with a little dandyism, fashion killed dandyism itself, since, by essence, it was condemned to be radical or not to be. Therefore it is not general socialization of the world (as one could imagine it in a society of rigorously uniform clothing, like the present Chinese society) that killed dandyism; it is the intervening of an intermediate force, between the absolute individual and the total mass: . . . modern democratic society constituted in fashion a kind of organism of equalization, destined to establish an automatic balance between the requirement of singularity and everyone's right to satisfy it. It's evidently a contradiction in terms: Society only renders viable sartorial innovation of a strictly regular duration, sufficiently slow so that it's possible to submit to it, sufficiently fast in order to precipitate rhythms of purchase and reestablish a distinction of fortunes between men.[21]

In the Soviet Union, the restricted scope of permissible, thus assimilable, stylistic innovations and the inefficiency of commercial mechanisms (which, in the West, undermined the dandiacal goal of *déclassement* by packaging shock effect as *haute couture*) may well have prolonged dandyism's survival *within* the realm of fashion, such as it was. Even something as officially sanctioned as a Soviet fashion show may have facilitated this, for the relationship between couturier runway and communal apartment hallway was utterly nonnegotiable. If a fashion show attendee wanted to disrupt visually based class identities (this being the supreme legacy of dandyism), it required the dandy's age-old project of self-fabrication.[22] In fact, this process of sewing one's own Western-influenced clothing so as not to look like three or four other people standing in the same queue for bread (or, paradoxically, shoes) became known as *samostrok*, a play on the Russian word for self-published literature, *samizdat*.

Granted, *samostrok* issuing from the typical comrade's sewing needle tended to be no more stylistically subversive than an American suburbanite's pantsuit constructed according to some perky Butterick pattern, but in the mid-1950s residents of Moscow, Leningrad, L'viv, Riga, and Tallinn began noting the appearance of small groups of *stiliagi* ("stylish ones"), young flaneurs who congregated in central urban locations, dressed in self-designed, self-made outfits that would have defied most suburbanites' notions of good taste. Routinely derided in the press and by passersby as "peacocks," "parakeets," and "monkeys," the *stiliagi* were undeterred from wearing cropped narrow-legged pants, oversized shoes, long checkered suit coats, wildly patterned wide neckties, and greased curly hair inspired by Tarzan movies.[23] According to a former *stiliaga*, the only substantive deterrent to their provocative form of display was, oddly enough, *cutting*, done in a most literal way by communist youth activists. Formidable bands of Komsomol zealots would stage "'cleansing' raids" in which "the main weapon in the struggle were pairs of scissors—pressing successive stilyagi up against the wall, [where] the guardians of our strict style norms would cut off a healthy lock of hair (so that the victim would have to head immediately for a barbershop) and then from below cut the leg of his narrow trousers (no joke)."[24] But even these attacks were of limited efficacy against the overall phenomenon because the social differentiation of the *stiliagi* was based on more than eccentric fashion. For example, they shared a passion for American jazz, obtainable on the black market in record format and disseminated among their ranks via *Roentgenizdat*, re-recordings dubbed onto used plastic x-rays (known as "ribs"). They also distanced themselves from respectable society by means of a deliberate manner of walking, "with the head thrown back, held high and bouncing around as if we were constantly on the lookout. And there was a reason for the stuck-up nose and the arrogant gaze; we considered ourselves much better informed than everyone else."[25]

"Everyone else" included the young Soviet women, fewer in number, who were equally well informed about Western fashion and music, the so-called *chuvikhi* ("stylish girls," derived from the slang of restaurant musicians). With customary dandiacal self-contradiction, the *stiliaga* considered the cropped-haired, short-skirted, high-heeled *chuvikha* to be of dubious moral character. Therefore he often shunned her company and, projecting the classic dandy's indeterminate sexuality, preferred dancing a modified boogie-woogie in cafés with his male peers. For all of this ostensible moral vigilance, the marginalized, homosocial, exclusionary milieu readily admitted members from one disreputable segment of Soviet society: *zolotaia molodezh* or "golden youth," the cynical children of elite government, military, and academic officials who enjoyed privileged access to luxury goods and information regarding foreign fashion. Like the NKVD agents of Stalin's era, *zolotaia*

*molodezh* were not only well-off but also they believed themselves im-
mune from prosecution. Consequently, this subset of *stiliagi* gained notoriety for their public violence, a trait that tends to classify them less
as dandies than latter-day "grey men," those dandiacal figures from
lower-middle-class London society during the 1850s and 1860s who
fraternized with criminals and other disenfranchised elements to such
an extent that there was little difference between them except for
wardrobe choices.

This intermingling of the "peacocks" and the Party-privileged confirms that if dandyism stands for anything, it is de-classing—putatively
an impossible task in an evolved communist society. The very existence
of the *zolotaia molodezh* demonstrates that class distinctions persisted
nonetheless, and as Albert Camus observed in an essay that considers
dandyism at length, "The spirit of rebellion can exist only in a society
where a theoretical equality conceals great factual inequalities."[26]
While this was intended as an indictment of capitalist democracies, it
applied just as well to the USSR, where, in addition to the pervasive oli-
garchical abuses, Russocentric policies consistently victimized ethnic
minorities in fourteen of the fifteen "fraternal" republics. One small
form of revenge available to residents of the Baltic republics, irrespec-
tive of their status within the union-wide oligarchy, was broader access
to international fashion trends. Estonia's proximity to Finland enabled
reception of Western television broadcasts, and a comparatively higher
proportion of Balts exiled to the West during World War II improved
the chances of their compatriots in Estonia, Latvia, and Lithuania receiving "stylish" family photos and perusing fashion magazines left behind by visiting relatives.[27] Balts, in general, had a reputation in the Soviet Union for being better dressed, and their relatively advanced fashion consciousness may have engendered dandiacal self-awareness and
behavior, specifically of the Brummellian sort, in which one's state of
being well-dressed was successful only insofar as it was effected with
restraint and nonchalance. Even the Latvian *stiliagi* were conspicuously
less flamboyant in behavior and more "tastefully" attired than their
Russian peers, whom they dismissed as being laughably unironic about
the very idea of stylishness in the Soviet Union.[28]

Yet the ability to better effect what Barthes calls the "institutional
singularity" of garments hardly constitutes dandyism. For preeminent
expressions of this sensibility in the USSR, one must turn to the work
of two Latvian artists who resisted not only the pallor of collectivized

society but also bourgeois values held by those émigrés who had transferred a certain material sophistication to their occupied homeland.
Andris Grinbergs and Miervaldis Polis, in distinctly different ways and
at different moments, revived a pre-Soviet presence of dandyism in Latvian culture that had been epitomized by the modernist painter Karlis
Padegs. Throughout the 1930s, Padegs provoked Riga's bourgeoisie
with spectacular yet refined formal dress, as well as pacificistic yet
grotesque paintings such as *Madonna with a Machine Gun*. Like the
fallen *komsomolets* Boris Kliuev, he was just as likely to answer to a
foreign variant of his name (Carl or Charles Padegs) as to the original
Latvian. Padegs died at age twenty-nine at the start of World War II,
and was thus spared the impossible task of sustaining his dandiacal enterprise during Latvia's Nazi and Soviet occupations.

By the late 1960s, Andris Grinbergs assumed Padegs's mantle, although audiences and means of provocation had changed considerably
after decades of sovietization. Formally trained in clothing design,
Grinbergs rebuffed cues from central fashion authorities and found inspiration in smuggled and stolen issues of *Vogue*. The Carnaby Street
look of Mary Quant, Jean Shrimpton, and Twiggy, which James Laver
once identified as "the New Dandyism," infiltrated Riga via a small
but incorrigible hippie community, of which Grinbergs and his wife,
Inta, were key figures.[29] Such acquisition of alterity from abroad is perhaps the most venerable dandiacal act, dating from the francophilia of
Beau Brummell's coterie and the subsequent anglomania of the Parisian
dandies, a practice about which Jessica Feldman observed, "Th[e] international proliferation of dandyism suggests the very displacement
crucial to 'placing' dandyism: it exists in its purest form always at the
periphery of one's vision, often in a foreign language or a text requiring
decipherment."[30] In the Latvian scenario, the international hippie hi-
eroglyphics of Flower Power face-painting were read with great surprise and minimal comprehension by the Soviet masses vacationing at
Riga's seaside resorts on the empire's periphery. Of course, the mentality that authorized their effete self-expression was even less understood, though this mentality could be said to have become increasingly
operant within the public domain of personal grooming, which produced in later Soviet times other startling aesthetic forms, such as bouf-
fant hairdos hennaed various shades of magenta, which dependably
identified its middle-aged wearers as ethnic Russian.

It is Andris Grinbergs's vocation to the cult of self, however, that best

qualifies him as a dandy. His thirty-year career of self-reflexive performance art contended from the outset with a number of dandyism's si-
multaneities, such as dependence on and rejection of audience.[31] The ambivalent motivations underlying either of these attitudes further define his
project as dandiacal: The public is included as the validating witness, yet
mockable standard; the public is rejected as uncomprehending, yet com-
prehending enough to endanger his freedom. Grinbergs revels in such ambivalent positions. Projecting homosexual desire from within the context
of a "happy" marriage and family (essentials of today's dandy, according
to Sollers),[32] his work subverts determinate sexuality less through overt
action than erotic solipsism.[33] Visibly feminized in the manner of most
male hippies (a tendency that scholars have long presented as evidence of
the hippie-dandy alliance),[34] Grinbergs first staged performances during
the early 1970s in which narrative direction and duration were determined by physical pleasure. Afforded and enjoyed by his collaborators—
variously male or female—any pleasure remained incidental to his own.
Although this eroticism has had more of a pan-sexual nature of late, his
performances always resisted any sort of gender-based essentialism by
showcasing his "painstakingly presented body" *as* the embodiment of individual difference.[35]

Furthermore, Grinbergs's individuality appears so different from
performance to performance that it confounds categorical definition.
Indeed, within a single performance, his character often tends to recon-
cile qualities that many would regard as mutually exclusive: conjugal
Christ or playful Baader-Meinhof terrorist or urbanite pagan diety (fig.
9.1). As these three examples suggest, Grinbergs's performance personae are studies in ontological extremity and improbability, either
ethereally of this world or solidly anchored in heaven. Even when his
characters stop short of outright self-deification, Grinbergs purports a
liaison with God so primary that, to borrow the words of Dolto, "His
always chaste heart only wants to manifest itself in his shamelessness.
Scandal is the Veronica's veil he uses as a [pocket] handkerchief."[36]
Such accessorizing—be it wanton or, given the *dayvear/eveningvear/
svimvear* environment, simply resourceful—destabilizes not only Grinbergs's identity but also that of the reflective audience. Whether disrob-
ing during a live, nationally broadcast television interview or directing
and starring in a film that the independent cinema authority Jonas
Mekas has championed as "one of the five most sexually transgressive
films ever made,"[37] Grinbergs creates what the scholar Emilien Caras-

*Fig. 9.1.* Latvian hippie gathering with Andris Grinbergs (white blouse) seated in center. Dome Cathedral, Riga, 30 June 1968. Black and white photograph. Photograph credit by Māra Brašmane. Reproduced by permission.

sus has termed a "complex of nudity," in which the dandy's fully dressed spectator begins wondering, "Am I really clothed? . . . Is my tie a tie, and my clothes really clothes?"[38] Radicalizing Hans Christian Andersen's underdressed emperor (that great catechist of clothing), Grinbergs currently claims the title of "Fashion Emperor," dispenses with the penitence altogether, and writes causeries about menswear for a Riga newspaper. It is a coda to a career that recalls the denouement of the legendary Jules Barbey d'Aurevilly, though Barbey d'Aurevilly would not have dared publish anything like Grinbergs's recent photo-fabrications that suggest that Latvia's presidential cabinet of ministers might look better dressed in Vivienne Westwood or ravewear.[39]

Once a collaborator in Grinbergs's early performance art, Miervaldis Polis brought dandyism into the *fin-de-Soviet* period, but as a prophet of the new cult of the divided self. His performance persona, a postmodern monochrome called the Bronze Man (fig. 9.2), has extended, in a perfunctory sense, the tradition of monochromatic dressing started by the Regency dandies "Blue Hanger" Lord Coleraine and

*Fig. 9.2.* Miervaldis Polis as the Bronze Man, posed in front of a communist slag man, a detail of the sculpture *Soldier-Liberators* at Riga's Victory Monument, 1991. Color photograph by Michael Lange. Reproduced by permission.

"Pea-Green" Hayne, exemplified in the modern age by Baudelaire's so-called "mourning" costume.[40] But insofar as the coloristic effect exceeds the limits of clothing and overtakes Polis's exposed skin, the phenomenon of the Bronze Man also recalls Gilbert and George's *Singing*

*Sculptures* of the late 1960s and 1970s, in which the artists appeared in public as metallicized twins. Since the mid-1980s Polis has furthered the British pair's sustained exercise in doubling when he began single-handedly performing as an ensemble with the help of what he calls his alter ego, a mannequin configured to look more like the human Polis than Polis himself (fig. 9.3). Issues of doubling are complicated further in that Polis has fashioned himself to look like Joseph Beuys in terms of everyday attire and affect. His choice of a Beuysian state of *déshabillé* accomplishes what Carassus terms "the double efficacy of the costume: it proves at the same time idleness and artistic effort."[41] The same could be said for the laborious yet languorous toilette of the dandy, and on this count Polis is paradigmatic in that his toilette (i.e., the punctilious application of gilding) exceeds the limit of his body, extending to his costume.

This tangible manifestation of divided subjectivity is, of course, rife with Lacanian psychoanalytic implications (not the least of these being a dubiously cordial relationship with the Other), a fitting, splitting

*Fig. 9.3.* Miervaldis Polis as the Bronze Man, posed next to his "alter ego" on a Riga street bench, 1992. Color photograph by Atis Ievinš. Reproduced by permission.

tribute to Lacan, who, not only according to Dolto, lived and died a true dandy.[42] His narcissistic bifurcation recalls, as well, Jean-Paul Sartre's words about Baudelaire: "[T]he effort to divide himself in two assumed its most acute form. His aim was to exist for himself as an object, to dress up in all his finery and paint himself in order to be able to take possession of the object, to remain long in contemplation of it and, finally, to melt into it."[43] Painting with a risk of melting is, in fact, fundamental to the Bronze Man, his metallic appearance inspired by the Bolshevik commonplace of coating plaster statues with bronze paint to simulate a more precious, permanent monument. Just as the impermanence of these Bolshevik monuments was inevitably revealed by the changing climate, the vicissitudes of Soviet Latvian history inspired Polis to stage, at various times and in different ways, the undoing of his own epidermal splendor. For example, at one point the Bronze Man peeled the veneer from his face and displayed it like a relic or a death mask. Thus flayed, Polis proceeded to paint hyperrealist images of this indexical sign, and by so painting his face's *un*painting he further replicated not only his likeness but also his notoriety. This unmasking recalls the self-appraisal of another twentieth-century dandy, Claude Cahun, who said, "Under this mask, another mask. I will never finish removing all these faces"; it also recalls Cahun's creative process, which Rosalind Krauss has termed "personhood exfoliating into persona."[44] Polis literalizes this process, and in doing so he implicates his cultural environment to an extent that is simultaneously self-effacing and self-aggrandizing. As Soviet-era art infrastructures crumbled completely, the Bronze Man appeared outside a newly privatized commercial gallery in Riga to be painted gypsum-white by Vilnis Zābers, the artist of the next generation who seemed most likely to inherit Polis's reputation as Latvia's cultural provocateur. As Edward Bulwer's literary dandy Pelham once said, "The political and social system is rotten; but it created me, and I am sublime."[45]

Inasmuch as all this gilding and tarnishing brings to mind the English anti-dandiacals' definition of fashion as a "'false varnish' applied to inferior goods,"[46] we witness Polis playing dandy as well as anti-dandy, perhaps the ultimate simultaneity. The dematerialization effected by applying gold to Polis's blatantly unfashionable clothing partakes in the operations of "base materialism" incumbent in Georges Bataille's concept of the *informe* (or the "formless").[47] The job of the *informe*, per Bataille, is *déclassement*, which we know to be the dandy's mission, and which Barthes tells us is accomplished sartorially by "breaking the garment . . . 'deforming' it . . . subtracting all value."[48] Polis does this as he enacts, in his own ways, the famous fantasy of Barbey d'Aurevilly:

> One day the dandies let their fantastic notions go so far as "threadbare apparel." . . . They had run out of impertinence, they couldn't go on. They found that which was so "dandy" (I know no other word to express it), to tear their clothes before donning it, the entire length of the cloth, until it was nothing more than a kind of lace—a cloud. . . . Here's a true fact of dandyism! The clothing counts for nothing. *It practically no longer exists.*[49]

Several years ago, when Polis took part in an artist-as-couturier project, his submission was, as one might say, formless. A luminous scrim covered the models' bodies from ankles to neck, allowing viewers to project their sartorial fantasies on this disconnective tissue.

It was also Barbey d'Aurevilly whose ruminations about self-portraiture included claims of experiencing himself "as divided, as existing in multiple versions."[50] Polis may be familiar to thousands of Riga residents as the Bronze Man, but he is even better known as a painter, and on canvas he exists in dizzyingly multiple versions. In his *Self-Target* series, painted and then shot with a high-powered rifle, Polis performs the role of Sartre's executioner-victim, but in his own manner. In his series of self-insertions into art historical masterpieces, Polis is the Baudelairean dandy who insinuates himself into an artistic genealogy that provides him company more befitting than that of his contemporaries.[51] Whether sheepishly peering out of Caravaggio's *Deposition* (fig. 9.4) or Raphael's *Sistine Madonna*, transplanting monumental likenesses of his bronzed thumb *à la* César onto images of urban landscapes, or morphing within a triptych from a van Gogh–like self-portrait into an image of himself executed with decreasingly agitated brushwork, Polis simultaneously proves his virtuosity as a painter and denies the painter's agency.[52]

His appropriative paintings corroborate Hal Foster's designation of appropriation art as the dandyism of the 1980s, but with significant qualifications.[53] First, and here one can speak of qualifications quite literally, Polis's technical achievements outstrip those of a Sherrie Levine or Mike Bidlo, who have tended to select the easily imitated for their subjects. Moreover, the art historical erudition manifest in his

*Fig. 9.4.* Miervaldis Polis, *Polis and Caravaggio*, 1996, gouache on offset lithography, 11 × 7.5 in. Collection of the author. Photograph by: Mark Svede. Reproduced by permission.

work is far broader. Yet, with a profoundly modest self-assessment of his painting ability and a profound respect for art historical arcana, Polis could never be described as arrogative. Second, by practicing appropriation art in Soviet society—and not as parodic *sots* artists like

Komar and Melamid—Polis confounds Foster's assumptions about capitalism's centrality in contemporary artistic dandyism. Finally, the nature of his appropriative work defies the increasing tendency toward cynicism that Foster detects in the New York variant of appropriation art during the Reagan era. In fact, Polis's best work is finely balanced between reverence and wit, a tightrope act that, over the years, has increased in both nuance and the importance of what is at stake. A collaged painting of 1997 titled *Papa* incorporates a portrait of John Paul II initially commissioned from Polis by Latvia's postal service, a self-addressed first-day cover bearing the papal stamp, two more of the stamps with the right-hand image overpainted with Polis's self-portrait, some *tromp l'oeil* tape and, again, that shabby gold surface we've come to expect from Bolsheviks and dandies. Polis is evidently the papist of our post-Soviet times, if not a post-Soviet papal contender.

As the components of *Papa* demonstrate, Polis is decreasingly dependent on the art of others to situate his own appropriative work within history. At the same time, it has increasingly become his art to appropriate the job description of others. For example, in keeping with the Restoration dandies' love of sport, Polis assumed the role of boxing impresario in a 1986 work conceived in collaboration with the photographer Atis Ieviņš, titled *The Unprecedented Event, First Time in the World, Boxing Match Between Women in Folk Mittens*. Polis debunked the cherished nationalist illusion of the Latvian people as a potentially homogeneous nation—geographically, psychically, or culturally—by pressing trifling ethnographic difference into service as a symbol of the antagonism between Latvians living in the USSR and those in exile, two camps whose views were often in such a state of occlusion as to make Sollers's bipolar dandy (i.e., the nationalist/antinationalist) an inevitability. The comical fight was refereed by a man who would become, in time, one of the first premiers of the newly independent Latvia, and though Polis could not have predicted this professional promotion, his choice of a career politician to mediate (or exacerbate) an East European ethnic conflict might well be termed clairvoyant.

If dandyism stands for anything, it is the mediating of differences, or, at the very least, transforming difference into a media spectacle. As the Soviet Union disintegrated, the Bronze Man met officially and publicly with Finland's premier Harri Holkeri months before Latvian government officials were able to make such contact, recalling the Brummellian quip

"Tis finer to be 'prime-dandy' than prime-minister." [54] That Polis, in his dandiacal persona, served as some sort of cultural attaché even before Latvia had reestablished its diplomatic corps complicates what Emilien Carassus, in *Le Mythe du dandy*, presents as an either/or situation regarding the dandy's truck with profundity:

> True or false depth, who could say? For he himself to be capable of saying, it would be necessary for him to leave his role of dandy, become an artist, ambassador—in short, "to produce something" in place of "producing himself". The true dandy, the pure dandy doesn't think that there is a good solution. He refuses to be caught by the lure of a monument that [the certain] believe is erected for centuries upon centuries; his patience doesn't devote itself to slowly polishing one of these perishable masterpieces by which artists imagine themselves to last eternally, his ambition doesn't impel him to leave on earth this scar that pretends to inscribe politicians or adventurers of history. [55]

The notion of the dandy as a consciously perishable monument is intriguing, given Barbey d'Aurevilly's assessment of Brummell as "a statuette of a man who did not deserve much more than a statuette" and, moreover, the rapidity with which monuments have risen and fallen in Eastern Europe during this century. [56] Miervaldis Polis, in his oxymoronic role as Soviet dandy, appears to have found a way to have his monument and leave it too.

This is no minor accomplishment in a culture that, in its later years, produced leaders like Leonid Brezhnev, whose overdecorated—*falsely* decorated—public image as a war hero appeared only slightly less moribund than the embalmed body of his venerated predecessor Lenin, entombed in Red Square. Of course, the very fact that the Father of the Revolution himself appeared in public year after year dressed in the same old suit never boded well for Soviet fashion. And like it or not, it always seems to come back to one's state of fashionability. In the end, the height of fashion among certain male inmates in the Soviet penal system was to wear tattoos caricaturing Brezhnev and other sclerotic, poorly dressed leaders whose ideological exertions served to imprison them in the first place. [57] Employing a genre that already confuses mutilation and decoration, the captive body elected to bear the likeness of its enemy as the mark of its own inferior social status. If dandyism stands for anything, it won't stand for this.

NOTES

1. Philippe Sollers, "Le Dandy," in *Splendeurs et misères du dandysme* (Paris: Bouexière and Favardin, 1986), 73–74. All translations from the French and Spanish are mine.

2. Jessica R. Feldman, *Gender on the Divide: The Dandy in Modernist Literature* (Ithaca: Cornell University Press, 1993), 2.

3. Anne E. Gorsuch, "Flappers and Foxtrotters: Soviet Youth in the 'Roaring Twenties,'" *Carl Beck Papers in Russian and East European Studies*, no. 1102 (1994): 11, quoting a 1931 published statement by an unidentified "worried communist."

4. Reprinted in T. Kostrov, "Kul'tura i meshchanstvo," *Revoliutsiia i kul'tura* 3–4 (1927): 27. Intended or not, the critic's example of the English name "Bob" delivered with a French accent is perfectly in keeping with dandyism's early trans-Channel manifestations. Dandyism's dependence on an "alien element" for purposes of differentiation and estrangement is further discussed below.

5. A more accurate term might be "gent," the "second-hand, shop-worn imitation of the dandy" first found in Victorian England. Ellen Moers, *The Dandy: Brummell to Beerbohm* (London: Secker and Warburg, 1960), 215; even "gent," however, belies the proletarian origin of such Soviet "dandies."

6. Matthew Cullerne Bown, *Art under Stalin* (New York: Holmes and Meier, 1991), 130.

7. "From this point of view, dandyism was an episode in a venture in which Baudelaire was continually coming to grief; he was Narcissus trying to mirror himself in his own waters and catch his reflection. Lucidity and dandyism were simply the forms assumed by the couple 'executioner-victim,' in which the executioner tries in vain to detach himself from the victim and to discover his own image in its shattered features." Jean-Paul Sartre, *Baudelaire*, trans. Martin Turnell (London: Horizon, 1949), 130. See also Michel LeMaire, *Le Dandysme de Baudelaire à Mallarmé* (Paris: Klincksieck, 1978), 31–32, in which LeMaire cites Sartre on how society delimits the dandy's efficaciousness as revolutionary and quotes Théophile Gautier on the futility of politics: "What's a revolution? People in a street who fire gunshots that break lots of window panes; there's little besides glaziers who find profit there." T. Gautier, "Préface," *Les Jeunes-France*, xv.

8. See Ol'ga Vainshtein, "Female Fashion, Soviet Style: Bodies of Ideology," in *Russia—Women—Culture*, ed. Helena Goscilo and Beth Holmgren (Bloomington: Indiana University Press, 1996), 70–71; and Victor Buchli, "Khrushchev, Modernism, and the Fight against *Petit-bourgeois* Consciousness in the Soviet Home," and Susan E. Reid, "Destalinization and Taste, 1953–1963," *Journal of Design History* 10, no. 2 (1997): 161–76, 177–201.

9. Martin Burgess Green, *Children of the Sun: A Narrative of "Decadence" in England after 1918* (New York: Basic Books, 1976), 50.

10. Ibid., 293. See Edward Mendelson, *Later Auden* (New York: Farrar, Straus and Giroux, 1999), 268.

11. Pío Baroja, *Un dandy comunista, la Novela Corta*, no. 51 (Madrid: Gráfica Clemares, n.d.), 14.

12. Wallace Stevens to Henry Church, 20 November 1945, quoted in *The Letters of Wallace Stevens*, ed. Holly Stevens (New York: Knopf, 1966), 518.

13. Green, *Children of the* Sun, 224 (describing Sir George Sitwell).

14. Similarly, the revival of dandyism in *la belle époque*, according to James Laver, had underlying causes "not so dissimilar from those operating in the first age of the dandies. An old aristocracy was being replaced by a new plutocracy, and it is in such periods that the dandy has a chance to flourish." Laver, *Dandies* (London: Weidenfeld and Nicolson, 1968), 95.

15. Baudelaire's "The Dandy" was published in 1863 in the essay "The Painter of Modern Life" ("Le Peintre de la vie moderne"), quoted in Laver, *Dandies*, 68.

16. Patrick Waldberg notes dandyism's origin in an England described as "utilitarian," an adjective that also describes the Soviet cultural climate in the wake of Stalin's death. Waldberg, "Dandysme et frivolité," in *Le Mythe du dandy*, ed. Emilien Carassus (Paris: Armand Colin, 1971), 295.

17. Françoise Dolto, "Le Dandysme et l'absence du père," in Carassus, *Le Mythe du dandy*, 308.

18. Green, *Children of the Sun*, 7–8.

19. Bortnyik's work is reproduced in S[tephen] A. Mansbach, *Standing in the Tempest: Painters of the Hungarian Avant-Garde, 1908–1930* (Cambridge: MIT Press, 1991), 76. The New Adam became a trope of revolutionary modernism everywhere, including the USSR, where it was perhaps best exemplified by Dziga Vertov's "perfection" of the human cinematic subject with enhancements afforded by montage.

20. Her statements, made in an interview with Laurent Bouexière and Patrick Favardin, appear in Françoise Dolto, "Figure de proue," in *Splendeurs et misères du dandysme*, 92.

21. Roland Barthes, "Le Dandysme et la mode," in Carassus, *Le Mythe du dandy*, 314–15.

22. This do-it-yourself phenomenon is shown in the documentary *Baltic Chic*, part of the 1984 BBC series *Tovarishchi/Comrades*, reedited and rebroadcast in 1990 on the PBS series *Frontline*. Because these fashion shows were attended by anyone possessing the five-ruble ticket, as opposed to the exclusively patron-and-press Western audiences composed of Blaine Trumps and Anna Wintours, chances improved that a Brummellian transformation

would occur (that is, an anonymous individual of modest attributes becomes a singular phenomenon). Vainshtein, in "Female Fashion, Soviet Style," also notes the impulse to make one's own clothing, and though she maintains that there were enough stylish clothes available for purchase, she acknowledges that the habit was necessitated by the unavailability of *unique* garments. If, as Vainshtein explains, "You could often find two or three women on any trolleybus wearing identical dresses," there was no chance of de-classing oneself in that situation (65).

23. One of the best accounts of this phenomenon comes from former *stiliaga* Alexei Koslov, quoted at length in Artemy Troitsky, *Back in the USSR: The True Story of Rock in Russia* (Boston: Faber and Faber, 1988), 13–15. The phenomenon was eventually romanticized in the novels of Vasilii Pavlovich Aksenov, most notably *Zvezdnyi bilet* (A ticket to the stars), originally published in the journal *Yunost'* (Youth), nos. 6–7 (1961).

24. Troitsky, *Back in the USSR*, 17. Eižens Valpēters, a former Latvian *bitnieks* (beatnik, successor to the *stiliaga*) confirmed, in a February 1998 interview in Riga with the author, that roving bands of Komsomol members had constituted a far greater threat to his circle's hip attire and hair than did state security agents.

25. Troitsky, *Back in the USSR*, 16.

26. Albert Camus, *The Rebel: An Essay on Man in Revolt*, trans. Anthony Bower (New York: Knopf, 1974), 20.

27. The peripheral location of the Baltics in the Soviet empire also enabled greater circulation of publications from the more liberalized Eastern Bloc countries than was possible elsewhere in the USSR. For example, the Polish magazine *Prze-kroj* (The Profile) was very influential in Latvia's underground youth culture of the late 1960s and early 1970s.

28. For a fuller discussion of this "intra-*stiliagi*" condescension, see Mark Allen Svede, "All You Need Is Lovebeads: Latvia's Hippies Undress for Success," in *Style and Socialism: Modernity and Material Culture in Post-War Eastern Europe*, ed. David Crowley and Susan E. Reid (London: Berg, 2000).

29. Laver, *Dandies*, 114, 116. A fuller discussion of hippiedom's affinities with dandyism can be found in Carassus, *Le Mythe du dandy*, 175–76. In what seems to be a developing watershed of retrospective attention for Twiggy from the Sovietologist crowd, Vainshtein ("Female Fashion, Soviet Style," 65) also notes the "ingenue" influence on Soviet women's hairstyles, makeup, and clothing. Grinbergs favored the more psychedelic aspects of youthquake fashion.

30. Feldman, *Gender on the Divide*, 2. This alterity was transmitted, in turn, to less peripheral parts of the Soviet Union by visitors to Riga who witnessed the hippies' public spectacle.

31.

The dandy rallies his forces and creates a unity for himself by the very violence of his refusal. Profligate, like all people without a rule of life, he is
coherent as an actor. But an actor implies a public; the dandy can only
play a part by setting himself up in opposition. He can only be sure of his
own existence by finding it in the statement of others' faces. Other people are his mirror. A mirror quickly becomes clouded, it is true, since
human capacity for attention is limited. It must be ceaselessly stimulated,
spurred on by provocation. The dandy, therefore, is always compelled to
astonish.

Camus, *The Rebel*, 51–52. For a general discussion of the concept of the cult-
of-self, see René Huyge, "Dandysme et culte de soi," in Carassus, *Le Mythe du
dandy*, 304–7.
    32. "A dandy must be married, father of the family and very happy in *mé-
nage*. The liaisons of the dandy are indiscernible. They yield the more nonsensi-
cal adventures." Sollers, "Le Dandy," 74.
    33. Feldman argues that this tendency, commonly and reductively believed
to be misogynistic, is, in fact, highly self-implicating for the male dandy.

[T]he literature of dandyism challenges the very concept of two separate
genders. Its male heroes, artists and their subjects alike, do more than
punish women or dally with them"*they relocate dandyism within the female realm in order to move beyond the male and female, beyond dichotomous gender itself.* How is dandyism displaced upon the female?
By a variety of methods, each as distinctive as the artist who invents it."

*Gender on the Divide*, 11; emphasis in the original.
    34. This is discussed by Carassus in *Le Mythe du dandy*, 175–76, referring
to uncited remarks by Roland Barthes.
    35. Feldman, *Gender on the Divide*, 5.
    36. Dolto, "Le Dandysme et l'absence du père," 311. Earlier in her essay,
Dolto states, "Without a father, he has no one between himself and God, how
astonishing the naive confusion that he makes between God and the demon
who carries his mask" (309). This identification of the dandy with the divine
had been remarked upon as early as Carlyle, who wrote of the "Dandiacal
Sect," whose members, devoted to self-worship, "affect great purity and sepa-
ratism; distinguish themselves by a particular costume . . . ; and, on the whole,
strive to maintain a true Nazarene deportment." Moers, *The Dandy*, 182.
    37. Concluding remarks made to the audience attending the world premiere
of Grinbergs's newly restored *Pasportrets* (Self-Portrait, 1972) at Anthology
Film Archives, New York City, 15 February 1996.
    38. Carassus, *Le Mythe du dandy*, 106.

39. Whereas Barbey d'Aurevilly's brief foray into journalism has been described as "supercilious" (Moers, *The Dandy*, 258), Grinbergs's work has been consistently, deeply provocative—not least of all because the only members of his readership who could possibly afford the Moschino or Yamamoto designs that he favors are the *biznesmeni* of Latvia's organized crime circles. In the mid-1990s Grinbergs also hosted a menswear series on Latvian TV Kanels 4 titled *Imperators* (Emperor), whose nonlinear, improvisational format was as iconoclastic as the clothing it showcased.

40. For these and other nicknames of Regency dandies, see Moers, *The Dandy*, 58–59.

41. Carassus, *Le Mythe du dandy*, 105. That Beuys had covered *his* head in gold leaf for the 1965 action *How to Explain Pictures to a Dead Hare* indicates the extensive folding and refolding of chosen subjectivity in Polis's work. Also on the topic of doubling, consider this line from Sollers's manifesto: "The dandy is the complete opposite of travesty. One sees him full of compassion for this impossible twin." "Le Dandy," 75.

42. Dolto, "Figure de proue," 88.

43. Sartre, *Baudelaire*, 135.

44. Krauss's statement, made during a 1998 lecture at the Wexner Center for the Arts, Columbus, OH, appears in her book *Bachelors* (Cambridge: MIT Press, 1999), 47, wherein Cahun is quoted from her autobiographical *Cancelled Confessions*, 29.

45. Edward Bulwer, *Pelham; or, The Adventures of a Gentleman* (1828), quoted in Moers, *The Dandy*, 76.

46. This attack appeared in the anti-dandiacal journal *Fraser's* in the early 1830s; see Moers, *The Dandy*, 171.

47. See Yve-Alain Bois and Rosalind E. Krauss, *Formless: A User's Guide* (Cambridge: MIT Press, 1997).

48. Barthes, "Le Dandysme et la mode," 312.

49. Jules-Amédée Barbey d'Aurevilly, quoted in Feldman, *Gender on the Divide*, 56. This fantasy is recounted as historical fact by Françoise Coblence in "Dandyism: From Luxury to Immateriality," in *Industrial Design: Reflection of a Century*, ed. Jocelyn de Noblet (Paris: Flammarion, 1993), 92, a misunderstanding that by no means reduces the force of Coblence's argument about immateriality and form in dandyism.

50. Feldman, *Gender on the Divide*, 72, who cites several remarks by Barbey d'Aurevilly, among them, "My life splits in two and in three on so many sides . . . understand this life up in the air" (Feldman's translation).

51. Sartre, *Baudelaire*, 140–46.

52. Polis's reworked *Sistine Madonna*, titled *Raphael and Polis*, is reproduced in *Nonconformist Art: The Soviet Experience, 1956–1986,* ed. Alla Rosenfeld and Norton T. Dodge (New York: Thames and Hudson, 1995), 179.

53.

Certainly there is a tension (or is it a compromise?) between commitment and dandyism through appropriation art at least. ("I appropriate these images," [Sherrie] Levine remarked in an early statement, "to express my own simultaneous longing for the passion of engagement and the sublimity of aloofness.") Yet this tension exists only as long as the political culture allows. As Reaganism spread in the early 1980s, the dandyish position became less ambiguous, more cynical, and the star of Warhol obscured all others.

Hal Foster, *The Return of the Real: The Avant-Garde at the End of the Century* (Cambridge: MIT Press, 1996), 122; 259 n. 45. Foster cites Levine as quoted in Benjamin Buchloh, "Allegorical Procedures: Appropriation and Montage in Contemporary Art," *Artforum*, September 1982.

54. Attributed to Mr. Beaumont, a dandy character from a Regency novel, by Moers, *The Dandy*, 38.

55. Carassus, *Le Mythe du dandy*, 61.

56. Laver, *Dandies*, 64.

57. One of the most extensive visual compilations of such Soviet prisoner tattoos is Dantsik Sergeevich Baldaev, *Slovar' tiuremno-lagerno-blatnogo zhargona: Rechevoi i graficheskii portret sovetskoi tiur'my* (Moscow: Kraia Moskvy, 1992).

BIBLIOGRAPHY

Baroja, Pío. *Un dandy comunista, la Novela Corta*, no. 51. Madrid: Gráfica Clemares, n.d.

Bois, Yve-Alain, and Rosalind Krauss. *Formless: A User's Guide*. Cambridge: MIT Press, 1997.

Bown, Mathew Cullerne. *Art under Stalin*. New York: Holmes and Meier, 1991.

Buchli, Victor. "Khrushchev, Modernism, and the Fight against *Petit-bourgeois* Consciousness in the Soviet Home." *Journal of Design History* 10, no. 2 (1997): 161–76.

Camus, Albert. *The Rebel: An Essay on Man in Revolt*. Trans. Anthony Bower. New York: Knopf, 1974.

Carassus, Emilien, ed. *Le Mythe du dandy*. Paris: Armand Colin, 1971.

Coblence, Françoise. "Dandyism: From Luxury to Immateriality." In *Industrial Design: Reflections of a Century*, edited by Jocelyn de Noblet, 86–93. Paris: Flammarion, 1993.

Dolto, Françoise. "Figure de proue." In *Splendeurs et misères du dandysme*, 83–95. Paris: Bouexière and Favardin, 1986.

Feldman, Jessica R. *Gender on the Divide: The Dandy in Modernist Literature.* Ithaca: Cornell University Press, 1993.

Gorsuch, Anne E. "Flappers and Foxtrotters: Soviet Youth in the 'Roaring Twenties.'" *Carl Beck Papers in Russian and East European Studies*, no. 1102 (1994).

Green, Martin Burgess. *Children of the Sun: A Narrative of "Decadence" in England after 1918.* New York: Basic Books, 1976.

Krauss, Rosalind. *Bachelors.* Cambridge: MIT Press, 1999.

Laver, James. *Dandies.* London: Weidenfeld and Nicolson, 1968.

LeMaire, Michel. *Le Dandysme de Baudelaire à Mallarmé.* Paris: Klincksieck, 1978.

Mansbach, Stephen A. *Standing in the Tempest: Painters of the Hungarian Avant-Garde, 1908–1930.* Cambridge: MIT Press, 1991.

Moers, Ellen. *The Dandy: Brummel to Beerbohm.* London: Secker and Warburg, 1960.

Reid, Susan E. "Destalinization and Taste, 1953–1963." *Journal of Design History* 10, no. 2 (1997): 177–201.

Rosenfeld, Alla, and Norton T. Dodge, eds. *Noncomformist Art: The Soviet Experience, 1956–1986.* New York: Thames and Hudson, 1995.

Sartre, Jean-Paul. *Baudelaire.* Translated by Martin Turnell. London: Horizon, 1949.

Sollers, Philippe. "Le Dandy." In *Splendeurs et misères du dandysme*, 73–76. Paris: Bouexière and Favardin, 1986.

Stevens, Wallace. *Letters of Wallace Stevens.* Edited by Holly Stevens. New York: Knopf, 1966.

Svede, Mark Allen. "All You Need Is Lovebeads: Latvia's Hippies Undress for Success." In *Style and Socialism: Modernity and Material Culture in Post–War Eastern Europe*, edited by David Crowley and Susan E. Reid. London: Berg, 2000.

Troitsky, Artemy. *Back in the USSR: The True Story of Rock in Russia.* Boston: Faber and Faber, 1988.

Vainshtein, Ol'ga. "Female Fashion, Soviet Style: Bodies of Ideology." In *Russia—Women—Culture*, edited by Helena Goscilo and Beth Holmgren, 64–93. Bloomington: Indiana University Press, 1996.

# Epilogue
## *Quentin Crisp: The Last Dandy?*

## *Rhonda K. Garelick*

On November 21, 1999, Quentin Crisp died in New York City at the age of ninety. With him goes perhaps the last link we had to the great nineteenth-century tradition of the English dandy. It was my great pleasure to meet and speak with Mr. Crisp just a few months before his death. He was an unforgettable character.

Quentin Crisp was calmly sipping a water glass of straight Dewar's when I met him at the Bowery Bar. He wore a felt cowboy hat over long, thin gray hair pinned up in loops, Gibson-girl style. The lace scarf around his neck was anchored with a large rhinestone brooch. His fingernails were longish and pointed, like a guitarist's, and his left hand, slightly paralyzed by recent neurological troubles, was further weighed down by a gigantic coral ring displaying, improbably, an engraved Star of David. On his lapel was a tiny American flag pin. I had made this appointment to discover whether this man was, in fact, the last of the great British dandies.

   At ninety, Crisp still has a remarkable cleanness of feature—high, chiseled cheekbones, sharp, aristocratic nose, strong chin. His cheeks were pale and chalky (the result, I realized, more of heavy face powder than of ill health); and his blue eyes were rimmed with black liner. He had been dressed and made up identically in May 1998, when I saw him perform his one-man show, *An Evening with Quentin Crisp*, at the Grove Sreet Playhouse in the West Village.

   This tiny gentleman (5'3" maybe) is a fixture of Manhattan's East Village and Lower East Side, where the usual passersby are in their

*Fig. E.1.* Quentin Crisp, n.d. Photograph by Greg Gorman. Reproduced by permission.

twenties, sport multiple piercings, and expose tattooed midriffs. But Quentin Crisp is well-known and well-liked here—a smiling hostess at the Bowery Bar led me right to him—perhaps because it's so clear that his very being connects the past of this neighborhood with its present. A foreigner who came to New York at the age of 75 to escape

the persecution he felt in his native England (tormented for his effemi-
nacy, he says, even into his old age), Crisp is not unlike the thousands
of Irish, Italian, Jewish, and Chinese immigrants who all settled in
this part of Manhattan. Crisp is also obviously an artist of the self, as
are so many of the area's elaborately adorned residents. And Crisp is
poor and struggling to make rent—like so many of his neighbors.
When I called him (his full name, address, and phone number are
clearly listed in the phone book), he instantly said yes to lunch, before
even knowing who, exactly, I was. He says yes to all free meals.

Quentin Crisp, né Denis Pratt, was born and raised in the middle-
class suburbs of London. After a tormented boyhood, detailed with remarkable and moving candor in his 1968 memoir, *The Naked Civil
Servant*, Crisp decided that the world needed to know and accept him.
He decided, that is, to be openly gay. "It seemed to me that there were
few homosexuals in the world," he writes. "I felt that the entire
strength of the club must be prepared to show its membership card at
any time. . . . I . . . made myself into a test case."[1] For Crisp, this meant
wearing heavy makeup, long hair, and painted fingernails everywhere
he went. In the London of the 1920s, this kind of flamboyance was not
only rare, it was potentially fatal. *The Naked Civil Servant* describes
the near-constant jeering, face slapping, molestation, and violent beat-
ings (more than once leaving him unconscious) that Crisp endured simply for having walked outside in his preferred attire.

Crisp believes that he survived these countless assaults because their violence was actually born of a need "to release . . . sexual curiosity in a
manner consistent with [a] heavily guarded idea of manliness." "My as-
sailants," writes Crisp, "did not apparently require my death."[2] This
deadpan irony recalls, of course, the impassive, biting wit of the dandies;
but the remark's very personal subject and still-apparent pain—both typical of Crisp's work—ultimately set him apart from dandyism. Dandies
do not recount painful memories. Nor do they, for that matter, write
memoirs.[3] As it turns out, Quentin Crisp is not exactly the last living
dandy, but rather living proof of dandyism's historical specificity. Put simply, Crisp proves that we have long passed dandyism's moment. His art-
ful self-construction and cool wit, while clearly descending from Brummell's or Baudelaire's, coexist with very undandy-like talk show–style
confession, a shameless love of all publicity, and sometimes shocking
frankness. (*Naked* even describes Crisp's long boyhood struggle with in-
continence—of the more unpleasant variety.) Crisp has made a very pub-

lic, mass cultural career out of his dandyist refinements; he calls it being in "the smile and nod racket." In addition to writing many books, essays, and reviews (a selected bibliography follows), he has been a performer of stage, television, and film. (His best-known films have been *Philadelphia* and *Orlando*.) He is a cult personality and America, in particular, loves him. The feeling is mutual. "I was by nature American," he says.

Talking to Quentin Crisp is a curious experience. He is exceedingly cordial and seems to have infinite patience. He listens quietly and answers all questions directly, often wittily. On the other hand, he evinces little human curiosity or engagement with the situation. He asked me nothing about why I had called or what kind of article this would be. He offered none of the usual pleasantries of greeting or parting. Crisp spoke to me just as he might have spoken from a stage, when taking questions from anonymous audience members.

More unsettling, however, was the fact that Crisp answered so many of my questions with remarks lifted directly out of his books. I had a vague awareness of this during our interview, guessing that about 25 percent of what he said was prefabricated. But later, after reading more of Crisp's *oeuvre*, I realized the proportion was closer to 75 percent. Perhaps this is because at ninety, Crisp has already addressed virtually any question one might think to ask him, from literature to American television to his (surprisingly old-fashioned) views on homosexuality. Crisp never acknowledged his self-quotation. Never once did he say, "As I wrote once in this or that book . . ." On the contrary, he managed to make all those quotations appear to fit quite spontaneously into our "conversation." In this respect, he reminds me of a talking, interactive wind-up doll. Balzac once wrote that a dandy resembled an "ingenious mannequin."[4] Once the mannequin enters the age of the mechanically reproduced icon, perhaps Quentin Crisp is what obtains.

Yet, despite his aloofness and that odd recycling habit, Quentin Crisp endeared himself to me. He was particularly frank and affecting when he discussed his painful youth. And his wit, while sharp, is never unkind or bitter. In fact, he is *nice*. And his charming willingness to oblige any stranger's curiosity makes him a rare celebrity, as does his obvious delight in such simple indulgences as a paid lunch.

I began our conversation by asking him explicitly about the dandyist movement of the nineteenth century, knowing that he had once written the preface for an English edition of Barbey d'Aurevilly's treatise on the subject, "On Dandyism and George Brummell."[5]

*RG:* What do you think about dandyism or the dandyist movement?

*QC:* Well, I once wrote the preface to a book by someone with a French name. I have read about dandies. They were a terrible lot of rogues. They never paid their bills. They always wound up in Calais. And Calais became known as the city where English dandies went. I think they were terrible people. I would hate to be that kind of dandy.

Dandyism is about 1810 to 1820 or 1830 when George IV was a dandy. Somebody once said that the aristocracy in England in the early eighteenth century was the freest group of people ever known. They really did exactly as they believed. I don't know why. It would have been Lord Byron who said that. He would have been there; he was a strange man. He cared about the Greeks. . . . I never knew why. Everyone thinks Greece was the cradle of liberty. It was the cradle of slavery. The Greeks had slaves. It was appalling.

*RG:* I saw your one-man show at the Grove Street Playhouse. Your remarks on style were intriguing.

*QC:* I believe in style, because style prevents you from being part of a group. It is bad to be part of a group, because in the end you are saying, "I am subservient, therefore, I am right and everyone else is wrong." Style prevents you from the worst aspect of fascism. We should never use the word "we," except to mean "you and me." If you say "we love football," that means you're going to Belgium to kill all the Belgians because you lost the match.

*RG:* I see you wear an American flag. Isn't that a form of saying "we"?

*QC:* I wear that in the hope of avoiding deportation. I've been here eighteen years. And when I've been here twenty, I can seek the next stage, being a naturalized citizen; and the exam is much easier. You see, I couldn't learn it all. I think you have a very difficult examination in American political history. A friend of mine applied. He was asked three questions. The second was, "What president succeeded Lincoln?" and he didn't know. The third was, "How many Supreme Court judges are there?" And he didn't know. And they said, "You don't seem to be taking your situation seriously."

*RG:* What is it you like so much about America?

*QC:* It's the people. They're exactly the opposite of the English. Whatever is favored in England is ignored in America. Whatever is worshiped in America is disliked in England. Happiness is woven into the constitution here. In England, you have something more sensible. Pursuit of happiness is frivolous. You're supposed to suffer in England. No one speaks to you in England. An Englishman asked why I lived here permanently. "Why," I said, "because everywhere I go everybody talks to me." And he said, "I can't think of anything worse."

People are my only pastime.

*RG:* That's a noble pastime.

*QC:* That's nice, I hadn't thought of that. I don't do anything for them; I just enjoy them. I've never been any other way. When I was a young man swanning about the West End I thought why doesn't anyone look at anyone else. It could all be one long party. Well, in Manhattan it is. In America, you can get a whole bus talking to one another if you want.

And people here send me the most extraordinary presents. I never got any presents in England, now I'm showered with presents. Some people who live in Canada send me whole boxes of food. Wonderful food. There are days when I never go out, I stay in and eat. I am a born freeloader.

*RG:* No, you're just very charming.

*QC:* Perhaps they go together.

*RG:* I would like to know if you have any disciples.

*QC:* I don't think so. I think I would know.

*RG:* It might be subtle.

*QC:* There may be people who quote the things I say, which would make them disciples in some sense, but I think they're only part-time disciples.

*RG:* Did you always want to be a performer?

*QC:* I didn't really want anything. I have no ambition. When I was young if you had asked me I would have said I wanted to be on the stage. But I didn't really want to act. I just thought I'd be there in the middle of the stage and all the lights would be on me. . . . That's what Marlene Dietrich wanted. She wanted applause. She didn't even want sex. Did you know that she actually said, "You have to let them put it in or they don't come back"? Such a wonderful thing to have said. She didn't want sex; she wanted praise. Sex smudges your makeup, disturbs your coiffure. She just wanted admiration. I saw her first American film in a tatty cinema called the Biograph in England. And the girl behind me said, "Ain't she stuck on herself?" and, of course, she was totally self-absorbed; and that I understand. She was the first person to use the word "image" in the American sense. She said, "I dress for the image." And she did.

*RG:* Besides Dietrich, who are your favorite personalities?

*QC:* There were stars when I was born. The greatest star ever was Brigitte Helm. Beauty is not a woman, it's a man's idea of a woman. And during the reign of Mr. Mayer it was a Jew's idea of an Aryan. They were all blond, they were all remote. Because glamour exists where all is present but all is not given. You married some nice Jewish girl, but you longed for a great blond Nordic horse who's going to put her boot in your face.

And Fritz Lang invented Miss Helm and put her into the first science fiction film ever made, called *Metropolis*. She had a straight line from her forehead to the end of her nose. And when he showed her the photograph [of herself in costume for the role], she knew who she was. You see, the stars didn't have to be able to explain what they were doing, they just had to embody what they knew their creator thought they were. Fritz Lang invented Miss Helm the mechanical woman and when she saw the photograph she could do it.

The world was very feminine when I was young. Movie stars meant a woman. Men were in support of. Except possibly for Rudolph Valentino. Now, I'm not suggesting he was kinky, but his appeal was very feminine, remote.

Then, movies were made for a middle-aged woman with a broken heart. Now they're made for boys of fifteen, and their heroes are men. And all they have to do is break everything, which is what boys of fifteen love to do. So their heroes are Mr. Stallone and Mr. Schwarzenegger who have only to walk down the street and the buildings crumble on either side.

*RG:* Is there anyone now who has star potential? What about Madonna?

*QC:* Madonna can never be a star because she lacks remoteness. The actual big stars are remote. Miss Sarandon is nearly a star. If she were given the treatment, Miss Sarandon could be a star.

*RG:* What do you think of drag and camp?

*QC:* I think it's sad that if one group of people envies another, given half a chance it will imitate the worst characteristics of the other. Men in drag never want to be *nice* women; they're always the bitchiest, most self-regarding people you can imagine. Lesbians who want to be men never want to be *nice* men. They want to curse and spit in public. I don't know why that is; but that's so.

*RG:* But, don't men in drag shows want to imitate the very qualities you admired earlier? Such as Marlene Dietrich's wonderful presence?

*QC:* I've never seen a man imitate a star so as not to send her up. You see, it's the mockery implied in drag that takes hold of you—and it never changes. Drag died in 1926.

If you saw a woman sitting here today, legs crossed, with a cigarette [*pantomiming with exaggerated haughtiness, eyes lowered, arm extended*], you would think either that that woman has been sitting here since 1926 or it's a man in drag—because women don't do that nowadays.

*RG:* Have you ever worn drag?

*QC:* I've only once worn drag when I was quite young, about twenty-two or twenty-three. I thought, "What would it be like to be a woman?" So I borrowed clothes from the girls I knew, put them on and went down into the street. You can only say the occasion was a success because nothing happened. They accepted me as a woman and took no notice. So I thought, well, that was that; there really is no difference, save the clothes.

If the [transsexual] operation had been available when I was less than twenty-six or twenty-seven, I would have had it.

*RG:* Seriously? You would have become a woman?

*QC:* Yes, it would have simplified my life. Whatever I did would have been taken for granted. Everything I did was in question when I was young. Even the boys who liked me in school would say, "Do you *have* to stand like that? Put your hand down!" They were trying to teach me, to make me be like a schoolboy. I never learned. If I had been a woman it would have been natural.

I have never understood why people who have had the operation tell everyone. Then they are outside of society just as before.

I would have told nobody. I would have gone to live in a town in the distant suburbs, run a knitting shop and never have told anyone my terrible secret. I would have joined real life.

*RG:* But wouldn't that have been boring?

*QC:* It would have been wonderful; nothing would have been an effort. I used to sit in my room thinking, "Shall I sit here freezing in my room or shall I go out and buy a box of matches?" And if I went out I had to go into a shop where a girl would say [*imitating a staring shop girl backing away in horror, voice quavering*], "I'll see if there's a box of matches, just a moment," and gone and said, "May! It's that bloke!" And May would have come in and said [*more pantomime, another shocked shop girl*], "I can't seem to find any [matches] anywhere."

Everything was an effort. But in America nothing is an effort, because if you look strange people think you're advertising something. And you are. You see that's the difference. Showiness, which is vulgar in England, is acceptable here. People here want the world's attention and they go about it any way they know how.

*RG:* And yet some of the greatest showmen and biggest personalities have been from Britain. What about Oscar Wilde?

*QC:* Oscar Wilde was a mess. And I think he chose homosexuality because it was a sin.

*RG:* You think it was a choice?

*QC:* Yes, he was married and had two children; so he was a perfectly normal man. He loved the idea that he was shocking. And his poems are terrible. When you turn the pages of a book of poems by Oscar Wilde, you meet every word you expect to meet in poetry: love, death, gold, stars, black sea, the sky, art. You know, he wanted to show off and he was *such* a hypocrite. He was standing at his trial bleating about love and dragging in the fair name of Plato when he had had the most *sordid* life imaginable. When I was young and swanning about the West End all the boys thought that Oscar Wilde was a great nobleman who had thrown his life away for love. Nothing could be less true. He consorted with East Enders who had been procured for him by Lord Alfred Douglas. He only knew the boys in Braille because he only met them in darkened rooms in Oxford where the curtains were never turned back. How sordid can your life be? It's too late to talk about love.

*RG:* He did write good plays, though, don't you think?

*QC:* *The Importance of Being Earnest* is wonderful and I've acted in it. I've played Lady Bracknell. It's so good because all the jokes in act 3 have been prepared in act 1. He cut out one act and it still hangs together. And when you say the lines you don't have to point them, as actors say, you don't have to make them funny.

*RG:* Do you read contemporary literature?

*QC:* I don't read at all. I used to read a lot when I was a child. But reading is a substitute for living and now I don't read because I can live. I don't really like the occupation of reading, putting one letter in front of another and forming a word and putting a word behind another to form a sentence and then summoning up the image that the sentence describes. On television it's done for you. Television is a substitute for reading.

I watch television in the evening. I like my programs urban, nocturnal, and frightening. I watch *The Practice, Law and Order, Homicide*. Because the only emotion we know we feel is fear.

*RG:* What do you mean?

*QC:* You try to feel grief. Your lover dies. People stand around and say how terrible for you. You look at the floor but you can't remember his name. But you know when you're afraid. That's what made the Second World War so great. You'd walk along the street; London was black; the ground shook with anti-aircraft fire. The people you were talking to today might be dead tomorrow. You'd look your last on all things lovely every hour.

*RG:* How would you describe your politics?

*QC:* I don't like politics. Politics is the art of making the inevitable appear to be a matter of wise human choice.

### NOTES

1. Quentin Crisp, *The Naked Civil Servant* (New York: Signet, 1968), 27.

2. Ibid., 62.

3. While, of course, Oscar Wilde did write a memoir with *De Profundis*, I would argue that he was not a classic dandy. I see Wilde as a transitional figure whose style merged the high-gloss finish of nineteenth-century dandyism and a more modern celebrity that combines the autobiographical with the purely theatrical.

4. In his "Treatise on Elegant Living" Balzac wrote, "In making himself a dandy, a man becomes a piece of bedroom furniture, an extremely ingenious mannequin that can sit atop a horse or on a divan . . . but a thinking being . . . never." Honoré de Balzac, "Traité de la vie élégante," in *Oeuvres complètes* (Paris: Louis Conard, 1938), 2:177.

5. Jules Barbey d'Aurevilly, "Du Dandysme et de George Brummell," in *Oeuvres romanesques complètes* (Paris: Gallimard, 1966), 2:667–733. English edition: *Dandyism*, trans. Douglas Ainslie, foreword by Quentin Crisp (New York: PAJ, 1988), 7–11.

### BIBLIOGRAPHY

Balzac, Honoré de. "Traité de la vie élégante." In *Oeuvres complètes*, 2:152–85. Paris: Louis Conard, 1938.

Barbey d'Aurevilly, Jules. "Du dandysme et de George Brummel." In *Oeuvres romanesques complètes*, 2:667–733. Paris: Gallimard, 1966. English edition: *Dandyism*. Translated by Douglas Ainslie. Foreword by Quentin Crisp. New York: PAJ, 1988.

Crisp, Quentin. *How to Become a Virgin*. London: Duckworth, 1981.

———. *How to Have a Life-Style*. London: Cecil Wolff, 1975.

———. *Love Made Easy*. London: Duckworth, 1971.

———. *The Naked Civil Servant*. New York: Signet, 1968.

———. *The New York Diaries*. London: HarperCollins, 1996.

———. *Quentin Crisp's Book of Quotations*. New York: Macmillan, 1989.

# Contributors

*Jennifer Blessing* is a doctoral candidate at the Institute of Fine Arts, New York University. She is working on a dissertation on Gina Pane and 1970s body art. Among the exhibitions she organized at the Guggenheim Museum, where she was a curator for eight years, is *Rrose Is a Rrose Is a Rrose: Gender Performance in Photography.* Her most recent publications include essays in *Veronica's Revenge: Contemporary Perspectives on Photography*, ed. Elizabeth Janus, with Marion Lambert (Zurich: Scalo, 1998), and in *Parkett.*

*Susan Fillin-Yeh,* an art historian, is Anne and John Hauberg Director, and Curator of the Douglas F. Cooley Memorial Art Gallery, Reed College, and has taught at Brown, Yale, and Hunter College. She has published extensively on Charles Sheeler, Georgia O'Keeffe, and other figures in early-twentieth-century American art. At the Cooley Gallery she has curated exhibitions of American modernism and photography, contemporary art, and environmental art. She is working on a book on the WPA.

*Rhonda K. Garelick,* an associate professor of French at Connecticut College, is the author of *Rising Star: Dandyism, Gender, and Performance in the Fin de Siècle* (Princeton University Press, 1998). Her work focuses on the relationship between literary and theatrical performance, and she has published articles on such topics as European drama, American television, and modern dance. Her forthcoming book, *Electric Salome* (Princeton University Press), examines the cultural legacy of the American dance pioneer and early filmmaker Loie Fuller.

*Joe Lucchesi* is assistant professor, department of art and art history, St. Mary's College of Maryland. He received his Ph.D. from the University of North Carolina at Chapel Hill. He has published on Romaine Brooks and the British artist Gluck and is the curator of the recent Brooks retrospective exhibition at the National Museum of Women in the Arts.

*Kimberly Miller,* a Ph.D. candidate in the department of art history at the University of Wisconsin-Madison, has done research on women, violence, and visual representation in the recent history of South Africa and on African American women artists. She holds a dissertation fellowship from the American Association of University Women, and previously held a Woodrow Wilson Dissertation Fellowship for Women's Studies. The research for her contribution to this volume was funded by the Smithsonian Institution, where she was a graduate fellow at the National Museum for African Art.

*Robert E. Moore* is an anthropologist and linguist who has conducted fieldwork at Warm Springs Indian Reservation in central Oregon since the early 1980s. He has taught at Reed College and New York University, and he currently works in "experience modeling" at Sapient, at Internet consulting firm in New York City. His recent research and writing have grown out of a series of studies of the cultural politics of heritage in contemporary Native American reservation communities.

*Richard J. Powell* is the John Spencer Bassett Professor of Art and Art History at Duke University. He is the author of *Homecoming: The Art and Life of William H. Johnson* and *Black Art and Culture in the Twentieth Century.* In addition to publishing widely on American art and the arts of the African diaspora, he has organized many museum and gallery exhibitions in the United States and abroad.

*Carter Ratcliff* is a poet and art critic. He is a contributing editor of *Art in America* and *Sculpture.* His most recent book is *The Fate of a Gesture: Jackson Pollock and Postwar American Art.* A selection of his essays on art is forthcoming from Cambridge University Press.

*Mark Allen Svede* is a doctoral student at Ohio State University and works as an independent scholar of Latvian art and material culture. His recent projects include restoring a Soviet underground film, compiling a monograph on Andris Grinbergs for the Soros Center of Contemporary Art, Riga, and coediting the catalogue for a forthcoming exhibition of Baltic art from the Norton and Nancy Dodge Collection of Nonconformist Art from the Soviet Union at the Jane Voorhees Zimmerli Museum, Rutgers University.

# Index

abstraction, 108, 113, 115, 116, 120
Adams, Maude, 13, 134
Africa. *See* Gelede masquerade
African American dandies. *See* black
  dandyism
Alcibiades, 6, 90
Ali, Muhammad, 228
Allston, Washington, 8, 9
Althusser, Louis, 4
American Indians, Columbia River region:
  bargaining for clothing, 74–78; bodily
  adornment, 73; clothing as optional,
  72, 74–75; and dandyism, 59–91; disease epidemics, 60, 67; generational differences in sartorial practices, 85–87;
  and hierarchical social order, 66, 82–83;
  languages of, 66, 70, 93n; leadership
  issue, 3, 70, 91–92n; literature of contact, 61–87; making and buying of
  clothing, 83–85; motivations for dandyism, 81–83; network of transcultural
  exchange and trade, 59–60, 66, 68–72;
  overview of dandyism, 60–61; period of
  dominance, 67–68; poverty of, 73,
  94–95n; rank-consciousness of, 66,
  82–83; as slaveholders, 66, 73–74; time
  period for dandyism, 60, 89; wealth
  among, 60, 66, 67, 70. *See also* Cooper,
  James Fenimore; Northwest Coast Indians; Plains Indians
Anastasio, Angelo, 71
Andersen, Hans Christian, 255
androgyny, 130, 133, 135, 136–37, 155,
  168, 172, 175, 195, 196. *See also* cross-
  dressing
*Anne of the Indies*, 187
*Antigone*, 51
appropriation art, 259–61

Aragon, Louis, 190
aristocracy. *See* class privilege
*Arrangement in Black and Gold*, 163,
  164
Artaud, Antonin, 193
Ash, Juliet, 7
Ashbery, John, 112
Ashue, Celia, 87–89
Astor, John Jacob, 62
*Astoria*, 62–63, 71, 92n
avant-gardism: and abstraction, 108, 116;
  and androgyny, 130, 135; and double-
  gendered images, 130, 136–37; and female cross-dressers, 130, 133–34; gender issues, 130, 132–34, 138; relationship to dandyism, 102, 130–31; and
  women artists, 132–33

Babcock-Abrahams, Barbara, 5
Baer, Jo, 118
Bakhtin, Mikhail, 4, 5, 22
Balanchine, George, 47
Ballets Russes, 47, 50
Balsan, Etienne, 40
Baltic republics, dandyism in, 252–62
Balzac, Honoré de, 21, 36–37, 90, 225
Baraka, Amiri, 23, 219, 220, 229, 235
*Bar at the Folies Bergère*, 132
Barbey d'Aurevilly, Jules: assessment of
  Brummell, 1, 3, 36, 103, 262; denoue-
  ment, 255; view of dandyism, 2–3,
  102–3, 259
Barney, Natalie, 153, 155, 169
Baroja, Pío, 246–47
Barthes, Roland, 4, 15–16, 17, 35, 250,
  252, 259
Basso, Keith, 65
Bataille, Georges, 188, 258